ARCHITECTURE OF THE ANCIENT CIVILIZATIONS IN COLOR

GENERAL EDITOR: BODO CICHY

Architecture of the Ancient Civilizations in Color

Mesopotamia, Egypt, the Indus Valley, the Megaliths
The Hittites, the Minoans, the Mycenaeans
The Etruscans, Central and South America

BODO CICHY

A STUDIO BOOK

THE VIKING PRESS · NEW YORK

BAUKUNST DER ALTEN HOCHKULTUREN

© 1965 BY BURKHARD-VERLAG ERNST HEYER, ESSEN

ARCHITECTURE OF THE ANCIENT CIVILIZATIONS IN COLOR

ENGLISH TRANSLATION COPYRIGHT © 1966 BY THAMES AND HUDSON, LONDON

ALL RIGHTS RESERVED

TRANSLATED FROM THE GERMAN BY A. K. BAKKER

PUBLISHED IN 1966 BY THE VIKING PRESS, INC.

625 MADISON AVENUE, NEW YORK, N.Y. 10022

LIBRARY OF CONGRESS CATALOG CARD NUMBER: 66-22245

COLOR PLATES PRINTED IN GERMANY BY DRUCKHAUS ROBERT KOHLHAMMER, LEINFELDEN

TEXT PRINTED IN HOLLAND BY MEIJER WORMERVEER N.V.

BOUND IN HOLLAND BY PROOST EN BRANDT N.V., AMSTERDAM

CONTENTS

LIST OF PLATES

Introduction

ANY DISCUSSION ON THE ARCHITECTURAL HERITAGE of the advanced civilizations of the ancient world, richly rewarding though it may be, is full of temptations and perils. Tempting because it humours the modern, frequently superficial, desire to trace the footsteps of ancient peoples with an almost treasure-hunting zeal, and thus to fall under the mysterious spell of those far distant periods of human life; dangerous because this superficial enchantment can never convey the true essence of a culture, and because we still do not know enough of the past to plumb the human spirit behind the visible phenomena and to exclude errors of judgement. Finally, the challenge is rewarding—and this alone makes the venture worthwhile because contact with the works of art of lost civilizations makes us realize to what heights the human spirit can rise, albeit in a form alien to our modern thinking. We should try, therefore, to approach the great achievements of the past with modesty and understanding.

Before embarking on this venture it would be well to remember that the ruined buildings which we shall pass on our journey, are nothing but mute and lifeless structures of earth, brick and stone. The walls may have cracked, columns fallen, the people who designed them, erected them and brought them to life may have gone, but the human spirit that conceived them lives on; the creative force that went into their making endures, triumphant and indestructible. For whatever is shaped by man is shaped by his will and is the realization of a vision.

By no means everything man has created from amorphous material can be called art. Only when the creative impulse reaches beyond utilitarian purposes and consciously or subconsciously enters into the realm of abstract beauty, when a work, whatever its nature, has aesthetic effect and spiritual meaning, can one speak of art.

This last point touches on a problem inherent in all architecture as opposed to the related arts of painting and sculpture, namely, that architecture even in its noblest form serves a practical purpose by its very nature. And be they temples or cathedrals, mansions or primitive huts, all buildings have one function in common—to form a shell around an enclosed space. Whether every stone, every corner is filled with a special significance or holiness, or merely serves the simple requirements of living, the intrinsic principle is architecturally the same. All building is subject to the same natural laws of stress and support, force and counterforce. But although hut and temple obey equal laws, nobody would value them alike, and the hut remains a simple device for the practical purpose of giving shelter. Temple and cathedral, however, although they obey the same basic structural laws, set out to impress.

The religious inspiration which is the very foundation of temple and cathedral architecture and which gives them their true meaning, can surmount triumphantly all natural limitations; a transcendent vision can create, with the means at its disposal, the harmonious proportions of form and mass that are the hallmark of a work of art.

This is not the place to discuss the distinction between the aesthetic and the purely functional, and in any event good architecture includes both these elements. Moreover architecture is intrinsically a matter of form and space, which means that it can be experienced but cannot easily be explained in words. Throughout its many thousands of years of history, architecture has always enlisted the help of sculpture and painting to make itself more easily understood. The mysteries of architecture are profound, and often the only way of penetrating them is through murals and sculpture. Together with literature and music, architecture is among the noblest expressions of human thought and self-realization, and as a creation of the human spirit it is irrevocably linked with the history of the human mind. Human thinking does not stand still; it is perpetually changing, new ideas are born, man is for ever directing his eyes towards a new vision, new ideals. Thus art in all its manifold expressions is in a continuous state of flux. The history of art, which means in effect its essential and formal changes in time and space, is the history of the human spirit expressed in image and form. Each work of art reflects faithfully the thoughts behind the creative impulses of a given period and a given time. This does not mean that the history of the human mind and its artistic achievements is the history of an unbroken evolution from primitive art towards the highly accomplished creations of our own time. It is possible only to speak of a continuous physical progress of mankind when referring to the technological development which is sometimes described as 'civilization' or 'material culture'.

A disinterested approach to art knows only enrichment through change; the terms used for material progress as such—'better, more suitable, more progressive'—cannot be applied here, for the creations of a 'spiritual culture' depend very little upon the concurrent material civilization. If this were not so, then this modern age would have some right to look down upon the cultural attainments of by-gone ages and measure their value in terms of the material situation of those times. But it would be presumptuous indeed to regard the noble thoughts and accomplished art of the Egyptians or Greeks as inferior to the achievements of our own epoch, even if ours is materially more advanced. The value of Sumerian, Egyptian, or Aztec arts is only measurable within their own sphere. These different spheres can have a fertilizing influence upon each other or can fulfil their span of life in isolation. They constitute the 'high cultures', and they each have their own specific spiritual qualities.

The history of mankind has witnessed the beginning, flowering and decadence of many cultures. And although each represents an unmistakable individuality, they also show many similarities because they all were and are the work of man. Every culture can be equated with its particular philosophy and religion, which means man's conception of the world, his relation to the tangible and visible in nature and his participation in those invisible and mysterious forces which animate his world and are the essence of his being. History teaches us that a culture can only live as long as its philosophy is vigorous, that a culture depends not only on the vitality of its people, its political power, its boundaries and its destiny, but much more on the range and missionary zeal of that people's beliefs and convictions. Western Christian culture is a momentous example. We soon discover too that no culture is unchanging or static, it alters continuously in its allotted time-span without losing its intrinsic spiritual quality.

What are the reasons for the differing aspects of human evolution and what was the historical trend that caused the narrow cultural limits of an early age to expand until we stand today upon the threshold of a world-wide civilization?

A complex question indeed, the answer to which lies in man's ability to react in an active, creative manner to the specific conditions and stimuli of his environment. He reacts to climatic conditions by making suitable clothing; through inventing and perfecting his tools he cultivates the soil and improves his diet and his chances of survival. He arranges his thoughts about the hidden forces of nature into a logical philosophical system. Not only can he formulate his reactions, he can communicate them to his fellow men and transmit them to posterity. He is able to record personal experiences, noting men's responses to a variety of stimuli, and from these observations he can formulate rules for behaviour. In this remarkable human quality lies the secret of the continuance, propagation and diversity of cultures. Man's ever-growing cultural achievements, material as well as spiritual, rest in the last resort on this faculty of the mind. Even so, the advance of civilization towards a cultural unity has been a slow and irregular process, dependent upon the evolution of mankind itself. Whilst today the human race, despite all its diverse traits, is closely interlinked, in the beginning there existed only small isolated communities, which, having no intercommunication, reacted upon their environment in quite different ways and developed into highly individualistic material and spiritual groups. It was through an ever-increasing commercial contact between these isolated cultures that in the course of many thousands of years conditions favouring a world civilization were established.

The cultures that evolved in the long history of mankind may be divided into three main groups: primitive, low and high cultures. The first take up more than 90 per cent of the millennia of man's life on earth, nearly all this time being occupied with the mere struggle for existence on the simplest material level. In these earliest primitive communities man had little time or opportunity to develop the life of the mind and spirit. The only difference between his world and the animal world was that man knew the art of kindling fire, he could make simple tools of bone, wood and flint and he could think, speak and therefore transmit his thoughts. But he remained in thrall to nature.

There are many indications that he reached a higher standard of living during the Palaeolithic age, when he had conquered the immediate, basic problems of self-preservation, and was now forming for himself an image of the world. This is shown by the burials and the provision of necessities for life after death, the dead being regarded as the life-givers and protectors of the new generation.

The true foundations of culture were not laid, however, until man had abandoned his passive, parasitic role and set himself against nature, becoming instead an independent being. When about 10,000 years ago he built himself houses, when organized communities lived together in villages, when plants were cultivated and animals domesticated, when he stored the harvest and engaged in barter it meant that he had finally left 'Paradise' behind.

Following his first steps in active intervention in natural phenomena, man began to reflect on forms of social behaviour. He conceived more concrete ideas about the forces of nature; for, now that he was no longer entirely at the mercy of nature, he was able to appreciate how dependent he was upon whether these forces were well or ill-disposed towards him. The change from the parasitic and roving life of the Palaeolithic food gatherers and hunters to the more settled life of the Neolithic period did not take place everywhere at the same time, but depended largely on differences in environment and climate, and therefore resulted in a great variety of cultures. The step from peasant cultures, practising a kind of primitive communism, towards the so-called 'high cultures' was taken for the first time when an urban population divided itself into social classes based on professions, and developed a powerful and influential ruling class.

This revolutionary transformation took place many thousands of years ago in the fertile valleys of the Tigris and Euphrates, the Nile and the Indus. It was accompanied by the first known religious systems and a clearly defined pantheon. Ideas, hitherto confined to the spoken word, could be perpetuated by symbolic signs—the precursors of writing. Great art made its first appearance.

The argument has come full circle. A discussion of the architecture of the ancient civilizations is pointless unless the influences and forces which conditioned the characteristic forms of this architecture are taken into account, and if one is not content with a catalogue of what still exists or can be reconstructed. To understand a work of art it is essential to see it against its cultural background. And this background has many facets, among them geographical conditions, historical destiny, ethnic and racial factors, and so forth. In the chapters that follow an attempt is made to find the fundamentals of the Sumerian, Egyptian and Aztec civilizations and to explain them as separate entities, eliminating as far as possible these background reservations and all unnecessary academic ballast. But clearly, it is not possible to do this without making comparisons with the achievements of better-known civilizations nearer in time to our own.

Mesopotamia *Plates 1 to 12*

EX ORIENTE LUX. These three words express the importance of the East in the history of the ancient world; for the East was the fountain-head of every cultural and religious endeavour of man in this part of the globe. It was here, or to be more precise, in the fertile valleys of the Tigris and Euphrates, the Nile and the Indus, that the first decisive steps were taken along the road that was to lead from the bondage of primitive existence to a way of life that can genuinely lay claim to the word 'civilized'.

All these early civilizations—the Sumerian, the Egyptian and that of the Indus valley—are of enormous antiquity. To take the case of the last-named, the astonishing fact recently came to light that there already existed in 2700 BC a highly developed culture in that region, though its preliminary phases have not been traced and it is only known at its mature stage.

There is, however, abundant evidence that in the southern part of Mesopotamia and in Egypt as early as the third millennium BC life had developed far beyond a primitive peasant or nomadic phase. So far advanced were these people living along the river banks that they stood on the threshold of true civilization, with city and state organization, religion and historical tradition which was already quite highly developed. Whether the Sumerians or Egyptians were the first to reach this stage will probably never be known, although archaeological evidence points to a Sumerian priority.

It would be interesting to know why these particular valleys favoured an early cultural development. What were the causes of this extraordinary evolution? Was it because the people living there were more highly gifted by nature? There is *a priori* no reason for coming to such a decision. Was it because of the great fertility of the valleys? But then, people have settled in equally fertile valleys in other parts of the world without making similar progress.

The cause must be sought elsewhere, namely in the general geographical situation and the changes in climate that occurred when the final ice age ended (about 10,000 BC).

Conditions in Europe after the ultimate retreat of the ice became less harsh, and flora and fauna more abundant. But the way of life of the small tribes and families living there did not change greatly—they continued to occupy caves and rock-shelters, to hunt and to gather berries and wild fruits. However, over the vast territory that stretches from North Africa across the Middle East to the Far East, the natural conditions changed more radically. The temperature rose steeply after the end of the pluvial period, which in the south coincided with the glacial periods of the northern regions. This caused the swamps and marshes gradually to dry up, the tropical forests to give way to brush, and the lush grassland to wither into dry steppe and inhospitable deserts. The rainfall became less and less, and in many places failed altogether. Fresh-water lakes and streams, once rich in wild-life, silted up into muddy wasteland, and except for a few cases, life became restricted to the narrow stretches of land along the main rivers. Owing to this the low-lying lands within easy reach of life-giving water became more and more coveted by an ever-growing population.

Climatic changes take place so slowly that this change in environment must have taken thousands of years to complete. Perhaps this was in the end the decisive factor in the shaping of conditions favourable to the birth of the early civilizations.

Man, confined to the relatively small fertile area and steadily increasing in numbers, had to give up his roaming existence and settle down to a sedentary life. Thus the nomadic or near-nomadic tribes of the Palaeolithic period were transformed into the peasant communities of the Neolithic or New Stone Age. Archaeological evidence, sparse as it is, shows that these peasant communities, which existed in Mesopotamia and Egypt from the seventh until the third millennium BC, met with many new prob-lems, and shows also how the cultural horizon widened, how new creative impulses were released and new techniques developed. Systematic cultivation of land and animal husbandry made it possible to sustain larger communities, store the harvest, exchange goods and provide for the future. Permanent dwellings appeared for the first time. In the common interest, people had to submit to law and order. This new way of life called for a new type of equipment, for more efficient tools and domestic articles (pottery and wood-work). Man began to speculate about the world around him, wishing to understand its mysteries and his own place in it, and to control his own fate as far as possible.

The transition from primitive peasant settlement to a more complex way of life took place during the fourth millennium BC in Mesopotamia, and in Egypt a little later. While in the early prehistoric settlements each family was more or less self-sufficient, in the more complicated urban societies sound planning of labour became a necessity. Each individual now formed part of a large unit, specializing in his own work, and his co-operation was of paramount importance for the proper functioning of the town and state organization. But organization on strictly utilitarian lines is not sufficient in itself to pave the way to a highly developed culture, and this is clearly shown from the early remains found at Jericho in Jordan. Here (and also at the site of Çatal Hüyük in Anatolia) traces have been found of fairly large towns with an estimated population of two to three thousand inhabitants. Beehive-shaped mud huts with pointed roofs were protected by an enormous city-wall—the earliest so far known. Although these people had no knowledge of the art of making pottery (one of the criteria generally postulated for a 'Neolithic' state) it is obvious that there was some kind of organization of the community, to enable the great 20-foot high rough stone wall and a moat 30 feet wide cut out of the solid rock to be constructed. The purpose of these defences was to protect the narrow, fertile strip of fields along the river Jordan against constant attacks by marauders and to defend some, as yet unknown, wealth within the city.

Within the town the dead were buried beneath the floors of the dwellings, a practice widespread among primitive peoples in this part of the world. Most surprising, however, was the discovery of ten heads severed from their bodies; the features of each face were modelled in clay over the upper half of the skull and the eyes indicated by inlaid shells. It seems reasonable to connect these painted skulls with some kind of ancestor-worship or fetishism, but in any case the practice is far removed from anything found in a higher level of civilization. It is remarkable that it is not until well into the Early Bronze Age (*c.* 3000 BC) that any signs of further development are to be found. Could it be that the people were not yet psychologically ready for it?

It took man a long while to reach a mental and spiritual level high enough for true culture to flourish—a step as momentous in his evolution as the transition from peasant to urban society. It is, therefore, no coincidence that these two developments went side by side. True, most of this process, so far away in time, is extremely nebulous, but through patient archaeological research and comparison with primitive societies of today it has been possible to follow the transition of the mentality of primitive man to full human consciousness; we now see it as the break-through from magic thinking to the ability of man to detach himself from his environment and discover his own individuality.

The understanding of primitive mentality is not an easy matter. In the beginning man did not think rationally or intellectually; he lived 'from the unconsciousness of instinct and intuition', as Romano Guardini once put it. Primitive man made, as yet, no distinction between inanimate objects and living beings, no difference between person and thing. The whole world, visible and invisible, material and spiritual still formed a unity in which man himself participated. All things were filled with mysterious life—'if a stone falls and hurts him, that is because an enemy sorcerer set it moving'. He existed only in the present—a present that was not yet linked with the past and the future, and thus he had no sense of time.

Very slowly man awoke from this dreamlike trance. Gradually he loosened the bonds that tied him to his world of magic. The all-pervading life-force became less abstract, crystallizing into innumerable supernatural beings, in animal, human or hybrid forms. These vaguely personified powers were still far removed from being true deities, but their evolution was a clear indication that man was beginning to distinguish between himself and nature, and to discover himself as a separate entity.

There is no means of telling when this momentous change in consciousness took place. Although the process of evolution is necessarily slow, man must have been almost at this stage before he entered into the settled life of the Neolithic period. There were so many obstacles along his path—he had to decide which natural forces were friendly, which were potentially hostile and must therefore be propitiated. It was important for him to know how his destiny could be influenced through spells and magical formulae.

On the other hand it is possible that man did not begin to personify the powers of nature until he had begun to take an active part in the shaping of his life by becoming a food producer instead of merely a hunter and food gatherer.

Birth and death came to be regarded as the two poles of life. The life-giving and life-renewing forces became man's first godhead—the Great Mother of All Things. Personified as a woman, often suckling a child, figurnes representing her have been found in many parts of the world. Here is the beginning of religion, but a very tentative beginning it was. Only with the development of urban societies, in which each member had his allotted place, did this vague divine life-giving principle, this all-embracing power, call for clearer definition. Man now conceived deities controlling every action and every natural phenomenon. Everything that happened was decided by the will of the gods, and the whole system of divine counsel could be expounded in songs, epic poems and myths. Myths tell the story of how these gods, freed from the anonymity of primeval chaos and given human form, live and act. By personifying the forces of nature as deities who could be appeased and placated, man freed himself from his position as the helpless victim of these forces; he now believed that he could actively influence his own fate by intercession with the divine powers ruling his destiny.

This was, broadly speaking, the course of evolution in Egypt as well as in Mesopotamia. That the Mesopotamian pantheon was populated by different deities, and that their religious institutions were different from those of the Egyptians is mainly owing to the difference in geographical position and political development.

The south-western part of Asia, the Middle East, saw the birth, rise and decline of some of the world's earliest and richest cultures, which lasted from the fourth millennium until the conquests of Alexander the Great in 330 BC. The whole area through which the Tigris and Euphrates and their tributaries flow, makes up the geographical entity known as Mesopotamia. In the east it is bordered by the Zagros mountains, in the north by the Anti-Taurus range and in the west by the Syrio-Arabian desert. Arabia with its endless wastes of sand and rock has never been able to support more than a nomadic population. Only the Yemen, parts of Hadramaut and a few oases offer more favourable living conditions.

In the wide sweep of the fertile crescent which runs from the Mediterranean coast along the foothills of the Anti-Taurus mountains to the river plain, cultures flourished and died, empires rose and fell, and memories of the Assyrians and the Achaemenid Persians live on for ever. But among all the Oriental cultures Mesopotamia proper—the land lying between the Two Rivers—bears the palm. This relatively small, extremely fertile area was not only the cradle of the oldest civilization, but influenced all other cultures around.

Our knowledge of the existence, nature and history of the Mesopotamian civilizations has increased so much as a result of the archaeological discoveries of the nineteenth and twentieth centuries, that we now have a relatively clear picture of what happened. Explorers and men of learning from many parts of the world have unearthed, often under conditions of extreme hardship and danger, a world almost forgotten for millennia, apart from some vague references in the Old Testament.

Modern research has proved that many of the happenings related in Genesis are not fiction at all, but based on the folk memories of nomadic Hebrew tribes. That same Ur of the Chaldees from which Terah led 'Abraham his son and all his family into the land of Canaan' was in reality one of the oldest and most venerated cities of Sumer. Many other places mentioned in the Bible have now been identified with still-existing mounds or tells, such as the ancient city of Erech (Uruk), Babel (Babylon), Assur and Nineveh. The Tower of Babel, 'whose top may reach until Heaven', was in reality a ziggurat, a high pyramid-shaped platform upon which stood a shrine. The simple Hebrew nomads saw in it a symbol of proud arrogance on the part of the Assyrians—'and now nothing will be restrained from them'. It is of particular significance that the Bible has been found to present not only verifiable historical events (such as, for example, the Hebrew exile in Babylon) but to have adapted many elements of tradition received from the earliest known advanced civilization of Mesopotamia, that of the Sumerians. The story of the Flood, for example, follows closely the Sumerian version which pre-dates it by more than two or three thousand years. The hero, who through God's will survived the Flood and became the ancestor of the human race, was already known in Sumerian mythology as Ziusudra, or as he is known in the famous Epic of Gilgamesh by his Semitic name, Uta-napishtim.

According to the Sumerian king-lists, kingship was in the beginning 'sent down from on high' and eight kings reigned for an incredibly long time until the Flood swept over them, just like the ten patriarchs from Adam to Noah.

What brings life and human interest into the study of these ancient civilizations is the vast number of clay tablets on which are recorded deeds of the kings in honour of their patron gods, correspondence between rulers and innumerable incidents of daily life. With only the sad remains of ruined cities as a guide it would be difficult to realize what a rich world of mind lay beneath the crumbling material evidence; for today these once-proud cities are no more than shapeless mounds rising up out of the empty plain.

Mesopotamia is not rich in natural resources; since there is little stone and no timber, the basic building material is mud. Bricks were made from clay and hardened by being left in the sun; baked bricks were used only in special cases, where a more durable surface was required. It is no wonder, therefore, that these houses, palaces and towering temples, all built of such a perishable material, should gradually be destroyed by wind and weather and even by man himself. The foundations of the massive walls have been preserved under a thick layer of clay and sand which was formed when the super-structure of the buildings collapsed, and it is possible to form a clear picture of the ground plan, and even of the building techniques. But while much knowledge is to be gained through excavation, written documents give us a much deeper insight into Sumerian culture.

Of these little clay tablets thousands have been found in palace and temple archives. The writing technique was quite simple: when a lump of clay had been moulded by hand to a convenient size, lines were drawn across it with the point of a sharpened reed and the letter signs (in the wedge-shaped script known as cuneiform) impressed into the damp clay; the tablets were then dried in the sun, ultimately to be filed away in the archives. Thus these people are able to speak to us across the great gulf of time. The letters or memoranda, sometimes very personal, give to these fossilized cities, temples and palaces a degree of actuality that even representational art cannot provide. We follow their devotions in hymns and prayers, read their legends and stories and learn of their trades at home and abroad. King-lists, charters, records and similar documents have brought at least some chronological order to the flow of events, a major difficulty in the study of ancient cultures. Without written records, the scholar must fall back on the fact that the deeper the excavated level the earlier it is, but the interval of time between these levels is often very difficult to assess.

The broad outlines of the history of the later Mesopotamian cultures have been worked out, but the most interesting part, the origins, remain tantalizingly hidden in the twilight of myth and saga. This much is certain, that at the dawn of the historic period (c. 2700) the southern part of Mesopotamia (Sumer) was inhabited by a number of different peoples, speaking either a Sumerian or a Semitic language, but linked by a common culture, and living together peacefully. Who were these 'Black-headed ones', as they called themselves and where did they come from? Strictly speaking they did not constitute a race, and apart from the fact that they were a non-Semitic, non-Indo-European group who portrayed themselves as stockily built, broad-headed, with a straight forehead and prominent nose, we know little about them. The current view is that the Sumerians originally came from the east, and this is supported by the fact that they themselves believed that their gods came down from the mountains in the east to teach mankind the ways of settled life and the secrets of the arts, and this myth could well be based on a distant memory of their actual origin.

From the latter part of the fourth millennium to the beginning of the second, when the Sumerians finally lost their political independence and merged entirely with the Semitic-speaking people, the story is fairly clear. The true historical period does not go further back than about 2700 BC when a king, En-me-barage-si, who can be identified with some accuracy in the part-mythical, part-historical king-lists, is actually mentioned in an inscription on a stele, which is now in the Baghdad Museum.

The king-lists themselves date from about 1800 BC and thus are post-Sumerian, but are presumably based on much older traditions. However, the dividing line between legend and history cannot be drawn with any accuracy, and there is no way of knowing whether a figure such as Gilgamesh, who built the mighty walls of Uruk and who was the hero of the great Sumerian epic, was an actual historical person or merely legendary.

Another outstanding figure was Mesilim, King of Kish, who intervened in a quarrel between two neighbouring city-states and set up a boundary stone to commemorate the fact. Although not mentioned by name in the king-lists, he can be identified with another ruler who is placed about 2600 BC. On the whole the chronological order remains rather vague, for whilst the Sumerian scribes diligently recorded the deeds of their kings and the sanctuaries and shrines they built, there is hardly any mention in these earlier tablets of events of the scribes' own day. It is no wonder, therefore, that different dates have been given for the many dynasties, while for the period before any written documents are available, the dates may vary by some centuries.

Excavation has shown that Sumer's 'foundation' phase began about 3400–3200 BC and ended during the first or second century of the third millennium. Uruk was by then a flourishing city, so that archaeologists have named this the Uruk period. The period before this, known as the 'Ubaid period, was still mainly based on a peasant economy, though the transition from peasant settlement to city-state was already taking place and prehistoric villages gradually grew into densely populated city-states.

The geographical situation of these cities played a decisive part in the shaping of urban life. The valley between the rivers was fertile, but the desert was never far away, so that enormous communal efforts were necessary to keep the fields irrigated and check the course of the rivers during winter. During the following period, the Proto-literate or Jemdet Nasr (the name derived from the main archaeological type-site which produced tablets showing early pictographic writing), evolution continued along similar lines and the trend was set for the future history of the land of Sumer.

It is strange that the Sumerians were never able to weld themselves into a single nation, even though the conditions were favourable, for they formed a natural community whose various elements shared the same views on life and religion. The area where they lived, no larger than Ireland, was dominated entirely by the Tigris and Euphrates; these, with their tributaries, not only provided the main trading arteries, but also offered a permanent water-supply on which the whole economy was based. Yet these people seem never to have had the will to unite, and this is understandable considering that the cities were preeminently sacred cities, each ruled by its patron god.

This patron god, who resided in the temple, was the undisputed owner of the city, its surrounding land and the people. As a consequence, there was much feuding between neighbouring cities. The fact that some gods ranked higher in the hierarchy was unquestionably reflected in the political importance of their places of worship. Uruk, the residence of Anu, god of heaven, owed its importance to the prestige of this patron god. The city of Kish owed its status during the Proto-literate period and for a long time thereafter, to its political control of Nippur, the seat of Enlil, king of the gods and the appointer of kings. Although the gods reigned in their cities, this did not prevent their regents from engaging in a very mundane pursuit of power. So the political centre of gravity continually shifted. Each in its turn, the dynasties of Uruk, Kish, Akshak and Ur waxed, only to wane again and vanish. The only king who was able to realize for a short while the idea of a united Sumer was Lugal-zaggesi, *palesi* or *ensi* of Uruk (*c.* 2500). Exploiting the unrest of an oppressed population, he united by brute-force most of the land under his domination. From the great walled city of Uruk he controlled all Mesopotamia, Ur was taken, he marched against Lagash and set fire to the town. Not content with his conquests, he pressed on towards the Upper Sea, the Syrian coast of the Mediterranean. How far his empire extended is not clear, but it never attained to political unity and lasted for no longer than twenty-five years, at the end of which he was defeated by Sargon of Akkad.

This Sargon had been a military officer who rebelled against his master and established his rule in the newly-built city of Akkad. His dynasty lasted for two centuries during which time the whole of Mesopotamia came under Akkadian rule, which even extended over the adjacent countries from the Persian Gulf, the 'Lower Sea', to the Mediterranean and the borderlands of Asia Minor.

With the coming of the Akkadians, Semitic-speaking people took over from the Sumerians. Though the culture remained essentially Sumerian, many fresh impulses came from this virile Semitic strain. Great changes took place in the political organization. Sargon established a completely new centre, Akkad, which was primarily the temporal capital of the king, rather than the seat of a local deity. The traditional image of the sacred city, was, however, not destroyed all at once, and although the kings now claimed divine descent, Sargon was wise enough to respect the old religious traditions, according to which the rulers were only the stewards or *ensi* and representatives on earth of the gods.

The reign of the Akkadians came to an end in 2285 BC. Enfeebled by internal strife, split by attempts to make Uruk again the capital, the country became an easy prey for the people from Gutium, a savage mountain tribe. The Guti, however, were more interested in luxurious living than political hegemony, and during the century of their rule the largest of the Sumerian cities were able to acquire considerable independence, so that when the time was ripe they had little difficulty in either expelling or subjugating the intruder.

Eventually the towns of the south mustered enough forces to drive out the hostile Guti and Utu-khengal of Uruk defeated the last king of the Guti, Tirigan, took him prisoner and 'upon his neck he set his foot'. The overthrow of the barbarians prepared the way for a splendid, though short-lived renaissance of Sumerian culture. It was Ur, however, and not Uruk which played the decisive part in the revival of Sumer's fortunes. As rulers of the country, they styled themselves 'Kings of Ur and Akkad' and like the Akkadian kings they were worshipped as gods. Under their rule, which lasted no more than a century, the arts flourished again, the temples were rebuilt in greater splendour than ever before, peace and prosperity reigned.

The lowland was continually threatened by nomadic tribes from the west and east. These were by now well established at Mari, and in the days of the last king of Ur III period, Ibbi-sin (2029 BC), many key-positions were already in Semitic hands. The dynasties of Isin, Babylon and Larsa, played an active role in the central region of Mesopotamia, and in the south the Sumerian cities were hard pressed by the Elamites. Ibbi-sin was defeated and died in captivity and in 2015 BC Ur was again destroyed.

'Oh Nanna, Ur has been destroyed, its people have been dispersed.'

The accent now shifts north and before long the Amorite kings of Babylon were dominating the whole country. But although Sumer had lost its independence, and its cities had been reduced to provincial towns, the civilizing influence of Sumer still extended far beyond its limits. There is no doubt that the achievements of the Babylonians, Kassites, Mitannians, Assyrians and Persians in the material and cultural spheres can be traced back to this highly gifted people. Sumerian art, architecture and religion have left their ineradicable imprint on all later civilizations.

Sumerian remained for long the sacred language of the temple, just as Latin is still used in some of our churches today. The cuneiform script, adapted to the Akkadian, Babylonian and Assyrian languages, was used all over the Middle East for trading and diplomatic purposes, even by the Egyptians and Hittites.

In this short resumé of Sumerian history, it can be seen how religion lay at the very centre of things. The Sumerian saw the hand of the gods in every aspect of life, he felt completely dependent upon divine will. According to the myths, man was created from the clay of the sweet waters of *Apsu* (the ocean surrounding the earth and the seat of the wise and benevolent god, Enki). But the gods had created mankind to be their servants. The lot of man was to attend upon his divine masters, to entertain them with offerings, song and dance. The gods had instructed their servants in the art of agriculture and cattle raising for that sole purpose. The relationship of man to god was that of servant to master, and this was as valid for the humble peasant as for the king and high priests. In this hierarchy the Sumerian kings were not absolute rulers in their own right, but received their power from above. They were regent *(ensi)* and when the *ensi* called himself *lugal* (king) in names such as Lugal-zaggesi, he did not forget to add the name of the god he served. The gods of other cities were not ignored and found a place in the common Sumerian pantheon, but their status was greater or less, according to the Sumerian assessment of the importance of their native city.

When the earth was created, it was believed, the gods divided the land and all its inhabitants between themselves. Every city thus had its own god who had precedence over all others there. The prosaic fact is that Sumerian towns were originally communities under duress. The artificial conditions caused by the necessity of maintaining irrigation channels brought the settlers together in jealously guarded, closely-knit societies. In religious terms this meant that the duty of every citizen was to guard the property of his god. That is why enormous walls were built to enclose not only the sanctuaries and living quarters, but also the cultivated fields (the city wall of Uruk is over 6 miles in circumference).

It was natural that within a sacred city of this nature the temple and extensive temple grounds should form the nucleus of the community. Here stood the shrine of the patron god with the palace of his *ensi*, the symbol of law and order. Here also, attached to the temple area, were the rooms for storing corn and other produce of the fields and rivers. And of this produce a portion was set aside for the maintenance of the gods and also of the many priests and temple personnel.

The priests and the *ensi* were entrusted with the administration, the management of the granaries, warehouses and workshops. They interpreted the wishes of the gods through dreams and divinations from the entrails of sacrificial animals.

It would have been all too easy to abuse this power. But in actual fact, it seems that at this early stage the priests were on the whole honest, being convinced that nothing was hidden from the all-seeing eye of their god.

Between the fourth and third millennium the temple administration had become so extensive that it was not possible to rely on memory and verbal agreements alone. In the cities, now comprising tens of thousands of inhabitants, it was imperative to keep permanent records. This is how, through simple pictographs indicating the number of jars of oil, grain and so forth, the art of writing came to be invented. This is not the place to discuss the full significance of this invention and its technical development, but the importance of its role in disseminating knowledge and perpetuating tradition can never be sufficiently emphasized. Events and ideas which in pre-literate times could only live on in the memory soon became mere legends, but written down, they could be understood by later generations as history, as something that once really happened. For the proper understanding of these people, written documents are of the greatest importance. Without these, much of the early cultures, especially in the case of Sumer, would have been forever lost. We could never have known about their hopes and fears, their ideas on death and life after death.

That they believed in some kind of life after death is evident from their graves and the many objects of daily use found in them. Forms of inhumation may not have been the same everywhere and may have changed over the centuries, but the dead were mostly buried with their most precious belongings, jewellery and ornamental weapons, and provided with food and drink for the long voyage into the next world.

The Sumerians were deeply disturbed by the sufferings of man and shortness of his life on earth—'As for mankind, numbered are their days'—and they craved to know what happened after death, about which they took an extremely gloomy view. They envisaged the dead arriving, after lengthy wanderings, in the underworld where the goddess, Ereshkigal, reigned with her court. Around this underworld flows the river Chubur (the Greek Styx), which can be only crossed with the help of a ferryman (the Charon of the Greeks). The dead can never return to earth and must dwell forever in darkness, 'where dust is their food and clay their meat, they are clothed like birds with wings for garments, over bolt and door lie dust and silence'. It is a depressing vision and accounts for the fact that the Sumerians continually prayed for a long life on earth, and turned to the god Dumuzi for succour. Dumuzi, originally a mythical king, was made immortal by Inanna, the goddess of love. As shepherd of the sacred herds of Inanna he is often depicted feeding his animals from the tree of life or protecting them against lions, the symbols of the forces of death and destruction. Dumuzi could likewise protect his supplicants. In the end, however, he himself descended into the underworld to join Inanna. From the union of Dumuzi, the earth, and Inanna, the new vegetation sprang every year. The marriage feast of Dumuzi and Inanna was celebrated annually with elaborate ceremony during which the *ensi* or high priest, representing Dumuzi, was united with the high priestess, his consort.

Sir Leonard Woolley found during his excavations at Ur a magnificent burial chamber of one of the early kings of Sumer, containing everything that he might conceivably need in the after-life. A slightly later date saw the nearby burial of the queen Shub-ad (or Puabi), attired in full splendour of golden headdress and necklace. Both the king and the queen were attended by courtiers, musicians with their beautifully inlaid harps, attendants and serving girls, soldiers in full armour and even draught animals. What precisely lay behind these strange and startling burials can only be surmised; it may have been the belief that the king, the representative of his god on earth, now entered like a god into the eternal life and that his dependents were happy to follow him there.

Whatever the Sumerians' belief in a future life may have been, we can learn little of it from their art and architecture. In contrast to the Egyptian pharaohs, the kings of Sumer never had elaborate tombs or temples built for themselves. The temple remained the house of the gods; royal graves and royal palaces remained simple, and in earlier times the palace was generally part of the sanctuary. It was only at a much later stage in history, when kings were worshipped as gods, that rivalry between the temple and palace began and the splendid palaces with their courtyards, audience halls, towers and decorated entrance gates were erected. Temple, palace and city building in Sumer reached its peak during the second half of the third millennium. Plates 1 to 4 show the formal features of Sumerian architecture, though they cannot do justice to the original grandeur of the buildings, which had to make up in sheer massiveness for the inadequacy of the available material. For, unlike Egyptian monuments built of stone, Sumerian architecture was fashioned from earth. It could not withstand the ravages of time, and centuries of wind, sun and rain have eroded these mighty structures, until they have become little more than shapeless mounds and rubble.

The history of the Middle East, after the overthrow of the Sumerian city-states, was determined partly by the Semitic Babylonians, Assyrians and Canaanites from the Syrian coast and the Lebanon, and partly by tribes of Indo-Europeans—the Kassites, Mitannians, Hittites and Persians. Apart from Babylon, the immediate successor to Sumer, the political and cultural centre gradually shifted northwards, and the land of

Sumer and Akkad was reduced to a provincial backwater, coveted only for the fertility of the soil. The later centres were Nineveh, on the upper reaches of the Tigris, the capital of Assyria, Hattusas (modern Boghazköy) the capital of the Hittites, Pasargadae, Persepolis, Susa and Ecbatana, the royal seats of the Achaemenid Persians.

The struggle for control of the Middle East continued as in Sumerian times, and years of confusion followed periods of consolidation; Babylon and the capitals of Assyria were the main rivals and each for a time became the centre of a great empire. Both Assyrians and Babylonians were essentially the cultural successors of the Sumerians and their literature, architecture, religion and script were modelled entirely on the arts of Sumer. The chief god of Babylon, Marduk, was originally the city god, but became the principal god of the entire kingdom. The Assyrians were more concerned with the material side of life and their magnificent palaces have become a by-word. Stone reliefs, depicting the victories of the kings, hunting scenes and a life of wealth and glory, lined their walls. These palaces and temples, of which so many detailed descriptions survive, were sacked and looted when the Assyrian Empire fell to the Babylonians in 612 BC.

After the fall of the Neo-Babylonian empire, the Achaemenid Persians created a powerful empire stretching from the Greek coast of Asia Minor to India, and from Egypt to the Black Sea. By importing builders and craftsmen from Greek Ionia, goldsmiths from Egypt, precious wood and stones from far and wide, the kings of Persia emulated and ultimately outstripped the wealthy and powerful Assyrians.

Thus it was that the heritage of Sumer spread across the whole of the Mediterranean and the Middle Eastern world.

Plate 1
Sheep-pen from a limestone trough from Uruk.
British Museum

The origins of Sumerian building activities are lost in the mists of early prehistory. Experience, however, teaches us that the earliest attempts at building were no more than simple shelters for man and beast. Man practised his skill on basic structural forms and thus became sensitive to space shaped by his own hands. A feeling for space alone is not enough for the creation of true architecture. Form must be enriched by the spirit and the primitive structure must rise above its purely utilitarian purpose if it is to attain monumentality. As soon as the early neolithic peasant conceived his world as one governed by living deities for whom he felt it his duty to build places of worship, this higher purpose found its first expression. Because the gods were superior to man and the rulers of his fate, the dwelling on earth where they manifested themselves was built larger, more beautiful and stronger than the huts of mortal man. However intricate architectural form may have become in its fully developed stage, man learned his trade by building huts, stables and granaries. The few remains of the earliest Sumerian period prove this point sufficiently.

The earliest temples in southern Mesopotamia are those which were found at the famous and time-honoured city of Eridu. Remains, probably dating from the pre-Sumerian period, go back to well into the fourth millennium BC. They were small, one-storeyed, buildings. The walls, made of hard packed clay *(adobe)* were built on a square or oblong ground plan, the corners orientated to the points of the compass. The numerous successive temples, all superimposed upon the earlier foundations, gradually became larger and more impressive. Because of the tradition that made it imperative to incorporate the previous foundations beneath those of the succeeding temples, it has not been easy to make out the ground plans, but all were rectangular and not circular, as the relief on the trough would seem to show.

This limestone trough, now in the British Museum, probably came from the temple of the goddess Inanna at Uruk, and dates from the end of the third millennium BC. The relief represents the sacred flock of sheep which belonged to the goddess and was a symbol of the eternal renewal of life. The bundles of reeds tied in this particular fashion on either side of the roof show that it is dedicated to Inanna. This hut, unlike the temples at Eridu, was made of bundles of reeds, the heads being tied together at the top to make a barrel-shaped building. In the deepest excavated levels at Ur, pieces of mud-plaster have been found, on the inner side of which were impressions of reeds tied together in sheaves. This would seem to indicate that the outer walls of the reed huts were strengthened with layers of mud—very likely painted. In the Epic of Gilgamesh, the hero lives in a similar reed hut, notwithstanding his high rank. Even today in the southern part of Iraq, the Marsh Arabs build reed huts very like those pictured on the trough five thousand years ago. The fact that this traditional manner of building has endured for centuries is, however, not so interesting as the fact that their outer appearance seemed attractive enough for the Sumerians to continue to reproduce this appearance in brick and stone.

Plate 2
The remains of the so-called Mosaic Temple
in the E-anna precinct at Uruk

Uruk, Erech of the Bible, was not only one of the most densely populated cities in the land of Sumer and its political capital, but by the turn of the fourth and third millennium, it was already the chief religious centre. The double city wall which encircled the town was nearly six miles in length and was fortified by more than eight hundred bastions or towers. According to the legends it was built by the hero Gilgamesh, King of Uruk. Most cities possessed a temple for their own patron god, but the city wall of Uruk enclosed two main temples: one of Anu, the god of heaven, and the great sacred precinct of Inanna, the queen of heaven. The cult of Inanna, later called Ishtar, and in her aspect of earth goddess (the heiress of the Great Mother Goddess of the neolithic peasants), seems to have had a greater appeal to the people that that of Anu.

Very little of the goddess' precinct, called *E-anna* (the house of heaven) has survived, in comparison with the other temples of Uruk, but fortunately the main architectural features and the decoration have been preserved to some extent and show clearly that the Sumerians were not content with simple masonry and flat surfaces, but were intent on bringing some relief to their flat-roofed, massive structures. Originally the mud-brick walls had had to be strengthened with buttresses in order to prevent erosion, but the effect of buttresses and recesses was so pleasing to the eye with their contrast of light and shade, that this device developed into a deliberate art form which is found throughout all Sumerian architecture—it was so popular that it was even used on inside walls.

In the relatively small mosaic temple *(plate 2)*, the walls were decorated with a delicate pattern of baked clay cones, painted with red, white and black. The walls were first thickly plastered with clay into which the cones were pressed making geometric patterns, triangles and lozenges. These patterns may well have been a reminder of the plaited wool or bark with which the inner walls of the reed huts were decorated.

Plate 3
The ziggurat of the moon god Nanna at Ur,
north-east façade

Building activities were renewed at Ur on a truly monumental scale after the long domination of the Semitic Sargonids and the reign of terror of the 'hordes of Gutium'. During the reign of Ur-nammu (2113–2096), the founder of the third dynasty of Ur, the most impressive and best preserved monument of late Sumerian architecture was built and dedicated to the Moon god, Nanna. It represents the apogee of architectural style already established during the Uruk period *(plate 2)*.

From the fourth millennium onwards temple building in general followed the same principles. The temple itself remained a compact rectangular structure made less heavy by buttresses, mosaics and mural painting. It dominated the city by its height, standing on an artifical platform. These platforms or terraces were a characteristic feature of all Sumerian temple architecture. The Eridu temples and the shrine of Anu at Uruk stood on a raised platform to which stairs gave access. These artificial mounds were called *ziggurats*, which means simply temple-tower.

The idea behind raising a temple above ground level is not quite clear, but there are a number of good reasons why the Sumerians should have done this. One obvious reason is to place the temple out of danger. The low-lying ground in southern Mesopotamia was always liable to be flooded, therefore, by placing the sacred building on a platform it would keep it out of harm's way. It is also true that a large building is made even larger by being placed on a podium giving it a certain grandeur. It may have been a reminiscence of the mythical belief that the gods originally came down from the sacred mountains to the east of Sumer and that the true habitation of the gods was on the mountain-tops. In later times the idea of a temple-tower seems to have been to accentuate the distance between god and man. However, not all temples were built on a ziggurat; very often there were smaller shrines enclosed within the sanctuary at ground level.

The ziggurat of Ur-nammu was built around the core of a much older temple platform going back at least as far as the Uruk period (3400–3200 BC). The whole building covered an area of 190 × 130 ft. According to present knowledge this is the first time that the stepped ziggurat appears, a principle which was adhered to until the last Neo-Babylonian towers. Originally this ziggurat rose to heigh of 60 ft and had three stages, access being gained by staircases. The outer walls show a distinct batter (a leaning inwards) and were decorated with buttresses. The small shrine which crowned the topmost stage has been completely lost, but it was probably a single white-washed chamber. It was probably the bridal chamber where the high-priest and priestess of Dumuzi and Inanna celebrated the sacred marriage during the spring festival. In a description of the ziggurat of Babylon, which rose in eight stages, Herodotus (I, 181–182) mentions that on the topmost storey was a great shrine, inside which stood a richly covered couch and silver table. But there was no statue. Nobody remained there at night but one woman chosen by the gods from all the women of the city.

On the north-eastern façade, three vast stairways led up to the first stage; they met at a partially preserved gatehouse. The outer casing of the body of the ziggurat was made of baked bricks set in bitumen, with 'weeper' holes at intervals to allow water to escape. The base of the ziggurat has now been reconstructed so that it is now possible to imagine just how monumental this structure once was.

Plate 4
Living and business quarters at Ur

The temple precinct was the spiritual, economic and political centre of the Sumerian cities, for the city god was the absolute master and there was no activity but in his service.

The temple, representing the deity, was the great landowner. However, the large household of priests and temple servants organized on patriarchal principles could never have existed without the support of a vigorous town and country population. The enormous size of the temple precincts, the vast area enclosed by the city-walls, and the harbour on the river, prove clearly that the more important Sumerian cities were far more than peasant settlements. Such immense structures as the E-anna sanctuary at Uruk *(plate 2)*, the defensive walls and other similar architecture at Ur, Kish and elsewhere can only be explained as the communal work of a people living closely united under a central government. It is not impossible that at Ur, which covered an area of 225 acres or at Uruk, whose walls enclosed a space of more than a square mile, there was a population of many tens of thousands.

There is not a great deal of information concerning the living quarters of early Sumerian cities. But from the excavations of the so-called Isin-Larsa town in the south-eastern part of Ur one gets a general impression of life in a Sumerian city. The living quarters grew up around the sacred precincts with narrow, twisting alleys and streets. The houses were built of sun-dried brick, mostly one, but sometimes two storeys high. They were mostly private dwellings, but there are indications of business premises, shops, private chapels and even a school.

As is still customary in the East, the houses faced inwards onto a courtyard and showed only blind walls towards the street. A narrow doorway led into the courtyard which gave access to the living rooms. This open court provided light for the otherwise windowless rooms and it was probably the site of the hearth, which was a prominent feature in every house. Sometimes there were stairs to the upper storey or a flat roof where the family enjoyed the cool of the morning and evening. The sanitation was quite adequate with toilets and bathrooms, while drains were kept in good repair. Larger and smaller houses stood wall to wall, huddled together in the manner usual over the whole of the Middle East and eastern Mediterranean.

Babylon, the never-to-be-forgotten city of the Bible, stands at the end of the glorious architectural history of the Mesopotamian world. Herodotus who visited the city in the fifth century BC wondered at its splendour: 'The Assyrians possessed many large cities, but the most famous of them was Babylon. It was the most beautiful of all cities that we have seen'.

Since the German archaeologist Robert Koldewey started his excavations in 1899 much of its buried splendour has come to light again. During the eighteen years of his work he uncovered the foundations of temples, city walls and gateways. Much has been recovered, but not enough to give a clear picture and we must still rely on literature for our main source of knowledge.

It was the Babylon of Nebuchadnezzar II (604–561) that Herodotus described. Under this ruler Babylon experienced a vigorous, although short-lived, cultural renaissance. Little is known about the building activities of the first Babylonian empire founded by Hammurabi during the nineteenth century BC, because its foundations now lie below the water table and are therefore inaccessible. Moreover the buildings of the Neo-Babylonian phase were built for the most part directly on the foundations of the older structures.

The enormous city wall some twelve miles long partly followed the direction of an earlier defensive wall. Again Herodotus says 'first there was a moat, deep and wide and full of water'. The space between these two walls was filled with rubble and further strengthened with reed matting. The outer body of the wall on the side of the moat and another on the inside were made of baked bricks. The inner wall was 26 ft thick, the outer 22 ft, while the over-all height was about 48 ft. The outer wall was fortified at regular intervals with towers and the battlements along the top were wide enough for chariots to ride along. There were nine main gateways, of which the most impressive was the Ishtar Gate *(see plate 6)*. The history of its building is remarkable: the level of the Processional Way leading up to the gate was raised twice during the process of building, and the parts already completed were buried under a thick layer of earth. Plate 5 shows the west wall of the inner gatehouse in its initial stage which was later raised to a height of 32 ft 9 in. The same bull and dragon motifs which were used in the final version appear here, but without colour and simply modelled in relief on to the brickwork. In the second phase, the relief was abandoned for flat figures in coloured and glazed bricks. In the final phase both techniques were combined, relief and colour. One can imagine that the patron, probably Nebuchadnezzar II, rejected the first two projects as unsatisfactory and decided on the third, more brilliant version. But it is hardly likely that aesthetic considerations alone inspired these costly alterations. The raising of the water-table may have necessitated the continuous rebuilding.

Plate 6
The Ishtar Gate, Babylon. Reconstruction of
the outer gate, now in the Staatliche Museen
zu Berlin

The Processional Way led from the high
temple-tower of Marduk through the double
Ishtar Gate to a ceremonial hall outside the
wall, in which the Babylonians and before
them, the Assyrians celebrated the New
Year festival. The hall has not been completely excavated.

The outer casing of the gate was finished
in glazed bricks with alternate rows of bulls
and mythical dragons *(shirrushim)* in relief
in white, yellow, brown and green on a deep
blue background. These symbols of the god
Marduk and goddess Ishtar, which give the
gate its name, face in the direction which
would be taken by processions to the temple,
as if they accompanied it on its way. The
authenticity of this reconstruction is based
on the evidence of extensive excavations.
The recovered material is in the Berlin State
Museum and is carefully pieced together.

The glazed tiles with animals in moulded
relief, were found *in situ*.

Plate 7
*The Funerary Monument of Cyrus, Pasargadae,
Persia*

Persia did not emerge into the clear light of
history until the time of the Achaemenid
kings, when it suddenly reached its political
and artistic peak. Cyrus II (559–529 BC) who
called himself "the Achaemenid" and is
generally know as Cyrus the Great, united
the Medes and Persians and became the
founder of the mighty Persian Empire,
which at its height stretched from Mesopotamia, Syria, to Asia Minor and the eastern
borders of classical Greece to India. This
huge empire, consisting of many different
nationalities with vastly divergent cultures
and traditions was open to the most het-
erogeneous artistic influences. Besides an
original Iranian (Urartian and Median)
heritage, as well as Egyptian and Mesopotamian art forms, Achaemenid architectural features show definite traces of Ionian-
Greek influences.

The funerary monument of Cyrus at
Pasargadae shows this Greek element,
especially in its steeply pitched roof. It is
probably that Greek workmen were brought
in to do the work. Artists and builders from
the whole of the ancient world were drawn
to Pasargadae, Susa and Persepolis to build
the magnificent royal palaces *(see plates
8–12)*.

Beside Greek influences, Mesopotamian
influences are discernible in the six-stepped
platform of massive limestone blocks on
which the monument rests. Like the
Sumerian and Babylonian ziggurats, it raises
the building above the ordinary human level
although Cyrus and his successors never
claimed divine status. They were content to
be called 'King of Kings'.

Strabo tells us that the words once inscribed at the entrance to the tomb read as
follows: 'O man, I am Cyrus, the founder
of the Persian empire. Grudge me not therefore this my monument'. It is no god that
speaks thus. Man speaks here to fellow man.
A man, moreover, who even in death still
clung to the enchantment of life. The
monument, now so stark, once stood, according to the Greek writers, within a
garden—'a paradise'—enlivened by water
courses and fragrant with flowers. Historically it is the prototype of the mausolea of the
later Islamic period, which also stood in
luxurious gardens, and which reached the
acme of perfection in the Taj Mahal at
Delhi.

Unfortunately the prayers of Cyrus went
unheeded. The grave was rifled after the
conquest of Alexander the Great and the
fact that it is fairly well preserved was not
due to the fame of the Persian king, but to
the belief after the Arab conquest (seventh
century AD) that it was the resting place of
the mother of King Solomon and conse-
quentially revered as such.

Plate 8
The main stairway leading to the palace-terrace,
Persepolis

Between 559 and 550 Cyrus built the city of
Pasargadae, where he had gained a decisive
victory over his Median rival, Astyages, but
his successors soon abandoned Pasargadae
for Ecbatana and Susa, originally an
Elamite city, which was situated more
favourably on the main trading routes. Unfortunately very little is left of these two
cities, so that our knowledge of ancient
Persian architecture depends mostly on the
ruins of Persepolis.

Persepolis in the Parsa-Persis, the heart of
the Persian empire, is situated about thirty
miles to the north-east of Shiraz on the
upper reaches of the River Pulvar. Darius I
(521–485 BC) chose it not only for his
residence but for a religious centre. The
Persian New Year festivals were celebrated
here. During the reigns of Darius, Xerxes I
(485–465) and Artaxerxes I (465–424) a vast
complex of splendid palaces, courts and
audience halls arose. All the wealth and the
immense treasures of the Persian empire
contributed to its magnificence, so that its
fame was widespread, and, when a century

later Alexander the Great visited Persepolis
during his victorious campaign he was
fascinated by its Oriental magnificence and
fin de siècle refinement. It was Romain
Ghirshman who first acknowledged the
religious importance of Persepolis.

The Palace was so planned that the accent
was placed on the processional way from
the propylaea towards the Audience Hall.
Behind the public buildings lie the private
apartments of the king, his courtiers, military
barracks, treasuries and store-rooms. The
whole area was surrounded by a 60-ft high
stone wall and was therefore an almost impregnable stronghold.

The palace area was built on a high terrace which was reached by an imposing
stairway on the north-western side. Like the
staircases of the Baroque palaces in Europe
more than two thousand years later, the
processions would move first in an opposite
direction, then turn to face each other, and
unite finally at the entrance—"Gateway of
all Lands". This march and counter-march
of the festive crowds with banners flying
and trumpets sounding must have been an
impressive sight. And the theatrical effect of
these monumental stairways was fully
realized just as it had been earlier in
Sumerian and Babylonian architecture.

Plate 9
The Gateway of all Lands, Persepolis

When the visitor to Persepolis had climbed
the stairs, he passed through the magnificent
gatehouse, built by Xerxes I, before approaching the famous Audience Hall, the
apadana. The gatehouse was a square
building in plan with a flat roof supported
by four slender columns with fluted shafts
and bell-shaped bases, surmounted by
vertical volutes and bull capitals. It opened
on three sides with narrow passages between heavy tongue walls. Enormous
winged bulls guarded the outer entrances,
while human-faced, bearded bulls stood at
the exits. The walls are covered in relief
carvings, which almost give the impression
of free-standing sculptures. This technique
had also been used in the palaces of the
Assyrian kings, but the fuller, less severe
treatment shows the more sensual Persian
approach.

At Persepolis, structural and sculptural
features are interwoven into one coherent
unity. The massive bodies are not added to
the limestone wall as a decorative layer that
could be removed easily, but they grow out
of the stone as if released from the solid
mass. This may be due to Greek influence,
as the Greeks were very much concerned
with the plasticity of the body and the
Ionian artists may have found here a com-
promise between the severe Oriental form-
ality and the Greek love of naturalism.

Plate 10
The palace of Darius, Persepolis

Because of the great material wealth of the Achaemenids, many different building styles converged at Persepolis. Buildings in marble or limestone on a square plan, following Egyptian and Greek techniques are found side by side with the age-old baked and sun-dried mud brick techniques—often in the same building. The arch was not unknown, but it was of only secondary importance and did not play a part in the main structural features. The ground plans were square or rectangular, hardly ever curvilinear. The main buildings, the Gateway of all Lands, the *apadana* and the throne room, were all built on a square plan; whether for technical reasons, or whether because it was meant to accentuate the centralizing effect of the square, is, of course, not known. In any case the Persian architects could not have been concerned with the optical effect of a square, for the many columns and pilasters completely dominated the spatial effect. The wealth of columns reminds one of Egyptian or Ionian-Greek temples, but the final effect is quite different. The Egyptians and Greeks spaced their columns strictly according to the structure of the main building, while the columns at Persepolis stand in monotonous rows throughout the whole building, and can be justified artistically only by their great height and the gigantic proportions of the room.

The palace façades, however, show a less tedious and better proportioned aspect, full of elegance. The *apadana*, the Audience Hall of Darius and the throne-room of Xerxes, both have high pillared porticoes and monumental stairways. The palace of Darius, standing on a high platform, also possessed a portico with columns on the north side. On the south side it was approached by an elegant stairway, on the smooth parapet of which a large army of guards and servants marched, carved in relief. From the left and the right they march towards the centre of the terrace, keepers and guardians of their king and his palace. The main interest lies, however, in its architectural features. Enormous monoliths are used to make door-jambs and deep-set windows. They give the impression of prefabricated units of concrete, between which the walls hang. The lintels show cavetto mouldings in the Egyptian manner, probably the work of Egyptian workmen. The palace of Darius was the first, and for a long time to come, the only example of window architecture in the Near East.

Plate 11
Artaxerxes I giving audience. From the north door of the throne hall, Persepolis

Every smooth surface on terrace walls and parapets was filled with figured reliefs in the Assyrian manner. The pious care with which even the smallest detail was treated is a heritage of Assyrian artists, though the subject matter is typically Persian in its courtly conventional treatment.

The main emphasis falls on the figure of the royal master, to whom representatives of his subject people bring tributes, gifts and adoration as culmination of the New Year ceremonies. The king, seated on the 'Throne of the Nations' is drawn on a larger scale than his subjects. He receives in audience an official, who approaches his master in an obsequious manner. Behind the king stand his courtiers and his weapon bearers. Two fire altars are placed before his throne. Median and Persian soldiers, the palace guard, fill the four lower registers of the relief, separated by bands decorated with rosettes. It seems that the Achaemenid kings were always accompanied on official occasions by a large retinue.

A very similar relief of Darius I, differing only in small details, was found in the courtyard of the Treasury and it was probably this that Artaxerxes copied; the effect of symmetry is very marked in Persian architecture and decoration. The stiff regularity of this relief produced by the vertical axis pointing towards the figure of the king, the monotonous horizontal rows of soldiers and the fact that the action takes place against a flat background, gives an entirely different effect from the Assyrian reliefs. The Assyrian artists tried to give the illusion of a spatial background, while the Persian relief is weakened by its undisguised flatness. It is possible however that this was done on purpose to stress the solemn atmosphere of the ceremonial scene.

Plate 12
The rock-cut tomb of Darius, Naqsh-i-Rustem
Darius I (521–485 BC), the founder of Persepolis and the first of the Achaemenid kings
to call himself proudly 'King of Kings',
built himself a remarkable funeral chamber,
hewn from the solid rock. His successors
Xerxes and Artaxerxes followed his example
and built similar rock tombs.

The tomb itself consists of a narrow
chamber, deep in the rock behind a cruciform façade. The horizontal arm of the cross
gives a good idea of a palace façade. A wide
door with a cavetto cornice above it is
flanked by two slender columns on each
side. They show the usual high, composite
capitals, the impost blocks of which are
shaped into the foreparts of two bulls. The
columns support an entablature which in an
actual palace would probably have been
made out of wood. Considering the weight
of the beams combined with the extreme
height of the rooms in the palaces at Persepolis (the *apadana* was 65 ft high) and the
natural length of the wooden beams, it was
inevitable that the large halls had so many
columns to support the roof.

The lower vertical arm of the cross was
left unadorned, probably to leave room for
cult festivities or memorial services.

The upper part shows the glorification of
the dead king. Darius stands on a large
dais which has elaborately turned legs
ending in lion's-claws. Two rows, each of
fourteen figures representing twenty-eight
subject nations upholding the king's throne,
carry the dais on uplifted arms. In his left
hand Darius carries a bow. He supports it
on his foot. This attitude is quite common
and may have had a special significance. His
right hand is raised in supplication towards
the god Ahurah-Mazda, the only god worshipped by the Persians according to the
teachings of Zoroaster. The god is depicted
in symbolic form of a winged sun-disk,
from which the head and shoulders of the
god rise up, accompanied by the moon. A
small domed fire-altar stands before the
king. The Mazdaians were fire-worshippers,
but it is not known whether the cruciform
façade had any special meaning, for it does
not appear anywhere else in Persian symbols.
It is only found here and in the similar
rock-graves of his successors.

Plate 1
Sheep-pen from a limestone trough from Uruk.
British Museum

Plate 2
The remains of the so-called Mosaic Temple
in the E-anna precinct at Uruk

Plate 3
The ziggurat of the moon god Nanna at Ur,
north-east façade

Plate 4
Living and business quarters at Ur

Plate 5
The Ishtar Gate, Babylon. West wall of the
inner gatehouse

Plate 6
The Ishtar Gate, Babylon. Reconstruction of
the outer gate, now in the Staatliche Museen
zu Berlin

Plate 7
The Funerary Monument of Cyrus, Pasargadae,
Persia

Plate 8
The main stairway leading to the palace-terrace,
Persepolis

Plate 9
The Gateway of all Lands, Persepolis

Plate 10
The palace of Darius, Persepolis

Plate 11
Artaxerxes giving audience. From the north
door of the throne hall, Persepolis

Plate 12
The rock-cut tomb of Darius, Naqsh-i-Rustem

Ancient Egypt

Plates 13 to 36

EMMA BRUNNER-TRAUT

AFTER THE PRIMITIVE BEGINNINGS of pre-history came the astonishing phenomenon of the marvellous flowering of Egyptian culture. For three thousand years this ancient culture flourished through political storms and upheavals, and even today its imprint is to be seen. What took place along the banks of the River Nile, in the year 3000 BC would seem like a dream today were it not for the incontrovertible facts.

At that time pyramids, palaces and dwelling houses arose, tombs for nobles and war-lords were built. Books of wisdom and moral precepts were written. An organized state was built up, surveyors and astronomers observed the annual floods of the Nile; the calendar was fixed; the art of writing captured the fleeting word and carried ideas from place to place and from generation to generation. Lyrical emotions were expressed in music and dance and many musical instruments invented. Painting, wall-reliefs and sculpture drew their inspiration from religion and their expression from a fixed canon of ideal proportions or classical composition. A complex mythology explained systematically the powers of heaven and of nature, in very much the same way as modern science attempts to classify these phenomena.

Of the earliest events in Egypt during the fifth and fourth millennia, very little is known. Some mural paintings, primitive sculpture, and a few examples of jewellery as well as pottery and stone vessels belonging to the Predynastic period have been found. The people lived in simple reed or palm-leaf huts, they buried their dead in shallow graves in a contracted position without any special orientation.

Suddenly a new era of progress arose embracing the whole of the ancient Orient, during which well-developed cultures appeared in the Far East, Mesopotamia, the island of Crete as well as Egypt. This happened about 3000 BC.

Unlike the others, the Egyptian culture developed in isolation due to the strength of its natural boundaries: the Mediterranean to the north, the deserts to the east and west, the cataract to the south. Egypt therefore maintained her characteristic features for an unusually long time, undisturbed by foreign influences.

According to Manetho, who wrote a history of the Egyptian people during the reign of Ptolemy I, thirty dynasties ruled over Egypt. This dynastic period is divided into the Old Kingdom, the Middle Kingdom and the New Kingdom—a division already made in antiquity. These three periods were interrupted by periods of political and economic decline, the first caused by internal difficulties, the second by foreign invaders. The Second Intermediate period, as the latter is known, was brought about by the invasion and subsequent conquest by the Hyksos, a people from the east. Finally at the end of the New Kingdom, Egypt came under foreign rule, and this continued under the rule of the Greek Ptolemies until Egypt became a Roman province just before the beginning of the Christian era.

On the architectural side, the Old Kingdom can be described as the period of pyramid building. A wholesome and orderly culture prevailed, based on an agricultural peasant society. The pharaoh was the sacred king to whose life-power the life of the people was entrusted. An absolute divine ruler, he exerted complete power over the land and its people. Even in the underworld his authority was equal to that of the gods. His residence was at Memphis in Lower Egypt, a large straggling place with courtyards and gardens. The most important monuments of this period are in the necropolises of Giza and Saqqara.

After long years of general disorder during the First Intermediate period, Egypt went through a new phase of unification, re-orientation and re-thinking. Literature and sculpture at this time showed a certain inwardness and spirituality. Man recognized his responsibility for his own deeds; the mood became introspective. Pharaoh lost much of his divine power; the local chieftains disputed his sovereignty. At this time the royal residence and tombs were located in Middle Egypt. The architectural style is on a less colossal scale, although the labyrinth of Amenemhet III must have surpassed the pyramids of Giza in both size and grandeur, according to classical writers. After the unrest of the years between the Middle Kingdom and the New Kingdom it became necessary to concentrate on military strength. Powerful fortresses were built along the eastern part of the Delta and on the Nubian border. The New Kingdom was a time of great expansion—Egypt came into close contact with the Asian civilizations and waged war in the east. Great prosperity followed the conquests and the sudden acquisition of wealth led to excesses deteriorating into decadence. The capital now moved to Upper Egypt, Thebes, near modern Luxor, where imposing temples and tombs were built by the kings. Nubia was conquered and temples were erected with missionary zeal as far south as the fourth Cataract. Amon was the supreme god, his priests constituted a state within the state. Finally after continuous wars, Egypt lost its independence and was conquered by the Assyrians, Persians and Greeks in turn.

This very short survey may serve as an introduction to a less superficial review of Egyptian history which follows.

THE OLD KINGDOM

The first historical ruler, Menes, achieved the unification of Lower and Upper Egypt, an event ritually re-enacted by every subsequent pharaoh. The heraldic signs of the two parts of the country, from the hieroglyph 'to unite', are symbolically added to the royal name. The history of these earliest kings is still steeped in magic and myth. The divine pharaoh was guided by the sun-god Ra, and there was no looking forward to the future since the eye was always turned upwards to the heavens. The result was a rigid conservatism. It is true that some innovations took place, but these changes were involuntary and the old traditions remained unaltered. Education was directed towards ensuring obedience to the existing order as given by divine counsel.

History, in its proper sense, began with the invention of writing. Labels and jar-sealing inscriptions, stating the date and contents, are amongst the earliest Egyptian written documents. Political events were recorded on ornamental slate palettes. These archaic signs were not yet written words in the strictest sense, but still pictures, and consequently their interpretation is extremely conjectural. The first monumental burial chambers also appear at this time.

In spite of a tentative beginning, this period witnessed an amazing progress. The Step Pyramid built by the architect Imhotep at Saqqara for Zoser, the greatest king of the Third Dynasty, rises to a height of 200 feet above the level of the plateau (*plate 13*). Imhotep's fame was so widespread that the Greeks still knew of him as Imuthes, the physician, philosopher and statesman. This monument is the expression of an immovable, unalterable order, of a continuity for all eternity. Egyptian representational art shows the same feeling for order and precision; the figures keep to a strict sequence, with the king first, then his wife, son and servants.

Egyptian script developed from the purely pictorial into an abstract alphabetical script, based on its phonetic values with the help of determinatives. The hieroglyphs, the sacred script, an elaborate manner of writing, was quite unsuitable for daily use. For writing on papyrus the scribes evolved a modified script in which the pictorial characters were abbreviated: the hieratic script. This script was simplified still further during the seventh century BC and is known as demotic writing.

The Fourth Dynasty was the time of the great pyramids of Giza. The kings Kheops, Khephren and Mykerinus (Greek translations of the Egyptian Khufu, Khafra and Menkara) built their vast funerary monuments on the edge of the desert, so defying mortality for all time. A large number of mastabas of courtiers are grouped around the pyramids. The mastaba (Arabic for bench), so-called because of its similarity to the benches outside modern Egyptian houses, is an oblong mound with articulated, panelled outer walls, built over a subterranean burial chamber. They stand in straight lines forming streets leading up to the pyramid. The interiors are richly decorated according to the rank of the occupant during his lifetime. Most of the outer casing originally consisting of slabs of fine limestone has now been stolen, but the painted reliefs have been preserved in several instances, particularly the well-known examples from Saqqara of the Fifth and Sixth Dynasty. Unas, the last king of the Fifth Dynasty built his pyramid at Saqqara and his tomb is the first to have texts carved on the walls of corridors and chambers. These Pyramid Texts consist of ritual and magical formulae; they supply the dead man with the words which will permit his entry into the Next World. Later on similar formulae for the well-being of the dead are found in burial chambers, and they were also written on papyri placed inside coffins.

Ti, Ptah-hotep and Mereruka did not pray in vain that their names might live for ever: they are on the lips of every Egyptologist, and the beauty of their tombs is truly immortal. The walls of the buried chambers were covered from floor to ceiling with gaily painted reliefs of a very high standard of workmanship, portraying scenes of daily life on earth. Starting from the entrance the scenes progress from life to death. Sport, amusements, music and dance, banqueting scenes are followed by fishing in the marshes and lakes, fowling with a throwing stick from a shallow boat. Labour in the fields, cattle raising, and milking, as well as the fattening of geese are pictured as aspects of a happy, active life. Cattle are driven through a ford, crocodiles charmed with magic words. We see the activities in workshops, the delivery of tithes, and the morning toilet of the master. Then his funeral procession approaches, the ritual journey of the mummy to mythical places, and at the very end a long processional march with funerary gifts and offerings. In this manner the dead man could be assured of his existence in the Other World. The value of these reliefs lies not only in their high standard of artistry, but in the clear light they shed on Egyptian life and thought.

Egyptian representational art, whether wall-paintings, high or low relief, treats its subject matter in an entirely different way from western art since the Greeks. An exhaustive treatise on primitive art would be out of place here, but as Egyptian art can be considered as the prototype not only of every later culture, including the pre-Greek cultures, but also of the art of primitives and children, a few words must be said about its theory.

Egyptian art does not seek to portray objects in perspective; it could more accurately be described as 'aspective'. The artist does not show the figure as it would be seen in three dimensions, but takes the figure apart and represents each part as he knows it to be. It is as if he walks round his subject and notes its details, sometimes from above, sometimes from the side or front. He then superimposes one detail upon another, in order of their importance. This pattern or canon soon became convention and all artists worked according to a set rule. The artistic value achieved within this convention depended entirely on the sculptor, quality of materials and local traditions. The basic principle of this type of representation remained constant: the head in profile, the eye shown in full-view on the face, the shoulders in frontal position, while the rest of the body shows a mixture of frontal and lateral views. A square table can remain a square, a round plate a circle, dimensions are never foreshortened or lengthened, because the objects are rendered flat as seen from above. Aspective art has its own rules. In perspective art the figure diminishes in size according to its distance from the viewer. This does not hold with aspective art, where there is no relation between the foreground and the background. The figures are represented according to their relative importance. A person can be large or small on the same picture, depending on his place in the story it tells. A king is shown large when a supplicant or servant stands before him, but small when he himself stands before a divine being. The artist enjoyed great freedom in his composition, and could show in the same picture objects in associations which would be physically impossible in reality. He could paint a lake floating in mid-air, if it was necessary for the composition to have a fish in that particular position. Libations poured from a jar could defy gravity and spread over the heads of several people. He could divide the composition if necessary and draw the same person twice in different places. In the story he has moved on and so is shown engaged in his next activity; two events happening simultaneously in cinematographic sequence.

These few remarks may suffice to sketch the theory of Egyptian art in which the basic principles remained unchanged from Predynastic times to the final decadence, although the style developed towards greater clarity and severity. The straight line, angles and corners are explored in all their potentialities and there is a tendency towards geometrical design and ornamentation, and at the same time a love for detail, a delight in elegance and flowing line, a balance between faithful representation and abstract treatment. Both sculpture and painting were applied to palace and dwelling house, although primarily reserved for temples and tombs. Because the ordinary dwelling houses were constructed of unbaked mud-brick they have not survived, and the paintings on floors, walls and ceilings have disappeared for ever. With the death of Pepi II, the last king of the Sixth Dynasty, who lived to the age of ninety, the Old Kingdom came to an end.

As long as the kings were strong personalities, the absolute monarchy could survive, but the local chiefs were always striving after independence and with the decline of dynastic power a state of feudal anarchy arose. Long years of internal struggles and chaos racked the land. The treasury was empty, the workmen on the necropolises of Giza and Saqqara could not be paid, bloody revolutions followed. 'What was above came down.' 'The land turned round like a potter's wheel, the Nile was red with blood.' 'The lord of the manor was his own messenger.' 'The serving girl was dressed in finery.' 'The man who had never possessed a harp, now played.' Tombs were robbed, official documents flung into the street. Nobody trusted his neighbour— 'A man killed his own brother.'

THE MIDDLE KINGDOM

The dark ages of Egypt during the First Intermediate period lasted for about two hundred years, until at last a prince of Thebes—Antef—succeeded in subduing the local chiefs and reunited the country. (*c.* 2133 BC). The old order had broken down, and a new spirit arose, fresh minds were brought to bear on the old problems. The period between the Old and New Kingdom was the time when philosophy and literature reached the highest peak. Apart from the already ancient Book of the Dead, there were books full of scepticism and disillusionment and collections of sayings all showing a *carpe diem* attitude of mind. In a dialogue between a man and his soul we read: 'Follow after pleasure and forget care.' Egyptian literature is full of admonitions and aphorisms. There was widespread belief in the judgment of the dead. Osiris, king of eternity, governor of the underworld, sat in judgment, weighing the souls of the dead against truth and righteousness. Before being led into the presence of Osiris, the dead man's soul made the 'negative confession'. If he passed the test he would be admitted into the fields of the blessed. If he failed, his soul would be cast out and devoured by a frightful monster. He would then really die for all eternity; but if his soul could counterbalance 'the feather of righteousness', he would take his place in the kingdom of Osiris and all would be well. This theme is repeated again and again in literature and in painting, gradually creating an intricate pattern round the theme of the life hereafter—with its ultimate expression in Dante's *Inferno*.

Egyptian literature consists of books of wisdom and moral precepts, semi-philosophical writing, comparable in its later form to Greek idealistic philosophy, and the fairy tale in all its aspects. Memories of a distant age can be traced in animal stories which embody the origins of fable, satire, humour and parody. These themes live on in the tales of the Arabian Nights and Bible stories, and hardly any Egyptian myth has not found a place in our own fairy tales. The gods of the Nile have come to us as animals or bogeymen, and miracle stories and tales of witchcraft and sorcery survive in fairy tales. Neither was the Egyptian at all averse to a funny story. The tale of the pharaoh who seeks amorous adventures during the night or gets drunk on colobi wine, relieves the overwrought atmosphere of submission and devotion. Egyptian poetry also is mainly concerned with justice and virtue. And it was especially during the uncertainty and despair of the dark ages that literature reached its peak.

During the Eleventh and Twelfth Dynasty also literature was of a very high standard and the sculptural arts reached an unprecedented perfection. One has to search far to find a nobler portrait than that of Amenemhet III at Cairo. This is the portrait of a man who combined the exalted dignity of a god with human compassion and justice; he has seen sorrow and carries the burden of kingship with the knowledge of his own human frailty.

After a period disturbed by feudalism and the power politics of the local princes, a unified Egypt emerged with less worldly wealth, but spiritually the richer. The pyramids, tombs and temples are smaller in size than those of the Old Kingdom, and the materials used are of inferior quality. Many of the pyramids of this period are badly damaged (Lisht, Dahshur, Illahun, Hawara) and only the crumbling mud-brick cores remain. The funerary temple of Amenemhet III at Hawara, famous for the 'Labyrinth', was used by the Romans as a quarry and little remains but debris. According to Strabo the building consisted of two storeys, was 200 metres long and had three thousand rooms. He thought it was more impressive than all the Greek buildings put together.

The tombs of local chiefs were cut into the rocks during this period. The rock-cut tombs of Beni Hassan, Mer, Assiut, Kau-el-Kabir and Aswan in Upper Egypt may not have reached the high standard of former times, but their wall-paintings give an interesting insight into the prevailing conditions: military prowess and sport now play a prominent part.

The limestone kiosk of Senusret I is architecturally interesting and deserves mention. It had been dismantled and used as a filling for a later pylon at Karnak. Later the stone was retrieved and the chapel was restored *(plate 18)*. This fate overtook many buildings of the Middle Kingdom: they were destroyed or dismantled and used as foundations for later temples.

The great engineering feat of the Middle Kingdom was the reclamation of the Faiyum. Dams and locks regulated the water level of the Bahr Yusuf, a tributary of the Nile branching off into Lake Moeris. Inundations were checked, the marsh turned into fertile land. There were already traces of settlements along the river banks dating from palaeolithic times, but in the reign of Amenemhet III the Faiyum was made into safe agricultural land, which even now delights the eye and stands out in the western desert as a garden of Eden, rich in olive groves and vineyards.

The principle deity of the Faiyum was the crocodile-headed water-god Sobek (Greek Souchos) and most of the temples were dedicated to him. Only names need be mentioned here: Kasr Karun, Dimah, Kasr-el-Sagha, Karanis and Biahmu, Crocodilopolis (Arsinoe), north of the modern capital Medinet-el-Fayum, Hawara, with the pyramid of Amenemhet III, Illahun with that of Senusret II and the nearby town of Kahun, finally Tebtynis and Medinet-Madi, the last three particularly invaluable as the provenance of thousands of Egyptian and Greek papyri giving a lively account of life in this province during the Greek and Roman periods. Also of great interest are the mummy portraits mainly from the area of Hawara. Painted portraits of the dead person were inserted into the linen swathing the head. This fashion dates from the pre-Christian era.

Egyptian influence had already reached the first Cataract at Aswan during the Old Kingdom, and the latest excavations have brought to light a settlement as far south as Wadi Halfa near the second Cataract, but this influence was the result not so much of conquest as of commercial activities. Cattle, skins, oils and fats, giraffe-tails, leopard skins and monkeys were imported from Nubia, as well as gold, frankincense and myrrh, ebony and precious stones. In exchange the Egyptians protected their neighbours against raids by the Blemmyes, marauding desert tribes. The Nubians also provided the Egyptians with soldiers. At this time also, Egypt extended its frontiers to Semna beyond the second Cataract, built a chain of fortresses upstream and founded the trading post of Kermah on the third Cataract.

During the Middle Kingdom it became customary to place small models of all that was necessary for the dead in after-life in the tombs. Wooden figurines of bakers, brewers, soldiers, millers and groups of agricultural workers now fill the showcases of our museums. Sometimes crude, but often of high artistic value, they elucidate much that remains obscure in painting. Jewellery of this period surpasses in refinement, taste and technical skill, the products of other countries of the same date.

Between the Middle and New Kingdom lies a second period of unrest and foreign occupation: a century of Hyksos rule (*c.* 1785–1680 BC). Horsemen of varied origin, probably under the leadership of the Churili invaded Egypt from the eastern Delta. 'Peoples of the Sands' or 'shepherd kings' entered the country and took the throne. They founded the town of Avaris, near the later Tanis in the eastern Delta. The invaders, called 'Hyksos' by the historian Flavius Josephus, remained for a century in control of the land, until the last kings of the Seventeenth Dynasty, Kamose, and his son, Ahmose, succeeded in expelling them. Among the unintentional benefits the Hyksos conferred were the horse-drawn chariot and some new types of weapons.

THE NEW KINGDOM

After the expulsion of the Hyksos and the stabilization of political order, the pharaohs expanded their influence far into Western Asia. The most powerful sovereign of this period was Tuthmosis III (1491–1436 BC) of the Eighteenth Dynasty. Seventeen times he campaigned in Asia, defeating the Syrian League at Megiddo and stemming the advance of the Mitannians from the north. He conquered Palestine and Syria as far north as Carchemish, and in the south he crossed the fifth Cataract below the Gebel Barkal.

His step-mother and aunt, Queen Hatshepsut, had long prevented his accession to the throne, a fact which so embittered him that when he finally came to the throne, he obliterated all mention of her reign from every monument (cf. page 113, *plate 25*). With the deletion of her name he destroyed, according to Egyptian belief, her soul.

In the flush of his victories, he did not forget the gods. On the contrary he paid them homage by presenting them with temples and prayers. Amon was worshipped as the principal god, and it was he who led the king from victory to victory. Pharaoh's great deeds, tributes paid by the vanquished and observations about foreign peoples were depicted on the walls of his temple at Karnak. He also built monuments at Medinet Habu in western Thebes, and at several places in Nubia as far south as the north Sudan.

Tuthmosis III, young, athletic and warlike, created the Egyptian empire. Of great personal courage, he nevertheless remained humble, giving the credit for his victories to the god Amon. His buildings do not overwhelm by colossal dimensions, but excel in elegant proportions and careful arrangement of details.

The pharaohs of the New Kingdom were more human than their fore-runners; the god-like aloofness had gone; there was scope for individual initiative. Egypt had crossed its own frontiers and had come into contact with other powers. Thus for the first time Egypt could see itself dispassionately, comparing itself with these other people, and although they considered them as 'barbarians', the people of the Nile adopted many new customs from Asia. Amenhetep III (1400–1362 BC) even took a Mitannian princess for his wife.

The reign of Amenhetep III was indeed prosperous. The conquests of Tuthmosis III brought booty and wealth into the country from north and south. Thebes, the capital, was rebuilt in unprecedented splendour. The ancient writers praise it unstintingly. Thebes, with its hundred gates became the hub of the world and Amon was its overlord. The human-headed Amon, king of the gods, with his high crown of feathers, symbol of life-giving breath, is sometimes depicted in the form of a ram, the animal symbolizing great procreative power *(plate 19)*. Amon was the spiritual father of the pharaohs, the creator of all things, the oracle-giver. His reign stretched to the very ends of the empire. Under his banner the land was liberated from the Hyksos, his worship overcame the heresy from Amarna, and after the conquest of northern Egypt by the Libyans, he still reigned in the Theban theocracy, in Ethiopia and during the Meroitic culture well into the Christian era. In his animal manifestation he found a place in the hearts of the simple people and as the Spirit and the Breath of him 'whose coming is not heard' although 'living in all things', Amon inspired profound theological speculation in the priesthood. His chief temple was at Karnak *(plates 19–22)* where the temple priests had amassed immeasurable treasures in his name.

The conflict between the hierarchy which exercised great reactionary influence, and the progressive party of the king became more pronounced under Amenhetep III. This Amenhetep, the Memmon of the Greek writers, erected in front of his mortuary temple on the west bank two huge statues, known as the colossi of Memnon *(plate 27)*. He also built a temple at Luxor, dedicated to Amon *(plate 24)*.

His son, Amenhetep IV, who changed his name to Akhenaton (1380–1362 BC), the 'heretic of Amarna', broke completely with the cult of Amon and caused the names of the old gods to be obliterated—in particular the name of Amon. Instead of the old pantheon consisting of many deities, he created a new religion based on the worship of the sun's disc, the Aton. His was a monotheistic creed, although the idea of one great god was familiar from quite early times in the Egyptian pantheon, the various deities of which were explained as manifestations of the one god. In order to break the powerful influence of the Amon priests and officials of the old order, he surrounded himself with *homines novi* and in the sixth year of his reign, moved his new capital to Tell el-Amarna, Akhetaten, the 'Horizon of the Disc'. Palaces and houses were richly decorated in a completely new and naturalistic style, and in the temples, of which there were at least five, Aton was worshipped with a religious fanaticism that had never been known before. A deep feeling for all things natural speaks out of this beautiful hymn to the sun: 'When day breaks, thou rejoicest and awakest and goest up to the horizon and givest forth thy rays. They stretch out their hands to thee in thanksgiving for their rising.'

Unfortunately for Egypt, Akhenaton was more a poet and visionary than statesman and while contemplating his god and his wondrous works, he did not heed the cries for help from his vassals in Palestine and Syria, where the Habiru (Hebrews) and Hittites were stirring up trouble. The Amarna correspondence shows how easily his Asiatic empire crumbled. While foreign affairs deteriorated rapidly, the opposition in Thebes grew. And when Akhenaton and his queen Nefertiti disappeared from the scene his successor Tutankhaton reverted to the cult of Amon, and renamed himself

Tutankhamon. The City of the Sun was abandoned. Thebes was restored and the powerful priests of Amon prevailed again. Had not the tomb of Tutankhamon in the Biban el-Moluk been found almost intact, with its wonderful treasures (now in the Cairo Museum), the young king would have been remembered only as an obscure pharaoh of whom little was known. He died in his nineteenth year. He is the only pharaoh whose tomb was left virtually undisturbed; all other royal mummies were rifled and removed from their tombs and some at least have found a last resting place in the museum at Cairo. But the tombs themselves remain among the most impressive sights in Egypt.

The kings of the Eighteenth Dynasty were buried in rock-cut tombs on the west side of the river opposite the capital, Thebes. The entrances to the tombs, or *tubes* as the Greeks once called them, are long shafts of up to 656 ft long and as much as 328 ft deep. Steps, or more often, only a steep ramp, lead to the antechamber and burial chamber. Because these tombs filled with treasures were a constant hunting ground for robbers, false shafts were often constructed leading away from the actual chamber. Nobles and officials also had rock tombs, and in the area of the Theban necropolis there are some five hundred of these tombs in all, beautifully decorated with wall-paintings and hieroglyphic texts.

The last king of the Eighteenth Dynasty, Horem-heb, again brought order to the troubled land, stamped out corruption, reorganized the priesthood and army, and strengthened the foundations of the empire. The kings of the Nineteenth Dynasty (1305–1171 BC), Ramesses and his successors, recaptured their Asiatic and Nubian possessions, although the situation in northern Mesopotamia and Syria deteriorated rapidly. New peoples appeared on the scene, made more formidable by the use of iron weapons. Seti I (1305–1290 BC) again waged war against Palestinian and Syrian forces and advanced as far north as Kadesh, at the same time forcing back Libyan invaders from the west. His temples stand at Abydos, Gurna and Karnak *(plate 21)*. The art of his reign combines magnificence with elegance, every movement is well posed, the lines flow softly, the composition shows the correct balance between full-ness and restraint, disciplined to a very high degrees.

The greatest builder of all in Egypt was Ramesses II (1290–1224 BC). He built the Ramses city in the Delta for which the Children of Israel 'toiled with mortar and brick and all manner of service'; at Luxor he enlarged the temple of Amon-Mut-Khons of Amenhetep III *(plate 23)*. In the necropolis at Thebes he built himself a funerary temple, the Ramesseum. His temple at Abydos follows the same pattern as that of Seti I; his rock-cut temple at Abu Simbel *(plates 32 and 33)* and that of his queen were stupendous; his colossal statue greets the tourist leaving Cairo's main station, while a still larger figure has not been restored to an upright position but still lies under the trees near ancient Memphis.

The temples of Ramesses II do not show refined workmanship, they impress by their sheer weight. Episodes of the famous battle of Kadesh, where Ramesses won a doubtful victory over the Hittites, are found in several of his buildings. Sixteen years after the battle of Kadesh the Hittite king, himself hard pressed by the Assyrians, signed a peace treaty with the Egyptian pharaoh, the text of which was carved on the walls of his temple at Karnak. Ramesses thereupon married a daughter of the Hittite king, Hattusilis III (1296 BC) and commemorated this event in the 'Wedding Stele' at Abu Simbel. The temple at Medinet Habu *(plate 32)* carries many inscriptions and scenes of the battle of Ramesses III against the 'Peoples from the Sea' who invaded the eastern Delta.

Notwithstanding these victories and consequently the constant homage to the gods, the sad fact was that the Egyptian kingdom gradually became weakened internally to such an extent that the whole of the Asiatic empire was lost and once more the country fell apart and was split into a northern kingdom centred around Tanis, and a southern state ruled over by the priests of Thebes.

The following period in Egyptian history, lasting from 1085 until 332, when Alexander the Great came to Egypt to consult the oracle of Amon, is one of steady decline. Libyans, Ethiopians and Persians invaded the country and seized the throne. But with the founding of Alexandria by Alexander the Great, Egypt became a centre of Hellenistic learning, until the Emperor Augustus defeated Cleopatra VII, the last queen of the Ptolemaic line in 30 BC and Egypt became a Roman province.

Although politically enfeebled, Egypt still produced considerable works of art. From this period date the temple of Dendera, and buildings at Karnak and Medinet Habu. The treasures on the island of Philae, Edfu, the best preserved of all Egyptian temples, the double temple at Kom Ombo and temples at Dakka, Esna, and Kalabsha show how great was the respect in which all later conquerors held the ancient Egyptian culture.

The royal tombs at Tanis of the Twenty-first and Twenty-third Dynasty have been discovered almost undisturbed and yielded many treasures, including silver outer coffins. The funerary chapels of the priestess-queens of the Theban priest-state during the Twenty-fifth Dynasty (751–656) are also of considerable architectural interest. It is here that for the first time in the history of Egyptian architecture the vault was used in public buildings; it had previously only been used for store-rooms.

Psammetichus I of the Twenty-sixth Dynasty built a long gallery in the Serapeum at Saqqara, 'the Place of Apis', while at the same time the Greek colonists were settling at Naukratis. The tomb of Petosiris at Gebel el-Tuna shows Greek influence in the more profane wall paintings, while the religious themes still remain Egyptian in style.

At the city of Alexandria Greek and Egyptian culture merged. Some of the greatest artists and scholars of the Hellenistic world worked in its famous library containing over a million scrolls which was burnt down at the time of Caesar. Tradition has it that St Mark preached the Gospels here, and some centuries later it witnessed the fierce disputes between Arian and Athanasian theologians.

Today the only sign above ground of the Serapeum built to the god Serapis—an artificial fusion of the old Egyptian deities Osiris and Apis—is Pompey's Pillar, 277 feet high.

Finally, in the year AD 641 the city fell to Islamic conquerors after a fourteen-month siege.

Here, where today the fellahin live and till the soil with ploughs identical to those of their ancestors five thousand years ago, kings once strode over the earth. Here, where the words of the Koran are written in the mosques, there was once one of the first fully Christianized countries in the world. This land which popular belief fills with mummies, cat-worshippers and ignorant superstition, was the cradle of western civilization. It was here that the first seeds were sown of our technical and intellectual achievements, soon to be transformed by Greek and Christian thought.

Plate 13
The Step Pyramid of Zoser, Saqqara

The Step Pyramid at Saqqara stands at the beginning not only of Egyptian pyramid building, but of all monumental architecture in Egypt. It represents the first tentative experiment of what was later to become the hallmark of Egyptian architecture. Unlike the later pyramids *(plate 16)* the Step Pyramid of Zoser was built not on a square plan but on a rectangular plan, measuring 345 × 414 ft, and it rose in six unequal stages to a height of over 197 ft. The earlier tombs had been bench-like mastabas on a square plan with slightly inclined walls. The mastaba was then heightened to four stages until the builders were bold enough to risk the final step: a pyramid of six stages incorporating the earlier experiments. It was a revolutionary step indeed to take, starting from a subterranean tomb of sun-dried bricks faced with limestone slabs, to a veritable mountain of stone, which would dominate the desert as majestically as the pharaoh ruled over his people.

This royal tomb is far more than a simple funerary monument. In its permanence it symbolizes the stable, unchangeable government, realized for the first time by Zoser and his counsellor and architect, Imhotep (page 63).

When Egypt emerged from the shadows of neolithic life (*c.* 3000 BC) the country was divided already into two parts—Upper and Lower Egypt—later to be unified under one crown. Two centuries later Zoser, the second monarch of the Third Dynasty, organized the central government. A North and South building within the temple precinct represented the sanctuaries of Upper and Lower Egypt. To the right of the picture a small chamber or *serdab* is visible where the seated statue of the dead pharaoh stood. As the pharaoh was the ruler of Upper and Lower Egypt, it was necessary for him to have two tombs, a southern and a northern tomb. Underneath the Step Pyramid itself were the burial chambers of the king and eleven members of his family, hewn from the solid rock. The many subterranean corridors and chambers are decorated with religious motifs and embellished with panels of colourful tiles which imitated the reed mats covering the walls of the royal palace. The mortuary chambers are faithful replicas of actual rooms that must have existed in Egyptian houses. Open doors are imitated in relief, papyrus bundles, originally meant to protect the exposed ends of the walls are reproduced as fine limestone columns.

After at least three more stepped pyramids were started but never completed, the stepped form was finally superseded by the true classical pyramid *(plate 16)*.

Plate 14
The enclosure wall of the mortuary precinct of
Zoser, Saqqara

The mortuary precinct contained not only
the central pyramid *(plate 13)* with *serdab*
and temple, but also an entrance hall, the
North and South Buildings with courts and
a larger ceremonial hall with throne and
adjoining vestry. There was also the main
court where sacrifices were performed and
finally the Southern Tomb. The whole of
this complex, covering an area of roughly
1800 ft in length and 985 ft in width was
enclosed by a 34½-ft high wall.

There was an entrance gate near the
southern corner of the east wall and thirteen
false doors carved in stone. Buttresses, 216
in all placed at regular intervals, and narrow
perpendicular niches are typical architectural
elements already present in early palaces and
royal tombs. These buttresses and recesses
give a lively interplay of light and shade.
The building technique is perfect. The small
limestone blocks are carefully dressed and
faultlessly joined without any form of
bonding. After 5000 years the wall is still
standing for the most part and where it was
damaged it has been carefully restored.

With its colour of burnished gold this wall
of Zoser's sanctuary contrasts vividly with
the sapphire Egyptian sky.

Plate 15
*The North Building of the mortuary precinct
of Zoser, Saqqara*

Within the precinct there are two rectangular
structures representing the government
buildings of Upper and Lower Egypt, each
with its own court. The court of the North
Building lies east of its façade. The walls of
the building are decorated with semi-engaged papyrus columns, the plant of the Nile
marshes, which became the emblem of
Lower Egypt *(plate 24)*. The calyx opens
out from a triangular stem on a circular
base. There are still traces of paint on the
stems. In Egyptian formalism these decorative elements are more than mere embellishment, they were laden with an inner
meaning, they are functional and convey a
message. Symbol is too feeble a word for
the meaning of the architectural elements.
To enable the pharaoh to find in the after-
life at least the semblance of the same
conditions he had known in the living
world, the North Building is constructed
with a façade which faithfully reproduces
the form of the pharaoh's home, but has no
interior. Similarly, the chapels of the Jubilee
Court are blind façades backed with a
rubble filling. Here a light arch in relief
reaches from side to side following the curve
of the roof.

Plate 16
Sphinx and Pyramid of Khephren, Giza

Facing eastwards, the sphinx lies as a guardian 240 ft long in front of the necropolis of Giza. A knoll of rock left by the builders of the pyramid of King Khephren gave the sculptors the idea for this majestic piece of work. The striped royal *(nemes)* headcloth, once painted, stands out from the head like two wings, which break the sunlight and add depth to the sculptured head. The Uraeus (snake) on the forehead, an emblem of royalty, and the nose have been severely multilated by the Mamluks who used the sphinx as a target for shooting practice. Sand and desert winds have eaten deeply into its surface. The Romans did some repair work and cleared the sand away, but it soon accumulated again.

A stele between the paws tells how Tuthmosis IV had a dream while resting in its shadow. The gods promised him the double crown of Egypt if he cleared away the sand.

With its lion body and human head, the strange creature became the embodiment of the Pharaoh Khephren who lies under the second of the great pyramids at Giza. The pyramid, 474 ft high, is, like the pyramid of Zoser, the spiritual centre of the royal funerary complex. It is the most impressive example of Egyptian discipline, of the triumph of the spirit over matter, and its pure abstract form is an everlasting source of inspiration.

The pyramid was built on a square plan, 690 × 690 ft at the base, with an inclination of 52°20'. The apex retains a part of the original casing of limestone and the two lower courses of the red granite casing survive at its base. The precinct of Khephren's pyramid also contained a valley-temple and a mortuary temple, connected with each other by a causeway. There was also a smaller pyramid within the wall. All these buildings served the funerary rites and the regular services held by the priests, while the pyramid itself was closed after the funeral and could not legally be entered again.

Brick ramps were used during the construction to haul the stones up on sledges or rollers with the help of oxen. When the final height was reached, the outer casing of polished stone slabs was put in place, starting at the top, while at the same time the supply ramp was dismantled as the work proceeded downwards.

The most important pyramids stand in a line from north to south on the edge of the western desert over a distance of more than sixty miles, but the Meroitic kings of the Sudan again chose pyramids for their tombs at the beginning of the Christian era.

Plate 17
The valley-temple of Khephren, Giza

When the king was laid to rest in the burial chamber of his pyramid the corridor to the interior was sealed off with large granite blocks and only tomb robbers later forced an entry. The king was supplied with all the comforts and needs for his life hereafter: his crown and sceptre, his throne and other furniture, clothes and utensils as well as food, oil and wine. For the intrinsic meaning of the pyramid was to provide a worthy resting place for the pharaoh, not for his own sake primarily, but to safeguard his people. Pharaoh was god incarnate and it was most essential for his divine power to live on for ever so that he could watch over his people and bestow gifts on them. It was therefore imperative to erect a fitting tomb for the divine king. The malicious stories spread by the Greeks about slave labour are completely untrue. The work of pyramid building was probably undertaken during the wet season, when the Nile floods the fields and agricultural work came to a standstill.

The period which elapsed between death and burial was about seventy days, that is, the time between the setting and rising of Sirius and the decan stars in the Egyptian night sky. During this period the embalming ritual took place in the valley-temple or was symbolically re-enacted there. After crossing the river, the funeral procession entered the valley-temple and when all the necessary ritual ceremonies had been performed by the priests, it moved on towards the mor-

tuary temple along a covered causeway. From there the coffin was borne to its final resting place and sealed away for ever. The daily service was held in the inner recesses of the mortuary temple on the east side of the pyramid.

The valley-temple was only used once— for the embalming and purification ceremonies. It is amazing that a structure of such an ephemeral function was built so strongly that in the five thousand years of its existence only the outer skin has been damaged. As with so many other features of funerary architecture, it can be taken as an everlasting imitation of a pavilion or purification tent, erected for this one occasion.

Built of granite, it covers an area of 148 ft square and its slightly inclined walls are 42 ft 9 in. high. There are two monumental doorways in the east wall, surrounded by a band of hieroglyphic inscriptions, and flanked by sphinxes. Immensely thick walls hide symmetrical entrance halls, an anteroom, a columned hall, corridors and chambers. The hypostyle hall of the picture is in the shape of an inverted T and was divided by sixteen monoliths in red granite. The only light came through narrow slits high in the walls. This dim light played on the twenty-three or more life-size statues of the king in diorite, standing on bases of honey-coloured alabaster. Traces of the square bases are still visible.

This megalithic architecture is not a primitive experiment, but is completely in accordance with Egyptian belief that pharaoh was master of all life, here and in the world hereafter.

Plate 18
The processional kiosk of Senusret I, Karnak

The elegant structure of Senusret I (1971–1928 BC) in fine white limestone had been used as filling in the pylon later erected by Amenhetep III, but has now been recovered by archaeologists and reconstructed. This most remarkable work of the Twelfth Dynasty is all the more precious because most of the Middle Kingdom buildings have been lost. The kiosk was originally used for a royal festival but afterwards the processions on their way to the temple rested here.

Comparatively lightly constructed, the shrine is surrounded by an open hall and stands on a raised platform. A ramp leads to the entrance with stairs on either side. A roll moulding frames the outer walls, crowned by a hollow cornice. The roof is flat. A pedestal, on which the barque with the cult statue rested during the stay of the procession, stands in the centre of the building. Reliefs and hieroglyphs in honour of Amon, the great god of Thebes and the fertility god Min, cover the walls. To understand the meaning of these kiosks in relation to the temples a few preliminary remarks are necessary.

The Egyptian temple was a divine dwelling, apart from the profane world. Its plan was determined by the hidden place of the cult statue into which the god was supposed to descend. Mural painting and reliefs explained the function of the temple. A temple complex consisted of four main parts: priests and people congregated in the outer courts during the festival when the barque with the cult statue appeared. Behind these were the store-rooms for robes and ointments, the treasuries and all that was necessary for the ritual. Then follow the cult chambers for the king, while the god himself resided in the innermost chamber. The statue of the god stood in the dark recesses of an inner shrine, aside from the main axis, hidden from profane eyes. For the cult statue was 'more secret than what is in heaven, veiled like the mysteries of the Underworld and hidden deeper than the dwellers in the primordial waters'.

A second chamber in the inner part of the temple lay along the main axis. This was the room where the heavenly barque rested on a base which suggests the sky. This chamber ideally determined the temple plan. It was beautifully constructed of 'hard stone from the red mountains and mounted with white gold'. The third room was the offering room where the priests prepared the offerings for the god and "called him to his meal". The boat played as important a part in the temple ritual as it did in everyday life. The river was the highway of all festival processions. Priests carried the divine barque on their shoulders or on a sledge to a larger boat that would take it on down the river, followed by the faithful. From time to time the barque was put ashore and more offerings were performed. The barque and the cult statue then rested in the kiosks along the processional route, of which this small building was one.

In its classic severity and decoration the kiosk of Senusret is a jewel of Egyptian architecture.

Plate 19
The first pylon of the Temple of Amon, Karnak

Karnak, the temple city of Amon, was for a long time the cultural centre of the Egyptian world. It was the meeting place not only of theologians, but also of artists and philosophers. All the treasures of the ancient world flowed into its temples; precious vases from Crete, tribute from Syria, gold and frankincense, myrrh and precious woods from Nubia. A wide avenue flanked by ram-headed sphinxes (Amon manifested himself in the form of a ram) led from the banks of the river towards the temple complex of which the picture shows the last-built but unfinished pylon. The avenue continues through the gateway for nearly half a mile past another six pylons; between the third and fourth pylons another avenue turns sharply to the south and is flanked by four more pylons.

The temple itself grew around its holy of holies in ever expanding halls and courts. Since its foundation during the Middle Kingdom period, it was enlarged by successive pharaohs who built their own cult chambers and chapels, halls and courts and finished with a new pylon.

The outer pylon, harking back to a Libyan plan, was never completely finished, so that it gives an interesting insight into the building techniques. The pylon or portal was 143 ft high, 370 ft long and 49 ft wide at its base, becoming narrower at the top. Four flagpoles of cedarwood were fixed in the recesss on each side of the gateway;

the slots in which they were placed are still visible.

The picture shows the southern half of the pylon and the wing of the much lower gateway. The interior face is still partly covered with the dried mud of what may be the original scaffolding (or the derelict remains of later intrusive buildings). This consisted of mud-bricks forming ramps on which the labourers went up and down. When finished, the wall was thus covered with a wide mud bank. This bank was removed layer by layer while the outer wall received its final finish from the top to the base. This second treatment was not finished here with the usual reliefs of triumphal processions and battle or festival scenes. From the roof of the pylon one can get a splendid view of the immense complex, the walls and colonnades, pylons and obelisks covered with hieroglyphs and reliefs, and also the sacred lake. There are smaller temples and chapels, some in ruins, some still standing, statues of gods and kings. New buildings were added even in Roman times. The whole of the complex is surrounded by a high brick wall. Processional ways often flanked by sphinxes lead towards seven entrance gates. An unbelievable luxury was displayed in the temples, the floors and walls inlaid with silver and other precious metals, the ceilings covered in painting, the points of the obelisks mounted in gold. The glitter and sparkle in the bright sunlight, must have given the faithful a tremendous excitement, for here they stood in the very presence of their divine masters.

Plate 20
The column of Taharqa, Karnak

The Nubian Pharaoh Taharqa (689–663 BC) built a hall with ten columns in the first court of the great Temple of Amon, behind the entrance pylon *(plate 19)*. Only one column is still standing. The abacus above the bell-shaped papyrus capital indicates that these columns once carried a roof. But as in Egyptian eyes the roof represented the night sky, this lonely free-standing column does not break the spell and seems with its superhuman dimensions to carry the intense Egyptian sky.

The column is 69 ft high and consists of 25 courses of carefully dressed stone for the shaft and five courses for the capital which alone measures $16\frac{1}{2}$ ft in diameter and has a circumference at the open cup of the papyrus of 49 ft. It is so immense that its true size can only be appreciated after the eye has been adjusted to the enormous dimensions of the whole temple complex.

The king erected the hall in gratitude for the divine benevolence during his reign. Several high river floods rendered rich harvests year after year. The water level can still be read on the gauge at the quay in front of the sphinx avenue.

No wonder that those years of abundance brought forth such papyrus stems!

Plate 13
The Step Pyramid of Zoser, Saqqara

Plate 14
The enclosure wall of the mortuary precinct
of Zoser, Saqqara

Plate 15
The North Building of the mortuary precinct
of Zoser, Saqqara

Plate 16
Sphinx and Pyramid of Khephren, Giza

Plate 17
The valley-temple of Khephren, Giza

Plate 18
The processional kiosk of Senusret I, Karnak

Plate 19
The first pylon of the Temple of Amon, Karnak

Plate 20
The column of Taharqa, Karnak

Plate 21
Detail of the great hypostyle hall of the
Temple of Amon, Karnak

The great hall of the Amon temple contains 134 sandstone papyrus columns arranged in sixteen rows. The area covered by the columns is 338 × 171 ft, while the great hall measures 17,600 square feet. The roof of the nave is 79 ft high and is 33 ft higher than that of the aisles. The columns of the aisles consist of half drums of 3 ft 3 in. in height and 6 ft 6 in. in diameter, while the circumference is 21 ft.

Those of the nave, with a diameter of $11\frac{1}{2}$ ft and a circumference of more than 33 ft, equal the column of Trajan in Rome or the Vendôme column in Paris. The central colonnade through which the processional way leads have capitals with open calyces, those in the aisles have the closed papyrus bud. The plant structure has been abandoned, the columns are not fluted or ribbed any longer but have a surface completely covered with hieroglyphs. Shaft and capital, abacus and architrave serve as surfaces for endless inscriptions. A prominent place is given to the names and titles of the royal patron, Seti I, in relief on the north side and on the south, those of Ramesses II are carved in sunk relief—a far inferior technique. Later kings also introduced their own cartouches, often erasing the earlier ones. The colours on the architrave are remarkably well preserved. The hall originally had a stone roof and received light through clerestory windows. The frame of one of these windows is visible in the picture above the cornice. The columns are standing so close together that they give the impression of a papyrus forest growing in a sacred field—the temple.

Nowhere else in the world has the creative impulse realized itself so powerfully in stone.

Plate 22
*Pier with emblem in the Temple of Amon,
Karnak*

Behind the sixth pylon in the Amon temple
(plate 19) there are two granite piers with
the twin emblems of Egypt; on the north
side the papyrus, the emblem of Lower
Egypt, on the south side the lotus, that of
Upper Egypt. Both piers once supported a
roof, but today they are mere picturesque
ruins under the open sky. They formed part
of the first hall of the Annals where
Tuthmosis III gave an account of the peoples
and cities he had conquered. The incised
reliefs on the east and west sides show the
king together with a deity. Visible in the
picture, he stands in the company of Mut,
the goddess of the heavens; lower down
Amon is protected by the winged royal
falcon with the ring of eternity in its talons.

The plant emblems are carved in unusually high relief standing out from the main
body of the pier like slender semi-engaged
columns as in the North Building at Saqqara
(plate 15). Under the horizontal cartouche
of Tuthmosis III the three stems rise up
vertically. Although severely stylized they
breath organic life.

The accent falls on the central flower; the
petals of the smaller plants meet over the
stem of the larger one. The ornamental
petals are deeply incised, their pure forms
have crisp lines of unbelievable beauty.

In the background is the obelisk of Queen
Hatshepsut between the fourth and fifth
pylons.

Plate 23
The Temple of Amon, Luxor

It is not only for material reasons that the mosque of Abu'l Haggag was built in the ruins of the old temple, for a spiritual tradition still links both sanctuaries across the millennia.

The Muslim saint's sacred boat is borne in solemn procession in the same manner as was Amon, the great god of Thebes, in his sacred barque on the shoulders of his priests. The minaret where the muezzin calls the faithful to prayers seems to vie with the obelisk where the sun god himself descended at the first light of every new day and lit its golden apex with his rays.

The second obelisk flanking the opposite side of the pylon was brought to Paris in 1836 and stands now on the Place de la Concorde. The baboons at its base who once greeted the morning sun in attitudes of prayer are now to be seen in the Louvre. The Romans not only rebuilt the inner chambers of the temple and made it into a cult chapel for the emperors, they erected altars nearby, founded a town and laid out two camp sites.

The name Luxor is actually derived from the Roman *castra*, in Arabic, *el Kusur*, which has since become corrupted.

The Amon temple at Luxor was built by Amenhetep III *(cf. plate 27)* on the site of an earlier sanctuary 'on the silver floor and a bed of incense' as the inscription says. The complex was 624 ft long and 180 ft wide. Ramesses II (1292–1225) added a hypostyle hall which gave it an overall length of 855 feet. A five-and-a-half mile long avenue of sphinxes connected it with the Amon temple at Karnak *(cf. plate 19)*. The pylon giving access to the temple precinct has only lately been excavated and some interesting carvings have come to light; on the inside wall the representation of a Min festival, no less accurately executed than the battle of Kadesh on the outside. An elegant temple of Tuthmosis III stands within the open court with a double colonnade. One of the most important features of this immense complex is the high colonnade of Amenhetep III (to the right of the picture). Seven pairs of $52\frac{1}{2}$-ft high papyrus columns with bell-shaped capitals tower above the ruins. The impost blocks still carry the heavy architrave. The colonnade is 171 ft long. A continuous wall originally hid the sacred precinct from profane eyes.

Tutankhamon decorated the wall with interesting reliefs: the procession bringing the cult-statue of Amon from Karnak to Luxor where the god liked to visit his most secret shrine. We see the sacred barque with the statue on the shoulders of the priests, its journey on the Nile, the kiosks where the statue rested, the jubilant crowds accompanying the procession along the river banks, whirling dancers and Negroes beating drums.

His consort Mut and their son, Khons, accompany the god in their own boats. One of the most interesting chambers is the birth-chamber in the innermost part of the temple. Scenes of the supernatural descent of pharaoh are depicted on its walls comparable to those at Deir el-Bahri *(cf. plate 25)*.

Plate 24
Temple of Amon, hall of columns, Luxor

Shown here is the north-west corner of the second hypostyle hall, with its columns of closed lotus buds, and the adjoining pronaos of the sanctuary proper. One of the columns of the 171-ft long colonnade of Amenhetep III *(plate 23)* can be seen in the centre background. The 32 columns of the pronaos although in ruins, are still an impressive sight. While the court with its sixty-four columns was used during religious festivals, the "consecration of the house", was celebrated in the hall with the thirty-two columns, according to the foundation ceremonies of the wall reliefs.

This hall was roofed over and was the first step towards the ever-increasing darkness of the inner chambers. It was in those hidden recesses that the sacred boat was hidden. The innermost dark chamber contained the cult statue of Amon and his retinue.

Under the soft healing light of the moon these ruins again become the dwelling place of a god, emanating a living force, while in the light of the Egyptian day, they blaze in jubilant glory.

Plate 25
The terraced temple of Hatshepsut,
Deir el-Bahri

This terraced temple, an architectural gem, is perhaps the most 'feminine' of all Egyptian temples. Originally planned as a pyramid temple lower down the valley, like its southern neighbour, the pyramid temple of Mentuhotep dating from the twentieth century BC (to the left of the picture), it grew into something quite different under the hands of Queen Hatshepsut. It rises in three stages with its back against the precipice of the mountain which rises vertically behind it.

The temple is reached from the valley up two long ramps with gentle grandients. These ramps link the three terraces and divide the temple along its axis into two symmetrical parts. Entrance halls with their fine limestone columns and mural decorations at the end of each terrace lead into the interior. The birth-chamber and the Punt Hall are of special interest. The Punt Hall shows Hatshepsut as the Queen of Peace, and the destruction of the birth-chamber makes it all too clear that a woman could not easily succeed to the throne in her own right. Hatshepsut was regent for her stepson Tuthmosis III, while he was under age, but later she proclaimed herself king and remained in power until her death. Although her right to succeed was doubtful, she kept her threefold claim to the throne: she assumed herself to be the natural heir, for her father had proclaimed her his successor; Amon had declared her king in an oracle; and finally, and this is the theme of her birth-chamber, she was the daughter of Amon. The reliefs tell of the council of the gods in heaven, the divine conception of the royal child and the birth assisted by heavenly spirits.

The reliefs in the Punt Hall show a trade expedition to Punt, modern Somaliland. The journey through the Red Sea brings an Egyptian emissary into the presence of the royal family. In exchange for weapons he receives gold, incense and myrrh. To the south of the Punt Hall lies the Hathor Chapel *(plate 26)* and to the north of the birth-hall a shrine dedicated to Anubis.

Three chambers behind the second terrace deep in the rock itself, are the holy of holies. The tomb of the queen lies on the other side of the mountain. It is 700 ft long and dug in the hill-side to a depth of 330 ft. The temple lies in a direct line opposite the Amon temple at Karnak. Once a year the god visited the temple of Hatshepsut on the day of the great festival, when the living visited their dead in the necropolis west of the river by torchlight and shared a meal with them with song and dance.

At the end of the night when the torches were doused in milk, the barque of the god and his priests and the boats of the festive crowds returned towards the rising sun.

The terrace-temple of Queen Hatshepsut was severely damaged by Tuthmosis III, the rightful heir *(plate 22)* and later by the iconoclast Akhenaton. There were originally twenty-eight more than life-size statues of the queen carved in veined granite, more than one hundred limestone sphinxes, twenty-two sphinxes of red granite and forty limestone figures of Hatshepsut as Osiris. One of the sphinxes is in Berlin, another in New York.

The whole temple complex with its pure white columns against the forbidding background of black rock, its entrance gates with the overhanging Persea trees, its formal ponds and sweeping stairways was the work of Senenmut, the architect and favourite of the only queen to sit on the throne of Egypt as pharaoh.

Plate 26
The Hathor capitals, Deir el-Bahri

The shrine of Hathor, goddess of love, music and inspiration is one of the southern annexes of the terrace-temple of Queen Hatshepsut at Deir el-Bahri *(plate 25)*. Hathor was also the goddess of child-birth. The warm Egyptian sun bathes two of the columns in a golden glow, whilst traces of paint enliven the carefully carved limestone.

The capital is in the shape of a sistrum, the jingling musical instrument used in the ceremonies connected with the goddess. The clanging of the metal strips imitated the rustle of the papyrus when Hathor, in the shape of a cow, moved through the reeds. The bell-shaped feature just above the head is a reminiscent of the papyrus, the cow's ears projecting out sideways in front of the heavy wig relate to Hathor as the nursing mother in her aspect as a cow.

The form of the Egyptian column is not determined primarily by its structural function, neither is the capital an unrelated decorative element. There is a close relation between function and form. The capital is usually in the form of a reed-bundle, but it may have the Hathor head when the temple is dedicated to that goddess or the dwarfish Bes-figures for the Mammisi or birth-house *(plate 36)*. It appears as an open flower when it symbolizes vegetative fertility *(plate 20)*.

Plate 27
The Colossi of Memnon, Thebes

Visible from afar, the two colossi stand 63 ft high in the fertile plain between the Nile and the western mountains.

In antiquity they counted as one of the wonders of the world and many stories were told about them. Nero and Germanicus visited them, Hadrian spent several days here with his wife and retinue. Egyptian and Greek tourists scratched their names on the foot of the northern colossus at the right of the picture, for it was this statue that caught the imagination. Around 26 BC a crack appeared at its waist during an earthquake which afterwards caused the statue to let out a mysterious singing at sunrise and sunset. The geographer Strabo was not the first to mention it; Pausanias and Juvenal before him spoke of the strange sound as a well-known phenomenon. When Septimius Severus had the statue repaired in AD 199 after his visit, the cracks were roughly filled with layers of stone blocks, and the singing colossus was silenced for ever.

The colossi stood as 'guardians of the gate' before a great temple of Amenhetep III of which, except for some traces of the ground plan, only a few stelae and sculptures remain, namely the famous 'Israel' stela in the Cairo Museum, a quartz statue of the king, two sphinxes with crocodile tails in alabaster and the large group of Amenhetep III with his queen Ti and their three daughters which is also in Cairo. It was the mortuary temple of Amenhetep III the father of Akhenaton. Both the temple and the statues were erected by the master-builder, Amenhetep, son of Hapu, whose wisdom, it is said, was divine.

The statues of yellowish brown sandstone have weathered badly. Both figures have lost their crowns, only the *nemes* headcloth, draped over the shoulders in pleats, is intact. The beard, a sign of royalty, is missing, the loin cloth is finely pleated. Two smaller figures stand beside the legs of the colossi; those of the royal consort Ti and Amenhetep's mother Mut-em-uja. The small size indicates their lowly status in relation to the pharaoh. At the side of the throne a sunk-relief represents two gods of the Nile tying the papyrus and the lotus, symbols of Upper and Lower Egypt round the hieroglyph for 'Unity'.

The name Amenhetep was pronounced by the Greeks as Mi-Amon which became 'Memnon' a name that reminded the Greeks of the Homeric hero Memnon, son of Eos and Tithonos, who came from Ethiopia to fight in the Trojan war. This Memnon was killed by Achilles and the sad song of the statue became the lament with which the hero greeted his mother, the rosy-fingered dawn, when her tears flowed as dew over her son as she rose in the morning. When sometimes the statue remained silent, it was because Memnon was angry.

The phenomenon of the singing has not been satisfactorily explained. Presumably it was caused by the sharp rise in temperature and the sudden change in humidity at daybreak possibly acting on reeds hidden by the priests in some part of the statue.

The Colossi of Memnon are the landmark for the necropolis of Thebes and during high water they stand in lonely majesty amidst the floods.

Plate 28
The Osiris columns in the Ramesseum, Thebes

During the pyramid building period, the pyramid and its mortuary temple were closely linked, but after the New Kingdom the mortuary temple was completely separate from the tomb.

The dead rested in their sarcophagi in the necropolis far out in the western desert and when the burial ceremonies were finished the tombs were closed for ever, while the mortuary temples stood on the edge of the cultivated fields. These temples are built on the same plan as the Amon temples, with open courts, roofed hypostyle halls and finally the sanctuary with the cult statue and sacred barque. Semi-engaged columns of the deceased king, as the mummified Osiris, holding in his crossed hands the crook and flail, with crown and beard as the emblems of royalty, often lined the open courts. The Osiris column is not a free-standing caryatid supporting an architrave, but follows the Egyptian principle in that it is bonded into the supporting pier behind.

In the Christian era Copts who inhabited the forecourt of the Ramesseum destroyed the pagan statues and damaged all that they could reach. As much still lay below the level of the sand, it is the faces in this case which have been mutilated.

The warm red sandstone ruins proved to be a real treasure house for the philologist, the historian and scientist. The tombs of a magician and travelling story-teller contained interesting papyri. The historian can not only find the annals of contemporary events in the reliefs, but the temple was used as a school and many important documents were stored in the library, while the astronomer can find his delight in the star-covered ceilings. Other interesting features are the enormous brick vaults where the wines and provisions of 'Osymandyas' as Diodorus sonorously called Ramesses II, were stored.

Plate 21
Detail of the great hypostyle hall of the
Temple of Amon, Karnak

Plate 22
Pier with emblem in the Temple of Amon,
Karnak

Plate 23
The Temple of Amon, Luxor

Plate 24
Temple of Amon, hall of columns, Luxor

Plate 25
The terraced temple of Hatshepsut, Deir el-Bahri

Plate 26
The Hathor capitals, Deir el-Bahri

Plate 27
The Colossi of Memnon, Thebes

Plate 28
The Osiris columns in the Ramesseum, Thebes

Plate 29
The hall with four piers in the tomb of
Ramesses VI, Thebes

In a hidden valley behind the deep escarpment bordering the Nile valley were hewn
all the rock-cut tombs of the New Kingdom
pharaohs of Egypt. Here, within these
'Royal gates' (Biban el-Moluk), are sixty-
four tombs in all belonging to the Eighteenth, Ninteenth and Twentieth Dynasties,
and covering a period of about five hundred
years. The subterranean corridors, some
more than 656 ft long, and chambers contained not only the sarcophagus with its
mummy, but were filled with figures of gold
and other precious metals, ivory and ebony
inlaid with lapis lazuli, carnelian, malachite
and turquoise, obsidian and rock-crystal.
Myrrh, frankincense and costly spices were
stored in jars and pitchers. There was bread
and wine and every necessity for the needs
of the dead king. Robes of byssos linen,
crowns and sceptres, thrones and bedsteads,
even chessboards, chandeliers, table silver
and toilet requisites filled the corridors, halls
and chambers stretching deep into the rock.

Here walls and ceilings were covered with
pictures painted in many different colours
on a thick layer of plaster. Above an ornamental dado one can see the journey of
the sun through the night and the sunrise
next morning, the dead king being re-
juvenated in his suite. Fire-breathing ser-

pents guard the doors leading from hour to
hour. The god sits in judgment at the hour
of midnight. The fate of the damned is
terrifying: they are beheaded and pierced
with sharp knives, they suffer tortures by
fire or are drowned and devoured by
demons.

The large figure of the king in company
with the gods or alone, stands out against
the background of underworld scenes. The
ceilings are decorated with constellations
and other heavenly bodies, and the ibis-
headed Thoth, crowned with the full and
crescent moon is depicted on a pier in the
foreground. To the left, pharaoh is seen
burning incense and bringing a libation to
the god in a shrine. The sun-disc runs its
course between the texts from the Book of
the Dead. Evil spirits snatch their prey,
beheaded sinners kneel, their arms tied
behind them (just above the dado) or stand
up (just below the red sun-disc). The
ceiling is covered with gold stars on a blue
field.

This tomb, called the 'Tomb of the
Transmigration' was built behind the tomb
of Tutankhamon and was the cause of that
tomb being found virtually intact. Ramesses'
tomb was built in the twelfth century BC
and the rubble from its construction was
thrown down onto the entrance to the
earlier tomb, completely hiding it until it
was found after much painstaking excavation in 1922.

Plate 30
The main gateway, Medinet Habu

The fortified complex at Medinet Habu is
the most southerly of the Theban mortuary
temples. Dedicated to Amon, it not only
contains a palace of Ramesses III, but it lies
close to the temple begun during the
Eighteenth Dynasty, a city with dwellings
for priests, officials and officers. There were
government buildings, store-rooms and
stables, Nilometers, fountains, ponds and a
sacred lake. The whole complex was surrounded by a brick wall 55 ft high. There
was only one entrance gate on the desert
side, while the high main gate gave access
from the riverside. The 72-ft high towers are
aligned with the main body of the wall and
enclosed the narrow entrance in a pincer
movement. A two-storeyed stronghold connects the two towers. Ramesses had seen
and copied this kind of fortification in Syria
on his campaigns.

The builder had an eye for perspective
when he placed the royal statues high up in
the recesses of the side walls. The king used
the main gateway for his private apartments, to judge by the wall reliefs. They
show him informally at his leisure with the
ladies of his harem, scenes not found anywhere else in Egyptian art except in the
wall-paintings of the Amarna period, when
a free and naturalistic style developed.

Medinet Habu is also interesting from the
historical point of view. It was the seat of
the government department which arranged
the transport of mummies from the rock-cut
tombs to a central point after the ransacking
of graves and conducted the legal proceedings against the tomb robbers. Later, Romans and Copts built dwelling houses within the walls; the second temple court
became a Christian church when the old
sanctuary of the Eighteenth Dynasty, built
half inside and half outside the walls, had
been deprived of its religious meaning.

Plate 31
*The mortuary temple of Ramesses III,
Medinet Habu*

The columns of this temple seem not to have the grandeur of the Old Kingdom columns, neither do they possess the severe nobility of the Middle Kingdom columns. They lack the charm of the early Eighteenth Dynasty and the haughtiness of Ramesses II, but on the other hand they are less rigid than the heavy cylindrical columns of the Ptolemaic kings.

The temple complex at Medinet Habu, the work of Ramesses III (1171–1085 BC), is one of the most important buildings of ancient Egypt, with its fortified entrance gate *(plate 30)*, its classic temple of immense proportions and its palace. Until Coptic times it was a living entity; old buildings were altered and new parts added so that the reliefs are of great interest both aesthetically and historically. The large forecourt (108 × 138 ft) behind an imposing pylon is flanked on the left by a portico with eight columns (shown here) and on the right are seven Osireid columns similar to those of the Ramesseum *(plate 28)*. The left hand wall (which is on the right in the picture) also forms the façade of the royal palace. Three doors lead from the court into the palace (extreme right of the picture). Pharaoh appeared here on the balcony, to review his troops, to grant honours and receive homage. On either side of the door

pharaoh is shown in the customary posture of a victor. He stands on a ledge formed by the sculptured heads of his defeated enemies.

The reliefs on the walls tell of the many victorious wars of the king and his defeat of the 'Sea Peoples'. These may have been Philistines, Lycians, Tyrrhenians and Siculi, Sardinians and Achaeans pushed by the Dorian migration, who came into the eastern and southern Mediterranean and threatened Egypt. The great power of Ramesses III warded them off and so naturally these events formed the main theme on the temple walls. However, many of these peoples were retained by the Egyptians as mercenaries and this created political factors which were a danger in the long run to Egyptian strength.

The architecture of this period shows a marked lack of inspiration; the former firmness, the boldness of proportions has gone. The columns of this age are thick-set and stumpy; the shaft sags though the naturalistic swelling at the base is made less heavy by the delicately engraved leaves. The incised reliefs and hieroglyphs are executed with care, as in the old tradition, but compared with the majestic style of Ramesses II, they can only be called meticulous.

How feeble and empty it all is! There is no strength in the movement, even though the workmanship is faultless through long practice. The open papyrus capital is inscribed alternately with cartouches and emblems, surprisingly detailed in colouring and engraving, but totally lacking in vigour.

Plate 32
Façade of the great temple in situ, Abu Simbel

Carved out of the massive Nubian sandstone cliff along the Nile at Abu Simbel stands the great temple of Ramesses II. It is so accurately orientated to the east that the first rays of the sun touch the cult statues in the holy of holies at the end of a 208-ft corridor. The temple is dedicated to Amon-Ra of Thebes and Re-Harakti of Heliopolis. Ptah of Memphis and Ramesses the deified builder of the temple were also worshipped here. A parapet divides the forecourt from the temple façade and terrace to which stairs, flanked by lustral basins give access.

The larger than life-size falcons and statues on the parapet give an idea of the gigantic scale of the seated figures flanking the entrance. The façade is cut out of the rock in the style of a free-standing pylon. A roll moulding frames the sides; the top ends in a hollow cornice and a frieze of baboons finishes it off. With outstretched hands the baboons worship the rising sun. The names of Ramesses II are inscribed in the cornice. These are also visible in relief above the door, where the syllable 'Ra' is represented as the falcon-headed sun god himself in an almost free-standing sculpture. The king approaches him from either side and holds up the figure of Ma'at, daughter of the sun and goddess of law and truth. On the lintel the king is shown laying the foundation stone of his temple in the presence of several gods.

Four colossal statues of Ramesses II are seated in front of the 109-ft wide façade, hewn out of the living rock, and standing 66 ft high. The figure on the left of the entrance was cracked in antiquity, presumably by an earthquake. Its head and shoulders lie in pieces on the ground. The figures on the right have been repaired, so that only the left figure is in its original state. On top of the headcloth they wear the double crown of Egypt, the uraeus on the forehead and the royal beard. The loin cloth has a deep fold in front and the hands lie palm downwards on the knees, feet close together. On the upper arms, the chest and between the legs the royal names are inscribed in cartouches. Greek, Carian and Phoenician mercenaries have scratched their names on the two statues on the left. Small statues of members of the royal family stand beside and between the legs of the colossi. The proportions are simple and clean. Only superhuman dimensions can make an impression in this vast and lonely landscape. The workmanship is superb with great attention to detail. The heads of the prisoners on the sides of the foot-rests are rendered with great skill, Negroes to the right and Syrians to the left.

At the time of writing, work is in operation to remove the temple piece by piece to a place high above the rising waters of the Nile, which will in the end completely submerge this site.

Plate 33
The hall of the great temple in situ, Abu Simbel

The majestic entrance to the temple leads first to a great hall lined on either side with eight vast Osiris statues, then into a smaller, but wider hall with four piers and finally through a narrow transverse chamber to the inner chamber with the quadruple cult-statue. On the north side are four, on the south side three chambers used as store-rooms and treasuries.

While the paintings of the innermost chambers are of a religious nature, the great hall is decorated with scenes of war. The north wall shows pictures of battles against the Hittites, the march of the Egyptian army, camp-life, a council of war, treason by two enemy-spies, the assault at Kadesh and the final victory through the personal courage of the king, aided by the great god Amon.

The hall itself measuring 58×54 ft, is an unforgetable sight. Columns nearly 32 ft high in the form of statues of Ramesses II divide it into three parts. Heraldic vultures with outstretched wings fly across the ceiling of the nave, those of the aisles are covered with the stars of the night sky. The gently rising floor leads towards the centre of the temple. Plate 28 shows similar Osiris columns in an open air temple, but the statues at Abu Simbel are not in the form of mummies; they are dressed in royal garments, the pleated loincloth with a long belt ending in the Uraeus snake. The royal name is engraved on the buckle as well as on the upper arm. The position of the arms is the same as in the Ramesseum—crossed over the chest, holding the crook and flail. The facial expression is serious but serene.

Plate 34
The Temple of Horus, Edfu

The temple at Edfu rises from the plain on the fringe of a small cluster of mud huts. The work started during the reign of Ptolemy III in 237 BC was finished nearly 200 years later in 57 BC. For the last time in the history of Egyptian building, the architectural principles conceived by the pharaohs were used in this building. The foreign rulers, although Greek by birth, bowed before the Egyptian spirit; even the Roman emperors admired and followed the style.

The temple is dedicated to the falcon-headed Horus, to Hathor of Dendera and Harmuchis, a youthful Horus, and was built on an ancient and hallowed site. Accurately orientated from north to south, the whole complex is 450 ft long. Behind the entrance pylon lies an open court (shown here) giving access to a roofed pronaos and inner temple, which consists of a wide hypostyle hall, two smaller anterooms and the sanctuary surrounded on three sides by chapels. The brilliant light of the forecourt gives way to an ever-increasing shade, until the shrine is reached hidden in deep gloom. In that mysterious place stood the cult statue behind its sacred barque. Where the chambers along the main axis become narrower, corridors and small rooms fill up the extra space between the temple wall and chambers. The whole of the complex is hidden within a high protective wall, which at no place touches the main building and therefore leaves a space for a corridor. Plate 35 shows

a part of this temenos wall in the background.

A stairway leads up to the top of the pylon, which is 118 ft high and 210 ft wide, and another flight of stairs leads to where the sanctuary of Osiris stood, and to the subterranean crypts and to the well—an essential feature of the Egyptian temple.

The temple is a sanctum in a chaotic world. It draws its strength from the primordial waters of Nun. Its three elements, floors, columns and ceiling, represent the living water, the vegetation and the sky. The breath of eternity has touched living nature and petrified it into everlasting stillness.

The open court is surrounded on three sides by a colonnade of thirty-two columns. The fourth side forms the façade of the pronaos which is slightly narrower and stands away from the outer wall. The winged sun-disc hovers in the centre of the architrave above the entrance. The roll moulding and hollow cornice are ancient architectural elements. Screens between the piers and columns depicting Ptolemy III Euergetes I bringing offerings to Horus and Hathor hide the divine dwelling from the public eye. The capitals are alternatively of palm leaves and composite flowers. The shafts of the columns are covered with inscriptions and representations of ritual acts in sunk relief.

The plate does not give any idea of the wealth of the pronaos itself, the beauty of its capitals, the ceiling decorations and the interesting murals, but of the two Horus falcons guarding the entrance, one still stands in forbidding majesty, crowned with the double crown of the Egyptian empire.

Plate 35
The birth house of the Temple of Horus, Edfu

The birth house which stands to the west of the entrance pylon of the Horus temple, and across the axis, was built by the same king who erected the screens in front of the pronaos *(plate 34)*. Ptolemy IX Soter II finished and decorated it. Although the forecourt and hall of the peripteral structure have been destroyed, the temple itself still gives a fairly clear picture of this kind of intimate sanctuary. An anteroom and hall with two chambers on each side lie in front of the main chambers.

The Bes figures on the abacus above the composite capitals to the left and right of the door, indicate the purpose of the building, for the satyr god Bes with a high crown of feathers, was the protector of mother and child. He can also be found on the legs of the bedstead and is also present in the arbour where the child was born. The Egyptian child was born outside the house in an arbour and thus the divine child was born in a small stone pavilion, a 'Mammisi', outside the temple. In the earlier temples, however, the birth chamber was hidden inside the main building. The birth pavilion stood in a circle of columns in imitation of the arbour. There are Mammisi at Dendera, Philae, Kom Ombo and Kalabsha, where the divine birth was yearly enacted in a 'passion play'. The divine child was born and nursed by goddesses, soothed with music and the sound of the sistrum. Wall reliefs tell how the creator Khnum formed the child out of clay on his wheel. The child and his '*ka*' (his spirit) are formed side by side on the potter's wheel under the hands of the ram-headed god, while at the same time he grows within the mother's womb.

Even the Roman emperors until Caracalla identified themselves with the gods of Egypt and claimed a supernatural birth, and were worshipped in the same manner.

Plate 36
The temple, Deir el-Medina

The workmen who cut and decorated the royal tombs of Biban el-Moluk lived on the western bank of the Nile opposite Thebes. Stone masons, sculptors and workmen settled in Deir el-Medina close together. They received their daily rations at the city gate, for they were virtually kept prisoner for fear of betraying the secrets of the royal tombs. When during the reign of the Ramesside kings their provisions were no longer delivered regularly or became inadequate, there were often strikes and insurrections.

The artists of the necropolis made their own tombs, small, but delicate and maintained with great care in the hillside nearby. Long after the settlement had been abandoned and when there were no more Egyptian pharaohs on the throne, the Ptolemaic kings erected a temple in honour of the venerated Imhotep and Amenhetep

the architect, son of Hapu *(plates 13, 23 and 27)* on the site of an earlier sanctuary. Ptolemy IV laid its foundations in the third century BC; Ptolemy VIII Euergetes II finished the work.

The elegant building was officially dedicated to Ma'at, the goddess of truth, and Hathor *(plate 26)*. It is built of sandstone blocks and surrounded by a high wall of sun-dried bricks. The temple consists of a transversal outer hall, a smaller rectangular pronaos and three chambers all parallel to the axis. Although small, the architecture and the themes of the relief are delightful. The illustration shows the pronaos with an elegant window high in the wall giving light onto the winding stairs in the southwest corner. Vultures with outstretched wings fly across the ceiling and protect the royal route through the temple. Reliefs show the king offering to the gods; an unusual image of the four winds can be seen on the architrave over the inner columns. The hieroglyphs on the ornamental field to the right of the window promise 'all life' and 'salvation'.

Plate 29
The hall with four piers in the tomb of
Ramesses VI, Thebes

Plate 30
The main gateway, Medinet Habu

Plate 31
The mortuary temple of Ramesses III,
Medinet Habu

Plate 32
Façade of the great temple in situ, Abu Simbel

Plate 33
*The hall of the great temple in situ, Abu
Simbel*

Plate 34
The Temple of Horus, Edfu

Plate 35
The birth house of the Temple of Horus, Edfu

Plate 36
The temple, Deir el-Medina

The Indus Civilization *Plates 37 and 38*

LESS THAN HALF A CENTURY ago, evidence was uncovered in western India of what had once been a great empire, the beginning of which is obscure, the end violent. It has left no sagas of past glories, no conspicuous monuments to draw the attention of later generations and fire the imagination; only long ruined walls survived to be used as quarries. The first inkling that an ancient culture existed came when baked bricks were taken from the ancient mound of Harappā for use on the East Indian railway between Karachi and Lahore a hundred years ago. Since then archaeological research has brought to light the indisputable fact that there existed as early as 2700 BC in the valley of the Indus and its tributaries in the Punjab, a civilization comparable to the historical cultures of Mesopotamia and Egypt. The River Indus formed the backbone of this culture in the same way that the waters of the Two Rivers and the Nile had conditioned the life of the other ancient cultures. The Indus civilization is typified by two of its largest sites so far discovered, the cities of Mohenjo-daro and Harappā, nearly 400 miles apart but easily linked together by waterways and the Indus itself. Each city has a circuit of up to three miles and each was overlooked by a towering citadel. This latter is a feature of Indus civilization sites generally, including the most recently-discovered city, Kalibangan, which lies 100 miles south-east of Harappā. This civilization covered a huge area, roughly from Sutkagen-dor 350 miles west of Karachi to the Gulf of Bombay in the south-east, and extended inland more than 750 miles up the Indus and its tributaries. These area limits are by no means definitive as much archaeological work is being carried out in India and Pakistan by highly trained and specialist archaeologists, as well as by British, French and American expeditions, and new sites are continually being discovered. Gradually a reliable chronological framework is being built up as more and more carbon-14 dates are obtained from sites excavated under carefully controlled conditions.

Peoples of many races and diverse origins, attracted by an abundance of game and the easily cultivated alluvial soil of the valleys, converged in the vast triangle bordered in the north by the Himalayas, in the west by the mountains of Baluchistan and in the east by the Great Indian desert.

Without any noticeable preliminary stage this culture seems to have been concentrated in large cities, all built on an identical plan. No temples or sanctuaries have been found, no buildings that could be definitely interpreted as having had any ritual purpose. Strange indeed, for the link binding early peoples together is more often than not a common religion. The people of the Indus, however, were not absolutely without religion, for figurines made in terracotta, copper and bronze have been found, as well as statuettes carved in stone, which probably had some religious significance. Painted pottery and carvings on seals and copper tablets show what could well be religious subjects. On one stamp seal a deity is surrounded by sacred animals. It would be difficult to see in the female figurines with their elegant bracelets, necklaces and loin-cloths, hair dressed high off the forehead, the ubiquitous Mother-Goddess. However, they cannot be mere dolls, children's playthings, but were probably servants of an unknown deity, forerunners of the later Indian temple dancers. Numerous scenes from the animal world shown on seals and tablets give an interesting insight on the natural conditions of the area. There are pictures of rhinoceros and gazelle, long since vanished, and their presence is proof that the land, especially in the south, had all the characteristics of steppe-country and that hunting was of great importance.

These pictures have a naturalistic setting; the subject is shown strictly in profile, with an additional object such as an altar or tree (tree of life?) and accompanied by some kind of hieroglyphic script. The same hieroglyphs appear throughout the whole of the Indus region, and have not yet been deciphered. It has been suggested that the short lines are the names of the owners to mark their property, or maybe they are prayers or spells, which is indeed more likely, for the seals were used as amulets and the same letters appear on the copper tablets.

The deeper symbolic meaning, however, remains obscure. A curious fact is that many pictures of water buffalos, elephants and bulls are found, but few ordinary domestic and farmyard animals. The bull may have been a sacrificial animal connected with a fertility cult. The carvings, especially of the humped cattle, are brilliantly executed. One of the animals most frequently seen on the Indus valley seals is the so-called 'unicorn', a single-horned animal as its name implies. What appears to be a single horn could, however, actually be a convention for representing this particular animal in profile, since this view is always chosen. Nevertheless, the other horned animals shown on the seals, such as the zebu and the goat, have both their horns shown. Invariably the 'unicorn' has a manger or decorative post in front of its, which may even be an incense burner. Variations in the style of depicting this strange object are so numerous as to make its precise nature very uncertain. Another interesting animal to be seen on the seals is the elephant. Sometimes he is shown with two curved lines on his back which have been interpreted as representing a backcloth. If this is correct it would seem that here is good evidence for the early domestication of the elephant in India. There exist, also, a few representations of a horned and three-faced male god dressed in rich attire sitting in the position of a yogi; sacred animals surround him. One cannot doubt his divine nature. He may be the prototype of the Indian god Shiva, Lord of the Beasts, he may even be Shiva himself. He is represented as the lord of all living things, the creator of the animal world, the originator of mankind, for beside elephants, rhinoceros, tigers and buffaloes, a little figure of a man appears. On the whole the scenes reveal very little about beliefs and cults, although they already seem to contain the germs of Hinduism. The Indus culture seems too sophisticated for primitive fetishism and nature worship, which is generally a feature of all early cultures.

Nevertheless, it remains a mystery as to why there are no cult centres or architectural monuments devoted to the gods and priestly hierarchy, for the Indus people certainly possessed the necessary technical knowledge and building experience. The reason must have been that these people venerated their gods not publicly, but in the privacy of their own houses. A comparison with Minoan Crete can be seen here (cf. page 213). It may well have been that the Indus people saw their deities in a natural setting and that they communicated with their gods under the open sky at an altar or sacred stone with prayers and ritual dance.

We are much better informed about the secular aspect of the Indus culture. Although there were many small settlements, life seems to have centred around the main cities of Harappā in the north and Mohenjo-daro in the south. In area and population these towns are comparable to the cities of Mesopotamia, and equal, if not superior to them, in general town planning and sanitation. But they lack the monumental architecture of their Sumerian counterparts. There are no temples and palaces, but high citadels with terraces, massive walls and imposing gateways. Platforms of mud bricks faced with baked brick revetments supported extensive buildings which may have been the seat of government. It is less likely that they represented the keep of a feudal overlord, or the habitation of a ruling priesthood. This much is certain, that it was here that the cultural life of the community was centred and here that the upper classes lived. The seals, copper tablets, bronze statuettes and jewellery found within the citadel area are of much better workmanship than those found in the lower parts of the city. As is usual in the Orient, there was a sharp division between the 'haves' and the 'have nots', the small ruling class and the mass of common, working people, who lived under the walls of the citadel in well laid-out and well planned quarters with wide, straight thoroughfares between. The houses followed the typical Oriental plan with blind outer walls, the living rooms arranged round an open courtyard or courtyards, and were sometimes two storeys high. Socially the urban population was strictly differentiated. The workmen's quarters in Harappā near the granaries were very small two-roomed huts huddled together, while small traders and craftsmen, prosperous merchants and business people, lived in well-built brick houses, varying in size according to the status and wealth of their occupants.

But the citadel was a unique feature in town-planning and it would be tempting to postulate a foreign ruling class and not an indigenous nobility. Whatever may have been the real situation, one thing is clear, that the inhabitants of Harappā and Mohenjo-daro were a level-headed people, intent upon practical matters. Never again has there been anywhere in India a similar interest in the well-being of the urban population. The drainage system was perfected to an amazingly high standard of engineering; waste water from the houses, nearly all equipped with bathrooms, was carried away through long underground drains made of clay with inspection holes at regular intervals. Modern-looking facilities for refuse disposal have been found and the rubbish was probably taken away by ox-carts with large wheels, such as exist in India today.

The civil administration must have been extremely efficient. Mohenjo-daro frequently suffered from floods and very often the living quarters were completely destroyed. But the houses were invariably rebuilt on the same street plan as before; obviously a strict supervision saw to it that the structural plan of the original street blocks was kept unaltered.

They also employed standard weights and measures, scrupulously observed by the merchants, although different from Egyptian and Sumerian systems.

The economy on which the thriving cities of the Indus valley rested was mainly agricultural, relying on the rich hinterland. An extensive trade developed not only inland along the navigable rivers, but on an international scale. Seals and ornaments of semi-precious stones of Indian origin have been found at Kish and Ur, and their presence there would be difficult to explain unless one assumes a fairly extensive trade between the two countries. The appearance of Indus artifacts in contemporary Mesopotamian cities has been of great value for the correct dating of the Indus valley culture. For their part the Indus people benefitted from the crafts and skills of Mesopotamia; the potter's wheel may have come from there as well as the technique of brick-making. Nevertheless, foreign influences were only superficial and it would be quite wrong to surmise a migration of a Mesopotamian or Elamite population into the Indus valley.

Both internal and foreign trade must have reached a considerable scale, for the larger houses possessed store-rooms and magazines, as did the Hansa towns of medieval Europe. Following this analogy it would be reasonable to assume a government by an exclusive plutocratic oligarchy.

The final conclusion must be that the Indus culture was static, there was no incentive to progress, and no revolutionary impulses. The conditions and pursuits of its people remained the same, they did not go out to conquer the world. The ten centuries of Harappan civilization ended with the coming of the Aryans, barbarians from the north, the burning of cities and ravaging of homesteads. Early excavators postulated a final catastrophe when they found some skeleton remains of people who had obviously met untimely ends. Unfortunately the published account of these first investigations left much to be desired in clarity, and interpretation is difficult. Some more skeletons have been found in the recently renewed excavations in the town area which support the theory of an invasion and final massacre. In one instance a group of five skeletons were found huddled in the dog-leg bend of a lane where they had died. All these remains have been found in the uppermost stratigraphical levels and, apart from one small group, were not buried or covered in any way. The indications, therefore, are that from this point onwards the site was not inhabited. Something upwards of thirty skeletons have been found at Mohenjo-daro, and so far, all of them come from the town area. It seems, therefore, that the invaders occupied the citadel area, clearing away the signs of massacre, and possibly fires in the town kept marauding beasts at bay so that the corpses in their last contorted attitudes were undisturbed. The collapse of the Indus civilization seems to have been complete and yet another culture sank into oblivion.

Plate 37
A street, Mohenjo-daro

A survey of the history and spiritual background of the Indus culture drew attention to the fact that its people, although skilful town planners, did not produce highly talented architects. No buildings of artistic value, comparable to those of Mesopotamia and Egypt have been found. In the field of town-planning the Indus people surpassed every other Oriental civilization, but it remains a mystery why there should be no evidence of any sacred building. The only ruins found after clearing away the rubble of thousands of years, are those of a highly organized society living in densely populated cities during the third and second millennia BC.

The main building material was baked brick. The sun-dried brick, so much used in Sumer at the same period, is hardly ever found, and then only for the core of the walls and for the huts of the poor. Presumably there were still enough forests in this district to provide the fuel for kilns for baking bricks, otherwise it would have been impossible to produce the millions of cubic feet of brick necessary for the building of the Indus cities. The walls, still many feet high, owe their excellent condition to this indestructible building material. This view of one of the narrow streets speaks for itself.

The lay-out of the streets was similar to that of most other Oriental cities, narrow alleys between houses with blank outer walls. The rooms of the houses were grouped around small inner courtyards which provided light and air, and were one or two storeys high. The sanitation was amazingly modern in design. The main drainage system ran under the paved streets throughout the town, to which the house drains were connected. At regular intervals there were manholes for cleaning and maintenance. The curious double slits in the wall to the right of the picture are rubbish chutes. The household refuse was thrown through the sloping edge into rubbish bins in the street below, and cleared away by the municipal refuse disposal service.

Plate 38
The Great Bath on the citadel, Mohenjo-daro

The exact purpose of the ruins shown in this plate is unknown, although it is evident that the structure, which measures 9 ft 9 in. deep and $42\frac{1}{2} \times 59$ ft in area, was a water basin or bath. Two sets of steps lead to the bottom of the pool and its walls are made watertight with bitumen. Some piers and walls in a poor state of preservation on three sides of the pool could be the remains of small rooms, changing rooms or monks' cells. The bath probably served for ritual ablutions and the cells could then have been changing rooms. This is made even more plausible by the fact that the religion of these people shows a certain affinity with later Hinduism: for example, in the sanctity of the cow and the existence of a three-faced god, seated in a yogi position found on Indus seals, who may perhaps be the forerunner of the god Shiva, or possible already Shiva himself.

The great bath is therefore of exceptional interest, because it is one of the few examples of formal architecture within the Indus culture and the only building to be found which may have had a religious meaning.

Plate 37
A street, Mohenjo-daro

Plate 38
The Great Bath on the citadel, Mohenjo-daro

The Megalith Builders

Plates 39 to 46

SIBYLLE VON REDEN

A CHAIN OF TOMBS, cult monuments and sanctuaries built of gigantic stone blocks stretches over a wide area, reaching from Asia in the east, to Europe in the west. Although not belonging to a common culture, they are collectively called 'megalithic' monuments, from the Greek *megas*—large, and *lithos*—stone.

Most of these monuments are of extreme antiquity, and date from long before the great buildings of Mesopotamia and Egypt. The earliest are found in Palestine and can be dated to the fourth millennium BC. Why these monuments were built and why they are so widespread is one of the most intriguing problems of prehistory.

Thousands of these mysterious relics of the past are found in Israel, Jordan and Arabia, around the Mediterranean and along the shores of the Black Sea; in west and north Europe and in the British Isles, although only in a few instances did they develop into true architecture. During the fourth millennium nomadic tribes living on the rocky table-land of Jordan built simple funeral chambers of four upright stones topped by an equally large block, and people in Spain and southern France still buried their dead in exactly the same manner during the twelfth century BC. These structures are called 'dolmens' after a Breton word meaning 'stone table'. The Oriental corbel-vaulted tomb with its false dome, built in diminishing layers, is another feature of megalithic architecture which fell into abeyance in Europe during the beginning of the twelfth century, only to be revived in Etruscan architecture.

The basic elements of these stone structures did not alter radically during the centuries, although there are variations on the original theme. Such was their sanctity that no basic change was allowed. Religious and ritual traditions have an extremely long life: for instance, neolithic flint knives were used as offerings far into the Bronze Age and the Roman augur used a copper ploughshare to delineate the circumference of a newly founded township.

One could ask whether a discussion of the problem of these vast stone monuments, thought by the ancients to be the work of mythical giants, really belongs in the realm of architecture at all. But as their connection with all later building in stone is apparent, a description of megalithic building is not out of place.

Obviously a deep religious feeling moved primitive man to raise these towering masses of stone. The Herculean efforts that went into the creation of these gigantic tombs must have been born of a faith 'that could move mountains'. Stone was for these people the symbol of permanence and mystical powers, and these titanic structures were his answer to death and dissolution.

The outstanding feature of these megalithic structures is their similarity and identical grave furniture. Would it be too much to surmise a common substratum of beliefs, deeply embedded in human experience, that stimulated peoples of diverse races and conditions? That peoples living under the scorching sun of the Orient or Mediterranean were moved by the same ideals as those in the dark and misty north, many thousands of miles away?

It is possible that the period of the great cults of the dead which have given us these earliest monuments in stone represented a special phase in the spiritual and social evolution of mankind. Man became more sure of himself when he had settled down as an agriculturalist. The more he was aware of his own identity, his own power and abilities, the more he may have felt his inadequacy in the face of death, and the fiercer may have been his reaction against the impermanence of life. It was indeed the primordial fear of death that motivated his belief in the power of the dead. Dark images of the 'living dead' already existed in palaeolithic times crystallized in the conviction that body and soul were inseparable. The preservation of the body in an indestructible tomb was the most essential condition for the continued existence of the human soul.

This may have been the ideology behind megalith building, but practical considerations also played a part. Concentration of power in a strong ruling class or even in the hands of one person, and unification of tribal families into larger communities during the Neolithic period made possible the great communal effort without which these enormous monuments could never have been built.

However, not all the people of the ancient world looked upon death in the same way as the megalith-builders. The peasant settlers in the fourth millennium along the River Danube cared but little for the dead, and in the Sumerian Gilgamesh Epic of the third millennium, death and the life hereafter are treated with a certain pessimistic resignation. But in the Mediterranean area a creed arose, promising after death not only resurrection, but a spiritual power far beyond that of the living.

The origins of this belief go far back into Palaeolithic times. People around the Mediterranean and in western and central Europe treated the dead with great respect and care. Interment in caves or rock-shelters was the general custom, and weapons and jewellery were placed in the graves. The dead were frequently sprinkled with red ochre, probably for the magical properties of its blood-red colouring. Sometimes the corpse was tied and bound. All this indicates an ancient belief in some kind of continuation of life after death.

During the earliest urban settlements of Jericho and Çatal Hüyük it was customary to bury the dead beneath the floors of the houses, and this remained the general practice in the Middle East for thousands of years. It was only when the imagination attached greater importance to the dead, that separate resting places were built for them, on which much greater care was ultimately expended than for the living. The family tomb of a great tribe, the collective graves of a whole village community, the last dwelling place of an overlord gradually became the sacred centre of the religious life of the community.

It seems that ancestor worship, so typical of nomads with their strong sense of tribal solidarity, was at an early stage connected with the cult of the great Mother-goddess. The great Mother-goddess, the embodiment of the eternal fertility of the earth, who gave and took away life, ruled as queen of the underworld as well as in the world of the living. In her chthonic aspect she was the goddess of death, while she also promised resurrection, because she herself was life. In an ancient *Rigveda* text the dead are addressed with these words: 'Bend down to the earth, thy mother, she will rescue thee from the void.' This clearly expresses an age-old belief in the recreative powers of the great goddess. Whosoever went down into her realm was endowed with her own life-giving force. He became wiser and more powerful than the living, whose protector and helper he could be if his grave had been tended with due care.

The cult of the dead in pre and early historic times was closely connected with fertility rites. The belief that the dead could send rain and command the winds was widespread. To sleep on their tombs could cure sickness and brought prophetic dreams. This aspect of a religion asking for a nearly superhuman effort in the service of the dead is, however, only of interest here because of its importance as the origin of sacred architecture.

The earliest stone-built cult centres were probably dedicated to the dead. It was only a step from prehistoric cave burials to the construction of rock graves, artificial caves, which were already in use during the fourth millennium BC in the eastern Mediterranean and spread from there to the west as far as the Iberian peninsula. They were shaped like baker's ovens—the entrance through a steep shaft. It is not clear, however, whether the idea of a stone-built tomb above ground, of major importance for later architecture, was conceived at the same time or later. But it could only originate in a country dominated by mountains and rocks, where the materials for this kind of building were readily available.

Even today one can be struck by the mystery and grandeur of mountains; the solid mass of rock, its often bizarre shapes and colours stir the imagination and create superstitious fears. For primitive man stone was the immovable foundation of his world. His deities and spirits lived on the cloud-covered mountain tops. Caves in the dark depths of the mountainside were his first sanctuaries, falling boulders were the sign of the anger of the gods. His first tools were made of stone. Stone was sacred, filled with mystical powers, no other material was fit to receive the dead. Stone not only protected the dead, it could take the place of his wasted body and could become the eternal, indestructible dwelling of his soul, from which mysterious forces radiated.

The idea of stone as the seat of numinous power is very ancient: a small rounded pillar placed in a shrine was worshipped at Jericho in the seventh millennium. It is not clear whether this was a phallic fetish or a symbol of the Mother-goddess. In any case it resembles the aniconic idols, worshipped as Magna Mater and the goddess of Love in Western Asia in Roman times. Tacitus remarks that the famous statue of Aphrodite in the temple of Paphos was nothing but a 'round block of stone in conical shape'. Even in Tacitus' day the epiphany of a deity could be experienced with the same religious fervour as in prehistoric times. The Kaaba at Mecca, the most sacred shrine of Islam, houses a black stone, the sanctity of which is much older than Islam itself.

Orthostats, conical in shape or stelae rounded at the top, called 'menhirs' (the Breton word for large stone) were full of symbolic meaning. They could be the house of a god, the bridge between heaven and earth, the immortal body of the dead or the abode of his soul; they could be phallic fertility idols, memorial or funerary objects and boundary stones. Placed in circles, squares or in long avenues, they led towards the entrance of an open air sanctuary, identical in pattern from Asia Minor to the British Isles. The sacred stone-circle of Stonehenge represents the finest architectural example of this type of Oriental idea *(plate 43)*.

Seeing the thousands of menhirs of different shape and size standing in orderly rows between the red and gold heathlands of Brittany, one cannot but fall under the spell of the magical atmosphere of ancient rites *(plate 39)*. The largest menhir of all times lies near Locmariaquer in Brittany. It is broken in four pieces and lies at the foot of a mound 427 ft long and 164 ft wide. The menhir itself is the traditional 'sugar-loaf' shape is 65½ ft high, 16½ ft in diameter and weighs over 34 tons. The stone face is carefully tooled and finished. It was no mean technical feat to erect this monolith. However, its use is not at all clear. It could have been the throne for the soul of a departed ancestor buried under the enormous tumulus, a monument of his worldly power, or it could have been erected for a deity, like the Egyptian obelisk of the sun-god at Abu Gurob.

The menhir is the simplest form of monument, but in the megalithic graves several different conceptions, traditions and building techniques can be recognized. Megalithic building is essentially a form of construction in which large blocks of stone are used and placed on top of, or beside each other, without any kind of bonding or mortar. The classical type of megalithic building was the table-shaped dolmen, although this was in Europe at least, a fairly late development. Three to six upright stones formed a small rectangular chamber, leaving an entrance space. When the last burial had taken place, the entrance was closed by another large slab and the whole structure covered by a protective mound. Today, when the earth has eroded away, the stones are left exposed. It seems that the graves were left open for a considerable time and that they were visited regularly for religious services.

The dolmen and the simplest forms of gallery-grave, with low narrow corridors leading to the actual burial chamber, are still so primitive that they look more like caves than 'houses'. But there are more elaborate constructions, the prototypes of which can be found in the round huts of the eastern Mediterranean and western Asia. These are the already mentioned corbel-vaulted tombs or 'tholoi' with a long corridor *(dromos)* leading into a round chamber. The corridor and the lower courses of the walls were usually lined with flat orthostats; the chamber itself was often built of small dry-stone masonry. A round or oval mound covered these tombs.

This kind of grave, the gallery grave, in which two different building-techniques were used side by side, was the earliest in western Europe, and is found especially in Spain and Brittany. Originally mostly built near to the seashores or on islands, they could have been the graves of sailors who explored the whole of the Mediterranean and ventured far into the Atlantic ocean during the fourth millennium. It may have been these people who colonized parts of western and northern Europe and initiated the more primitive peoples into their religion.

Vaulted burial chambers are rare in the later megalithic period, but those which do exist are built with great care and are beautifully finished. They may have been the graves of royal families, probably the descendants of the first colonists. Technically the most advanced is a 'tholos' in southern Spain, the 'Cueva del Romeral' near Antequera. It is 145 ft long, and is cut into the natural rock. The walls are partly built of dry-stone masonry and partly megalithic. The long corridor leads to a finely worked circular burial chamber. The inner walls are corbelled and rounded-off to give a smooth surface, instead of the usual overlapping ridges. Behind the large chamber lies a smaller cell, also beehive-shaped. The whole construction is very similar to the Mycenaean royal tombs *(cf. plate 61)* but in comparison with the greatest period of Mycenaean culture, the Cueva del Romeral seems barbaric and primitive. Moreover, it is probably older than the Mycenaean tombs, the best of which belong to the thirteenth century BC.

Another monument of major importance is New Grange in Ireland. It was undoubtedly the tomb of a royal family equal in importance to the famous Atreidae. It lies under a tumulus of white stones, 295 ft in diameter and 39½ ft high; the base is revetted by huge blocks. Thirty-five menhirs form an outer circle around it. A narrow corridor, 65½ ft long in dry-stone masonry faced with stone slabs, leads to a central chamber with a 20-ft high vaulted roof. There are three smaller cells grouped like clover-leaves round the central chamber. A shallow stone basin stood here when the tomb was opened about 300 years ago with eight small conical stones arranged round it. Similar basins, probably meant to receive the ashes of the dead are still standing in the side chambers.

Most of the megalithic tombs in Europe belong to the category of the 'passage grave', although their ground plan consisting of a chamber reached by a corridor has many variations. Sometimes the chamber is very large with a short corridor and portal, whereas other tombs have long passages with side chambers. One of the best examples is the West Kennet Long Barrow near Avebury in Wiltshire. After passing through a semi-circular forecourt with a façade of upright stones one enters a passage 43 ft long. From either side of this corridor two pairs of side chambers open out, like transepts of a church. The tomb, dated to the third millennium, apparently stayed open for hundreds of years and was used as a religious centre, for many gifts and offerings of different periods have been found. After the final burial had taken place perhaps about 1600 BC the forecourt was blocked with two megaliths weighing nearly twenty tons, and the whole tomb buried beneath an earth and chalk barrow. The skeletons of forty-six people were found when it was excavated in 1955–56, together with animal bones and much pottery.

These mausolea, such as West Kennet and others, prove their dual purpose as communal graves and sanctuaries, for often the actual tomb was surrounded by a ditch and a ring of stones indicating the sacred area where offerings have been found. There were libation shafts and trenches, menhirs and stone stelae engraved with the signs of the goddess of death, spirals, concentric circles, meanders and eyes, etc.

With the beginning of the Bronze Age the passage graves fell into disuse throughout Western and Northern Europe, only to be replaced by the 'gallery grave'. Here, the chamber itself was long and narrow, without any corridor, and divided into compartments by dividing walls or large slabs of stone. These elongated chambers were often 98 ft long with a short entrance set in the centre of the longitudinal side so that the structure became T-shaped. But the gallery graves were comparatively small and low, often only 65 or 98 ft long.

In the Paris Basin and in central Germany, the *allées couvertes*, a type of subterranean gallery grave, faced with neatly polished, smallish, stone slabs, became customary.

The megalithic structures on the whole are on a massive scale. There are stone blocks weighing up to 100 and 150 tons and the energy used in the transporting and building of these resting places for the dead, must have bordered on frenzy. The difference between the humble primitive huts of the living, remains of which have been found in Brittany, and the eternal dwellings of the dead is immense. Stone and earth weighing up to 8000 and 10,000 tons were shifted and very often the enormous monoliths had to be brought from far away, because the material used was not always available locally. This mammoth work must have been the voluntary collective effort of a community, seething with religious fervour, or the labour of serfs in the service of a ruling class.

The final phase of the megalithic culture drew to a close towards the end of the second millennium. Some of the great monuments of this period were never covered by earth and must be considered as temples in honour of the dead. The 'Roche aux fées' in northern Britanny, a rectangular construction of 41 slate blocks of a deep purple colour belongs to this category. A monumental portal leads along a passage into the main chamber 13 ft wide and divided by stone slabs into several sections. Four enormous stone slabs nearly 65 ft long were sufficient to cover the roof of the monument.

The overwhelming size of the architecture of the final phase perhaps reflects the power and wealth of a king or priest-king ruling over a large and relatively prosperous community. Business relations between West and East were well established;

there was a lively trade in metals, amber and other raw materials and considerable wealth had been accumulated. Many of the large collective burial places belonged to village communities; the eleven gallery graves under one Long Barrow at Barnenez in Finistere were definitely a village cemetery. Nevertheless most of the imposing tumuli of Neolithic times were probably erected as graves for a ruling class, who could summon a labour force and direct the organization necessary for the transport and erection of the sarcen and blue stones of Stonehenge, the menhirs of Locmariaquer and other monuments.

Another aspect of megalithic building developed meanwhile in the eastern Mediterranean: the cyclopean type of architecture. This represents the same impulse to build in extravagant dimensions. In this case, walls were built of enormous undressed stones, accurately adjusted without the help of mortar. This technique had been in use in Palestine and Cilicia for defensive buildings since early in the Neolithic period and the later Mycenaean citadels are its most famous examples. According to Pausanias they were built by the Cyclops because in his day nobody thought it possible that these enormous masses of stone could have been moved by human hand (cf. *plate 64*). The prehistoric "nuraghes" of Sardinia, powerful conical-shaped towers and fortresses are no less impressive than the Mycenaean palaces (*plate 46*).

The *Talayot* on the Balearic islands and the *navetas* also seem to be connected with a cult of the dead. Talayots are short stumpy towers and navetas are boat-shaped megalithic burial chambers. The round towers of Corsica belong to this group and are now known to be communal graves and sanctuaries. It would be interesting to know whether the *specchie* in southern Italy also were funerary monuments, but this requires more research. These and other cyclopean structures not yet explored on the Mediterranean islands and in ancient Palestine seem to indicate that this technique was spread by seafarers, possibly proto-Phoenicians, during the second millennium.

Except for Stonehenge, whose architecture may possibly be attributable to Mycenaean overlords, because of the carving of what seems to be a Mycenaean axe on one of the upright stones, megalithic building developed only on one occassion into true architecture, namely on the small islands of Malta and Gozo. During the third and second millennium a distinctive temple-architecture developed here in which the traditional elements of megalithic temple and tomb building took on a completely new form. The Maltese temple was elliptical, constructed on a simple trefoil plan, to which later apses were added. It is a fine example of native culture combining worship of the gods with a cult of the dead.

The controversial problem of the origin of Megalithic building has by no means been satisfactorily solved. Ever since classical times people have been speculating about these mysterious gigantic stone constructions. Where did the people come from? It has been argued that they originated in the eastern Mediterranean, or the Iberian peninsula, or even in Jutland where extremely large and very early megalith graves have been found. Egypt is often hailed as the cradle of megalithic culture.

The sacred architecture of Egypt certainly is on a very large scale and the elaborate Egyptian death cult seems closely related to megalith ideology, but their monumental architecture, artistically and technically far advanced, is the creation of a mature culture. Mastabas and pyramids can in no way be a later stage of the dolmen. It is possible that Egyptian tombs, temples and obelisks may have influenced the more primitive Mediterranean peoples, but they were definitely not prototypes.

The Palestinian dolmens and passage graves covered by earth were much older than the pyramids, but the latter are the ultimate realization of a stone dwelling for the dead with its covering tumulus. Egyptian funerary architecture, however, first developed in the marshy lower regions of the Nile, which is poor in natural stone. Palestine, the bridge between Africa and Asia, where since Palaeolithic times races and cultures have met, has always been the cradle of religious ideas. It would indeed not be too far-fetched to imagine here the birthplace of a world-wide religion, long before Mosaic monotheism and Christianity, a religion that stimulated mankind in its earliest stages to gigantic efforts in honour of the dead. In Palestine the care and veneration of the dead was of very high antiquity. An early monumental tomb containing several burials was discovered a few years ago on the Lake of Hulah in Galilee, which must be dated to the seventh or sixth millennium BC and most of the funerary furniture in west and north European graves is identical to that from Palestine. Cyclopean building technique in Palestine can also be traced back to the Neolithic period. Wherever its roots may lie, it was there that man began to think in terms of stone building, and the methods of the megalithic builders are the beginning of all architecture in stone. Dolmen and domed tholoi and the sacred precinct with its circle of menhirs, are the prototype for a sanctuary in monumentally enclosed space.

Plate 39
The dolmen at Kercadoret, Brittany

The dolmen of Kercadoret consists of six upright stones with the flat sides facing inwards, and a vast capstone. The short corridor which led up to the chamber has completely disappeared. The holes between the uprights were filled with smaller stones, rubble and clay and the whole structure, about six feet high, was buried under an artificial mound. These roughly built passage graves and the still simpler dolmens without passages are found over a large area of Europe and the Middle East, from Palestine to southern Sweden.

Archaeologists, thinking in terms of the evolution of architecture from simplicity to complexity, formerly equated primitiveness with antiquity and saw in these dolmens the beginning of megalithic grave architecture. Modern research has however, established that this is not valid for European megalithic graves, since, in the regions of the oldest known megalithic structures, the Iberian peninsula and Brittany, vaulted tombs, which are technically speaking the most advanced, proved to be the earliest, while the dolmens belonged to the final phase of megalithic building. The dolmen at Kercadoret does not belong to the earliest Armorican stone graves, but is a native interpretation of the stone tomb introduced into Brittany towards the end of the fourth millennium by Mediterranean peoples. The native builders had as yet no experience in stone building and were unable to reproduce the highly developed tomb structures of the new settlers. In any case, the corbelled burial chamber remained the exception in northwest Europe where it was always the simpler construction that was preferred.

The many different forms of passage graves in southern Brittany stem either from practical considerations or the fantasy of their creators. The dimension and shape of corridor and chamber and their relative positions within the tomb varied considerably. Some graves became very complex monuments through the addition of extra cells alongside the corridor; some were elbow-shaped with the corridor and the long narrow chamber placed at right-angles to each other, but this shape does not occur frequently. The real hall-mark of the European megalithic graves is the use of giant stones.

The dolmen of Kercadoret may have been the modest grave of a peasant family, but the higher the family rated in the social strata, the more monumental the grave became. The gigantic funerary monuments in the neighbourhood of Morbihan suggest a sacred precinct, where only the highest of the land were buried. Here also are the largest alignments and menhirs. The accumulation of megalithic graves around Carnac and on the peninsula of Locmariaquer also suggests a sanctuary, for there are no traces of towns or villages. Near the dolmen of Kercadoret there are a number of passage graves built of large stones. The granite capstone of the grave of Mane Rutual is $37\frac{1}{2}$ ft long, 14 ft 9 in. wide and $1\frac{1}{2}$ ft thick, and weighs over 49 tons. Capstones of a similar weight are no exception in northern Europe. The largest of the three capstones on a 82-ft long passage grave near Antequera in Andalusia has a volume of 1836 cubic ft and weighs over 167 tons.

The enormous blocks were sometimes transported over large distances, probably with the help of wooden rollers, but without metalled roads. Another method of transport was to make clay slipways on which the stones, already on rollers, could slide. Manpower and draught animals were used as well. A description of the moving, in 1885, of a lintel weighing ten tons to the churchyard of a French town gives an idea of the efforts required in moving such vast stones. The stone had only to be moved less than two miles along an existing road, but eighteen horses were needed and the whole operation took three days.

Plate 40
Dolmen de Soto, Trigueros, Spain

Seafarers from the eastern Mediterranean reached the Iberian peninsula during the fifth and fourth millennia BC probably bringing with them the knowledge of agriculture and stock breeding. After this the connections with the East remained close, and then the later discovery of silver and copper mines made the peninsula highly important to the Bronze Age cultures of the Aegean and the Near East. Southern Spain and Portugal developed into centres of overseas trade. Many small fortified towns sprang up near the mining areas.

During the Neolithic period, the cult of the great Mother-goddess arrived in the Iberian peninsula in the wake of the colonists, and by the beginning of the Chalcolithic period a fully-developed cult of the dead had been established. Near the settlements extensive necropolises with collective chamber tombs constructed of stone beneath a mound, or rock graves came into being. Ingeniously constructed passage graves in dry-stone masonry with corbelled roofs, the sides reinforced with stone slabs now appear; these are the earliest forms of graves, and this idea may well have been imported from the East. These tombs occur mostly near the sea and along the estuaries of the main rivers. Megalithic graves also

appear in these regions, but passage graves remained the most popular kind of tomb inland until well into the second millennium BC, and it is more than likely that the megalithic architecture spread from Spain where it reached its zenith, over the rest of north-western Europe.

The dolmen de Soto belongs to a group of grave monuments dating from the period when mining and trading in metals was at its height around 2000 BC. It represents the prototype of west and north European megalithic building. Trapezoidal in plan, it is nearly 69 ft long and lies under a tumulus 246 ft in diameter. Granite blocks of 20 tons were transported over a distance of $23\frac{1}{2}$ miles. The earth for the tumulus also seems to have been brought from some distance away. Seventeen of the stone slabs of the chamber, where eight bodies in a contracted attitude were found, are engraved with stylized human figures, weapons and mysterious symbols. One of the reliefs is that of the dolmen idol, the schematized figure of the owl-faced goddess of fertility and death. No wonder that folklore has woven so many legends around these monuments. Although the dolmen de Soto is architecturally not of the same standard as the still larger Cueva de Menga, or the Cueva del Romeral that seems to foreshadow the Mycenaean tholos, it belongs nevertheless to the most impressive achievements of the European megalithic structures.

Plate 41
The 'Visbeck Bride', Germany

The so-called 'Visbeck Bride', a hunsbed
on the Ahlhorner Heath, belongs to a class
which includes a number of megalithic
graves in Oldenburg in north-west Germany. The original Long Barrow had disappeared, and only the inner structure of
boulders, 269 ft long and 29–33 ft wide, with
the flat side outwards, now remains. The
single burial chamber is much damaged. A
second similar hunsbed, the 'Visbeck
Bridegroom' lies nearby, 373 ft long and
also with only one passage. The actual
burial chambers are relatively small (23 and
33 ft long) compared with the enormous
superstructure. Presumably the barrows
were meant to contain more than one
chamber; a 111-ft long hunsbed near
Kleinenkneten actually contains three separate passage graves.

The communal effort necessary for the
erection of these massive funerary monuments must have been immense. The
bouders were often six feet thick and had to
be transported over long distances. Enormous masses of earth were heaped up to
provide the barrows. The burial chambers
had an extra revetment of smaller stones. On
the undisturbed hunsbed at Kleinenkneten
this covering is still intact. The 'Visbeck
Bride' was probably the burial site of a
powerful local family rich enough to afford
such a monument; it is less likely to have
been the collective burial place of the entire
village. Several smaller megalithic graves
nearby form together a kind of cemetery.

The megalithic culture reached Oldenburg during the third millennium BC. The
remaining sixty-five graves are only a small
proportion of the original number and make
this province in north-west Germany one of
the richest in megalithic monuments.

Plate 42
The Hunsbed at Borger, Holland

This hunsbed at Borger is the largest of the fifty-four Dutch megalithic graves found along the Hondsrug in the province of Drente, a ridge of hills formed by the terminal moraines left by the retreating ice-cap of the glacial period.

Opened up in 1682, mainly on the instigation of a well-known poetess, it was the first prehistoric excavation in Holland. The imposing structure is orientated on an east–west axis. The short entrance passage in the centre of its long side gives it the shape of the letter T, and is similar to those frequently encountered in the north German graves. It is 74 ft long, 7½ ft high and its maximum width is 13 ft 3 in. Rough, undressed boulders are used in the construction. Of the uprights twenty-three are still standing, the two end stones and most of the capstones are in their original places. A trilithon construction formed a primitive portal. The passage leading towards the entrance consisted of only two stones and was probably never roofed over. The building technique was as follows: The prehistoric builders first made a mound of earth in the exact measurements of the planned grave chamber. Separate holes or a continuous ditch were then dug in which the upright and end stones were tightly rammed. The sides of the stones smoothed by glacial action, faced inwards. The gaps between were then filled with small stones and clay and the base of the structure reinforced by an extra course of stones. The next step was to bring the oval mound within which the burial chamber would be hidden, up to the height of the uprights and to construct a firm ramp of sand and gravel on the narrow sides of the structure. The capstones were levered up to their required height along the ramp, stakes being driven into the soil to prevent the boulder from rolling back. After the capstones had been put in place, the original mound of earth was dug out from the chamber, the floor of which was plastered and covered with a layer of fine gravel. The structure was then ready for the burial, after which the chamber was carefully closed and the whole structure hidden beneath a vast tumulus. The base of the mound was reinforced with a row of large boulders, this time with the smooth side outwards.

Most of the hunsbeds seems to have been used for several centuries, and according to the latest research they appear to be much earlier than previously thought. They were probably built somewhere between about 2500 and 2200 BC.

Plate 43
Stonehenge, Wiltshire, England

The impressive ruins of Stonehenge consist of a series of stone circles around an inner horseshoe of bluestones, and represent the high-water mark of megalithic architecture in north-west Europe. The monument lies in the midst of an area with a large number of barrows and other similar structures.

Stonehenge as we see it today was not originally completed in one building operation, but consists of a number of building phases, and probably reached its final stage in about 1500 BC. Archaeological research of the nineteenth and twentieth centuries shed new light on the history of the stone circles and revealed that there were at least three major building periods to be distinguished.

The earliest phase, Stonehenge I, dating from the beginning of the second millennium, consisted of a ditch with a bank outside (a feature of most of the henge monuments in southern England) and the so-called 'Aubrey Holes'. A sandstone menhir 20 ft high, probably one of a pair of entrance posts, now lying on its side, and the Heelstone outside the bank, probably also belong to this period. The occurrence of graves and offering pits points to some sort of funerary cult at Stonehenge. During the eighteenth century BC additions were made to the earlier sanctuary probably by the western European people who settled in southern England at this time. The Beaker people, as they were called, erected a double circle of eighty-two bluestones (spotted diorite), a stone only found in the Prescelly Mountains of Pembrokeshire, 186 miles away. This circle was, however, later dismantled and the stones used in a subsequent structure. At this time also, the Avenue leading from the River Avon to the north-east entrance was constructed.

The middle of the second millennium BC was a period of great prosperity for southern England which was the centre of an intensive trade between the west country and the Continent, and to this period belongs the final phase of Stonehenge, when a circle of thirty greyish-green sarcen stones was set up. These uprights originally supported a continuous ring of lintels three feet thick. The lintels interlock and fit in to the uprights by means of a knob (tenon) and a corresponding cup (mortice). Inside the ring of trilithons stands a horseshoe of undressed bluestone with its open end to the north-east. The horseshoe seems to have had a special significance for it is repeated at the centre of the structure by nineteen carefully dressed bluestones. The so-called 'Altar Stone' a 16-ft long block of sandstone, now embedded in the soil, belongs to this period.

Some aspects of the construction of Stonehenge still remain a mystery. The advanced technique of tooling a material harder than granite demanded great skill, and endless patience. The subtle entasis of the sarcen uprights, the curving and slight upwards broadening of the lintels, add to the optical illusion of height and balance. The standard of workmanship found here is excellent when compared to the crudeness of other megalithic monuments in the British Isles.

During an intensive photographic survey in 1953 a number of very eroded carvings of axes and a dagger were discovered on one of the uprights, and this gave rise to the hypothesis that Stonehenge was the work of foreign builders from the Mycenean cultural sphere. There is an undeniable likeness between the stone circles and those around the royal graves at Mycenae, and many objects found in the area of Stonehenge prove trade connections with the Cretan-Mycenaean world. It is not at all unlikely that some great chief of the early English Bronze Age appointed an architect from afar for this immense project, where, according to the latest estimates 1500 workmen must have toiled for more than five years.

Plate 44
View of the entrance into the sanctum. The Middle Temple of Hal Tarxien, Malta

The temple complex of Hal Tarxien, covering an area of nearly two and a half acres, consists of three parts dating from different periods, and a small trefoil building of considerably older date. The wide portal of the west temple, the last to be built, which forms the entrance to the whole enclosure, and the megalithic enclosure-bank have disappeared, but the bases of the stone inner wall remain. Here and there they still support parts of a superstructure consisting of oblong blocks. The middle temple, set obliquely behind the anterior building, is possibly of the same date as the temple at Hagar Kim. Its three oval-shaped compartments along the main axis decrease gradually in size. The first of these functioned as a forecourt. A round hearth stone and a large stone basin seem to indicate cult-proceedings. This was probably the only place open to the general public. The entrance to the inner halls has a symmetrical arrangement of projecting piers and recessed walls set on a low stepping stone. A barrier blocks the entry into the holy of holies, decorated with a spiral design symbolizing the threatening eye of the goddess of death and the apotropaic power of the eye makes the screen all the more effective. A similar symbol occurs once more at the entrance to the side apses of the furthermost oval, carved four times on two finely polished screens against a trelliswork background. The trellis effect was achieved by innumerable little holes. The workmanship of the inner chambers is of a higher quality than that of the forecourt. The stone plinths of the apsidal walls are accurately fitted and a block still standing on one of them is slightly tilted forwards with a wedge. It is possible that it formed the lower course of a true vault and that the apses of the later temple had domed instead of corbelled roofs.

The third hall of the middle temple possessed a niche in the centre of the back wall in which cult objects probably stood. These statuettes of crude and shapeless goddesses and phallic pillars have been found in great numbers in the immediate neighbourhood. Entry into the inner sanctum where only the priests were allowed was by way of a secret passage inside the yard-thick walls. Stairs to the top of the apse walls are still extant. The Maltese sanctuaries possessed several arrangements for oracles and other mystic proceedings. A secret chamber has been discovered with a long narrow opening into the forecourt of the Hal Tarxien temple that may have served as an amplifier for the voice of a priest.

The two earlier megalithic sanctuaries, although they are built on a simpler plan with rough undressed stone, convey, nevertheless, a certain dignity and grandeur. The later west temple dating from the sixteenth century is elegant in proportions and possesses a wealth of ornamental reliefs on the stone blocks and altars, accentuated by red and white paint. The numerous covered niches and cells which played an important role, as in all other later sanctuaries, are remarkably small. The high standard of workmanship is all the more astounding as the islanders had no metal implements and all the work and elaborate carving was done with flint and stone tools and animal horns. The ornamentation of the west temple shows a marked Cretan influence in its predilection for spirals and tendrils. Finely executed reliefs of sacrifical animals occur only once in this temple and once in the middle temple.

The west temple was the latest and most ornate building of the mysterious megalithic culture on Malta and Gozo, which left more than thirty gigantic sanctuaries, but hardly any traces of the daily life of the population whose creative activities seem to have concentrated entirely on the service of the dead and their long since forgotten deities.

Plate 45
Talayot sa Nova, Arta, Mallorca

The conical towers *(talayots)*, which are found on the Balearic islands are reminiscent of a very old Oriental technique that was the prototype of the cyclopean architecture of the whole Mediterranean area.

Its characteristic conical shape is achieved by a gradual diminishing of the courses towards the top. Tombs in dry-stone walling of a similar shape were already built on the Sinai peninsula during the second half of the fourth millennium, not larger than two or three metres in diameter and equally high. The talayots also seem to have been grave and cult buildings, for traces of burials and offerings have been found. They were about 13 to 16½ ft high and had a diameter of up to 33 ft. The ground plan is circular or rectangular and construction only sometimes cyclopean. Besides the corbelled roofs there occur also flat roofs, supported by a central column. The larger talayots have a second storey above the main hall with a corridor; others have an inside staircase to a roof terrace. Many of these towers stand on a podium.

Other megalithic structures are the *navetas*, stone graves in the shape of an upturned boat, a distinctive type of pillared hall, menhirs, circular or semicircular stone enclosures, vaguely reminiscent of Stonehenge and fortified villages within cyclopean walls.

The Balearic megalithic culture belongs to the Bronze Age period which started on the islands in the middle of the second millennium and continued until the last centuries of the pre-Christian era as part of a general western Mediterranean culture. Its affinity with the Sardinian *nuraghe* culture or the Torre culture of Corsica is undeniable.

It is not known which seafaring people were responsible for spreading the cyclopean technique throughout the western Mediterranean but it was the architecture and religious ideas of those people that conditioned the prehistoric island cultures and also left their mark in southern Italy in the form of the *specchie*, those enormous monuments in stone.

Plate 46
The nuraghe at Sant' Antine, Sardinia

The *nuraghe* of Sant' Antine is one of the last cyclopean fortifications bult on the island of Sardinia as a stronghold against the Romans. It is dated to the fourth or third century BC. Punic engineers from the Carthaginian ports on the island may have helped with the construction of the citadel with its many towers, terraces and courtyards, a safe refuge for its people in times of war, and a strategic base for a whole regiment. But the prototype for the nuraghe was established probably a thousand years earlier. The rough dry-stone construction of polygonal stones gave way to regular courses of dressed blocks. The preference, however, for colossal blocks, especially for the base remained, and even a construction as late as the nuraghe Sant' Antine was still constructed without the use of mortar to bond the blocks and with smaller stones and clay to fill in the gaps. The centre tower, at present still standing 59 ft high, retained the earlier truncated conical shape and within its walls were the same circular rooms and corbelled roofs as of old.

The nuraghe can be considered as the prototype of the defensive stronghold. It shows a nearly unbroken façade with only a few openings in the walls, which are 16 to 49 ft thick. The doors are so low that one had to stoop to enter or even crawl on hands and knees. Sometimes they were high up and could only be reached by wooden or rope ladders. The early nuraghes had no doors at all but only a subterranean entrance. To the right of the entrance corridor there is often a small apartment for the guard who could challenge any intruders on their unprotected side. A spiral staircase or ramp inside the strong wall led to the battlements.

If by any chance the enemy broke through, he was then severely hampered by the narrow stairs and galleries within and was unable to attack in full strength. The defenders for their part were in a favourable position to ward off a large number of attackers with a relatively small force.

Originally the nuraghe may have been built as the stronghold of a family and served as a refuge for the many tribal feuds. In later times they were centres of larger settlements, where the scattered population could find shelter with their goods and livestock in times of danger.

During the eighth century BC they were extended to include annexes and smaller towers and linked together with very thick walls honeycombed with passages and galleries. Store rooms, cisterns and wells, even forges and smelting furnaces made it possible to withstand a long siege. When Sardinia was threatened by the Phoenicians, Greeks and Etruscans, the inhabitants, by nature rather individualistic, seem to have joined forces against the foreign invaders. Nuraghes were built at every possible invasion point. The coast was dotted with watch towers and warning fires were lit from nuraghe to nuraghe over Sardinia.

The most impressive military installation is situated on top of a plateau $7\frac{1}{2}$ miles long and $2\frac{1}{2}$ miles wide with a 1954-ft high escarpment. This natural stronghold, large enough to give shelter to the greater part of the population with all their stock, was fortified by twenty nuraghes overlooking every path of ascent. It is amazing how many of these cyclopean towers there are on the island; about three thousand are still in a good state of preservation. In construction the Sardinian nuraghes are a reminder of the Mycenaean citadels. Both archaeological finds and legends speak of the foundation of Mycenaean colonies on the island, but eastern Mediterranean settlements on Sardinia go much farther back in time. It is probable that the first conical towers are from a much earlier colonization and that the cyclopean construction spread from Syria and Palestine over Corsica and the Balearics, bypassing Greece.

Plate 39
The dolmen at Kercadoret, Brittany

Plate 40
Dolmen de Soto, Trigueros, Spain

Plate 41
The 'Visbeck Bride', Germany

Plate 42
The Hunsbed at Borger, Holland

Plate 43
Stonehenge, Wiltshire, England

Plate 44
View of the entrance into the sanctum.
The Middle Temple of Hal Tarxien, Malta

Plate 45
Talayot sa Nova, Arta, Mallorca

Plate 46
The nuraghe at Sant' Antine, Sardinia

The Hittites *Plates 47 to 50*

FRANZ FISCHER

THE HITTITES arrived at a relatively late date on the historical horizon of the ancient Orient. The cultures of the Nile, the Two Rivers and the Indus were in full bloom when these people appeared on the extreme borders of what was later to be the centre of their world, and only after several generations of assimilation did they achieve an independent civilization. The coming of the Hittites brought the first known Indo-European speaking peoples into Western Asia, and thus began a series of events of great significance to the history of Europe.

The existence of the Hittite people has only relatively recently been discovered, although the name was known from the Bible. In the Old Testament under this name they figured as one of the many tribes inhabiting northern Syria, and gained considerable importance during the time when the kings of Israel hired Egyptian and Hittite troops to disperse the Syrian army. A completely new light was thrown on them when Bedouin Arabs found at Tell el-Amarna in 1887 the famous clay tablets containing the archives of two Egyptian kings, Amenhetep III and Akhenaton, of the fourteenth century BC. Among the many documents were several letters addressed to Syrian and Palestinian kings in which a king of the 'Land of Hatti' is mentioned. These letters are written in cuneiform script in Akkadian, the diplomatic language of that time; the name 'Hatti' has also been found written in hieroglyphs on Egyptian monuments and is read as 'Cheta'. The exact location, however, of the 'Land of Hatti' could not be deduced from the letters, but it seemed certain that behind the Egyptian name lay hidden the name of a people known to us from the Bible as the Horites. The existence of the 'Land of Hatti' was consequently much earlier than suspected from the evidence from the Old Testament.

Among these documents also, were two tablets written in an unknown language in recognizable cuneiform script from a king of the land of Arzawa, and simply called the 'Arzawa letters'.

A few years after the discovery of the Amarna archives, another interesting find of tablets occurred, this time in the small Turkish village of Boghazköy on the Anatolian plateau. The Berlin Assyriologist, Hugo Winckler, recognized them as written in the same cuneiform script as the Arzawa letters from the archives at Tell el-Amarna. He then decided to go to Boghazköy himself to see whether there were any more tablets to be found which would give a clue to the whereabouts of the 'Land of Arzawa'. He had hoped to find at Boghazköy one of the main Arzawa cities. The name of Bogazköy was already well known. In 1834 the French scholar, Charles Texier, had come across the ruins of an ancient site and the nearby rock-gallery of Yazilikaya with its carved reliefs. Winckler's new excavations (1906–1912) brought to light thousands more of these clay tablets—a whole royal archive in fact. Most of the tablets were in the script and language of the Arzawa letters, but some, however, were written in Akkadian, which could readily be understood. Parts of this correspondence were about a century later than the Tell el-Amarna letters, and what was more important, showed that the ruins of Boghazköy had no connection with the land of Arzawa, but that it was the capital of the 'Land of Hatti'—Hattusas. Hugo Winckler had discovered the capital city of the Hittites.

From the evidence of the Armana correspondence and the archives of Boghazköy, we can form a fairly clear picture of the Hittite state during the fourteenth and thirteenth centuries. From a relatively small state centred within the bend of the Kizil Irmak river, the classical Halys, the kingdom soon extended its influence into northern Syria and clashed there with Egyptian spheres of influence. The title of its ruler showed that the Hittite 'Great King' considered himself equal in rank to the Egyptian pharaoh and the Babylonian and Assyrian kings, whom he addressed as 'my brother' and with whom he exchanged presents, as was the royal custom. The Great King of the land of Hatti was one of the great powers during the fourteenth century.

While the Akkadian correspondence was a source of information about the relations between the Hittite kingdom and its neighbours, the Arzawa letters informed us about the internal conditions of the state and people. Dr Hugo Winckler was already well on the way to deciphering the language, which he now called 'Hittite', when he died in 1913. Two years later Friedrich Hrozný could prove that the Hittite language belonged to the Indo-European group of languages, but the question of whether it really belongs to the so-called 'centum group' has still not been satisfactorily decided; it may belong to an earlier stage. Hrozný's discovery came as a surprise for, at the time, it was not thought possible that tribes speaking an Indo-European language had advanced so far west as early as the second millennium BC. But it has now been proved beyond doubt, and has given rise to a new branch of study known as 'Hittitology'.

There is one difficulty, however, in the Boghazköy archives; there are documents in languages other than Hittite and Akkadian. Some letters are written in Luvian and Palaic, languages closely related to Hittite. Moreover, traces of an older non-Indo-European language have come to light, which seems to have been that spoken by the indigenous people living in those parts before the Hittites arrived on the scene. The later Indo-European language of the texts was spoken around Nesa, a city which has not yet been definitely located, and therefore ought to be called 'Nesian'. But the name 'Hittite' is now so firmly established that it cannot be changed without causing confusion. The older language therefore is called 'Proto-Hittite' or 'Hattian'.

The existence of an earlier and a later language surviving side by side are a further proof that people speaking an Indo-European language did not settle in Anatolia as a political unit, but infiltrated into an existing society whose name they adopted. They donned an alien mantle which they wore as their own. If the Hittites were not indigenous in Asia Minor, where did they come from? There are two possibilities. In the south-east, the subcontinent of Asia Minor is linked with both Syria and Mesopotamia, but because these people were speaking Semitic languages during the third and second millennium, this possibility must be ruled out. To the north-east lies the Armenian highland of northern Iran, the Caucasus and the Eurasian steppes. To the west, Asia Minor is divided from Europe by the Sea of Marmora, the Dardanelles and the Bosphorus. As narrow seas never prevented movements of population, a western origin for the Hittites cannot be totally ruled out. It is now generally assumed that the Hittites arrived in the Anatolian plateau region somewhere around the turn of the second and first millennia, a date so early that the fourteenth and thirteenth-century texts retain no mention of any legends to do with their distant homeland. It is, however, most probable that they came from the north-east.

The first mention of Hittite names is found in the records of the Assyrian traders who settled in Cappadocia about 1900 BC in search of copper and silver, which is found abundantly in Asia Minor. They lived in separate quarters assigned to them by the local rulers under whose protection they stood. One of the most important trading centres (*karums*) was in the city of Kanesh (modern Kültepe, near Kayseri). In the houses of the merchants large numbers of clay tablets have been found containing transactions and correspondence in Assyrian cuneiform script. Hittite names are mentioned opposite their Assyrian equivalents, and the names of religious festivals which served as terms for payment and delivery dates. This can only mean that as early as the nineteenth century some Hittite families were already established in this district, and were wealthy enough to partake in foreign trade.

It is in the same period—about 1800 BC—that we hear of the exploits of one Anittas, king of Kussara. Kussara was a town in central Anatolia, probably south of the Halys, but its exact situation is not known. Anittas succeeded in subduing most of the rival cities, after his father had already conquered Nesa, a city of such importance that the new people called their language Nesian. Anittas made Nesa his residence, built an entrance gate on which all his victorious deeds were recorded and dedicated the spoils of his many conquests to its patron god. The connection between Kussara and Nesa is not quite clear, but four or five generations later, King Labarnas, who is traditionally considered the founder of the Hittite kingdom, is also mentioned as king of Kussara. It is, however, doubtful whether Anittas was a forebear of Labarnas.

Labarnas was a great war-lord; he extended his kingdom from the Black Sea to the Mediterranean; his residence was still at Kussara. His successor, however, made the ancient city of Hattusas his capital, although Anittas in his time had conquered and utterly destroyed it, even laying a curse upon it. 'May the great Weather-god slay whoever shall be king after me and rebuild Hattusas.' The Weather-god did not strike, and Hattusas was rebuilt, but the reason for moving the royal residence from

Kussara to Hattusas is a mystery. The first king to reside in the new capital took his name from the city and is known in history as Hattusilis I.

The people of Hatti were now well established in the ancient world and under this name we know about them from the Bible.

By tradition Labarnas and Hattusilis I were the founders of the Hittite Old Kingdom. While the conquests of Labarnas were restricted to the Anatolian tableland, Hattusilis I expanded his empire southwards and besieged Aleppo. His successor, Mursilis I, captured it and pressed on towards Babylon, where he brought the Amorite dynasty of Hammurabi to an abrupt end in 1595 BC. The young state, however, could not yet stand the strain of such far-flung expeditions and on his return Mursilis was assassinated by his brother-in-law. This sorry deed initiated a time of palace revolutions and anarchy, the central government was weak, and the conquests south of the Taurus were lost. The nomadic tribes of the highlands rebelled and invaded the valleys of the lower Halys and the Hurrians from northern Mesopotamia and Syria made several incursions across the mountains into Hittite territory.

It was only about 1500 BC that King Telepinus brought order to this chaotic state of affairs. To put an end to any rival claims to the throne, he decreed a remarkable law of succession: the king had the right to designate his successor and the Council of State was obliged to abide by the king's decision. In this way the succession remained linked to the dynasty, but the eldest son need not necessarily be the heir to the throne. If there was no prince of the first rank, then a son of the second or other wives could become the heir; if there was still no successor, then the husband of a daughter could be nominated.

The king was not an absolute ruler, for the council of elders or nobles had to sanction the royal edicts and could sit in judgment over the royal family itself. It was not by the will of the gods that the king ruled; he was the *primus inter pares* of a powerful aristocracy and was subject to the code of law. This concept of royalty is characteristic of Indo-European communities, and in complete contrast to the Oriental monarchies where the king was the representative of the gods on earth, whose will was law. This strict rule of succession consolidated the internal situation considerably and the kingdom regained much of its former strength. After three generations, a period about which not much is known, the Hittites again attacked Syria shortly after 1400 BC.

The real founder of the Hittite Empire, or New Kingdom, was Suppiluliumas (1380–1346 BC). He subdued the small Syrian states as far south as the Lebanon and intervened in the internal troubles of the kingdom of the Mitannians, who lived in northern Mesopotamia on the upper reaches of the River Khabur, and who, for a long time, had been a threat to the Hittite kingdom. The king of the Mitanni did not offer much resistance and subsequently held his lands in fealty from the hands of Suppiluliumas, while his ties with the Hittite dynasty became stronger through his marriage to a Hittite princess. Suppiluliumas had acquired a secure frontier against Assur.

This was a far-seeing measure against possible Egyptian aggression, for since the campaigns of Tuthmosis and his successors during the end of the sixteenth and beginning of the fifteenth century the Egyptians claimed suzerainty over Palestine and Syria as far as the Euphrates, and although Amenhetep IV (Akhenaton) gave up most of his Asiatic possessions, this favourable situation could not last very long. Egypt would certainly reassert her claims in the foreign field. Mursilis, Suppiluliumas's son, successfully consolidated his power against potential Egyptian threats so that his grandson, Muwatallis, inherited a strong empire supported by vassal states. About 1300 BC he shifted his capital from Hattusas to another town nearer the Taurus passes, and from here he marched towards Kadesh in Syria. Here he fought the famous battle against Ramesses II in 1286 BC, which ended inconclusively, both parties claiming victory. The Hittite army took the Egyptians by surprise and nearly annihilated them, but at the last minute Ramesses extricated himself by sheer personal courage. The Hittites for their part were not strong enough to rout the Egyptian army and the ensuing stalemate left an unaltered but tense situation. Twenty years later Hattusilis III, the brother and second successor of Muwatallis, concluded an 'eternal' peace treaty with Ramesses II.

The signing of a peace treaty was something quite new in history. Contrary to Oriental custom, the Hittites were accustomed to sign treaties with neighbouring states to guarantee alliances and end conflicts. Often a treaty confirmed the vassalage of a partner. The idea of waging war only until the adversary was ready to come to terms and submit to a binding agreement, was introduced by the Hittites to the ancient Orient, and they succeeded even with the Egyptians. The treaty of Kadesh was the first peace treaty between two world powers. Hattusilis III shortly afterwards gave his daughter in marriage to Ramesses II to ratify the treaty and relations between Egypt and the Hittites remained friendly until the very end of the Hittite kingdom; one of the main reasons for this was the threat of the growing strength of Assur.

The attention of the Hittite king was constantly directed towards the south-east. This is understandable. Syria was not only a rich country, but it was economically far in advance of the Anatolian plateau and culturally superior. Moreover it was natural to follow the long established trade routes to the south and east. Expeditions to the west, on the contrary, mainly served the purpose of warding off and pacifying unruly tribes. From the middle of the thirteenth century onwards more energetic military operations became necessary against their western neighbours. In the south-west lay the land of Arzawa, already mentioned in connection with the Amarna letters. This area owed allegiance to the kings of Hatti, but was continually threatened by the people of Ahhiyawa, a name reminiscent of the Homeric Achaeans. The Hittite kings were compelled to send several military expeditions far into the western coastal districts, but were not successful in pacifying the area. The situation deteriorated rapidly, for new peoples had arrived against whom the Hittites were powerless. A century earlier the Mycenaean culture of Greece had spread over the Aegean islands.

Their influence expanded rapidly and they had established a foothold on the western seaboard of Asia Minor. Mycenaean seafarers reached the coasts of Cyprus, Syria, Palestine, Egypt, Cilicia and southern Italy.

The 'Peoples from the Sea' as they are known, in alliance with the Libyans, invaded the Egyptian delta but were repelled by Merneptah in 1225 BC and the people of Ahhiyawa fought a naval battle near Cyprus against the Hittites. Ramesses III at last defeated the 'Sea Peoples' on the Palestinian coast in 1183, but, 'the Land of Hatti withstood them not.' This is the only direct mention of the sudden decline of the Hittite kingdom. Shortly afterwards Hattusas was burned down after fierce fighting.

These turbulent Aegean migrations caused considerable disturbances in Asia Minor. This was the time of the fall of Troy and tradition has it that the Phrygians, who flourished around 700 BC in Asia Minor, crossed at that time from Thrace into Anatolia. From the tenth to the eighth century small independent kingdoms kept alive the name of the Hittites. They seem to have assimiliated fugitives from the central Hittite country, who preserved Hittite traditions and culture. An inscription at Karatepe in Cilicia shows Hittite connections, and it was through Cilicia that the Greeks came into contact with the Hittites and learned much from them.

All these small kingdoms eventually came under Assyrian rule and later were overrun by Aramaeans. Hittite mercenaries served everywhere in the Middle East and these were the Hittites known to the Israelites.

The history of the Hittites is filled with the clash of arms and military glory, typical of an aristocratic society; but by borrowing and assimilating cultural elements from the great cultures of the Orient, they created a distinct civilization of which at some future date we hope to know much more.

The Hittites used an intricate hieroglyphic script for inscriptions on rocks and freestanding monuments, and probably also on tablets of wood. But this script only dates from the late Hittite period when international contacts may have acquainted them with Egyptian hieroglyphs. It is only recently that these Hittite symbols have been successfully deciphered and that it has become apparent that hieroglyphic Hittite was related to Luvian, another Indo-European language. The art of writing was borrowed from the Babylonians, and they not only employed the Akkadian language for diplomatic purposes but even adapted the Akkadian cuneiform script to suit their own language. When the Hittite kingdom came out of its isolation and joined in the community of nations, it became necessary for them to write down the many treaties and international agreements in their own language.

It was the duty of the scribes, instructed in special schools, to keep the chanceries up to date and record the royal edicts. The schools kept in close touch with their pupils and sometimes personal relations between teacher and pupil break through and enliven the official correspondence. Laws, codes and even actual court cases were recorded, epic poems and popular myths were written down. The Epic of Gilgamesh and other heroic tales were translated into Hittite; but religious texts form the major part of Hittite literature, with inumerable ritual instructions, oracles and omens. Although the texts are incomplete they still convey an impression of the intimate relation between the people and their gods, a relation of trust as between king and vassal, master and servant. Numerous ritual instructions tell of the desire to learn the wishes of the gods so that they might be obeyed. The kings give account of their deeds in the form of Annals, and these royal records are one of the first attempts at historical writing in the modern sense of the word.

The finding of a description of an elaborate funerary ritual for a king and queen has been of the greatest value, because there is no known royal tomb of the period, nor do we know anything about Hittite graves in general. The king and queen were exalted above ordinary mortals in so far as they 'became gods' after death and were thereafter worshipped as gods. The funeral ceremonies lasted for thirteen or fourteen days and the body was cremated. Traces of cremation have been found at Hittite sites next to inhumations, but it is not at all certain whether the practice of cremation was confined to the ruling classes.

The Hittite pantheon knew many gods; local deities kept their own cult; Hurrian and other deities were also worshipped. The texts speak of the 'Thousand gods of the Land of Hatti'. The principal deities were Arinna, the sun-goddess, venerated as 'Queen of the Land of Hatti, Queen of Heaven and Earth' and her consort the great weather-god, Teshub, also a vegetation and fertility god. On the walls of the rock sanctuary of Yazilikaya, the names of the gods are carved in Hurrian and some deities have Protohattic names, whilst there is a conspicuous lack of true Hittite names. The texts mention cult-statues in human form, executed in precious metals and ivory. Stone pedestals found in the temples testify that they must have been more than life-size, but as they were made of such costly materials, they were an easy prey for temple robbers, and not one single statue has survived. Some idea of what these statues may have looked like is given by the few figurines in gold, silver and bronze and even rock crystal which have been found. Looking at the large reliefs on the gateways of Hattusas and the procession of gods at Yazilikaya *(plates 49, 50)* one can imagine what a wealth of monumental sculpture must have been lost forever.

The principal deities at least were worshipped in temples. As was the custom in the East, the temple grounds were extensive, the temple itself surrounded by narrow chambers, storage rooms and magazines grouped around a paved court. The architecture of the Hittite temple however has some characteristic features. The entrance was through a triple gateway into a large rectangular court, determining the axis of the whole structure. On both sides are narrow passages which could only be reached through the main gate or the inner shrine. The court was terminated by a row of columns. Having passed through the end colonnade, one would turn right to reach the cella, which was not in alignment with the rest of the building but stood in one corner. The entrance to the inner shrine again was through a side door, so that the cult statue was hidden from the direct view of the worshipper. This is known as the 'bent axis approach'. The statue itself was placed before the end wall of the cella, illuminated by brilliant light filtering through two small windows set slightly behind the statue. This is a typical feature of Hittite temple-building, for in Oriental temple architecture the statue stood in a windowless holy of holies, hidden from profane eyes, and in the Greek temples the statue was visible for everyone to see from the entrance gate. In contrast to this, at Yazilikaya, the cult-statue stood under the open sky.

The civic architecture of the Hittites was equally well-planned. The citadel of Hattusas was built on a man-made platform, on which the royal apartments were arranged around an inner courtyard, separated from an outer court for official reception and administration. The superstructure of the walls was of brick, but for the foundations of city and temple walls undressed stone blocks were used without mortar in the method known as cyclopean. Only the jambs of the entrance gates were constructed of carefully worked monoliths *(plate 48)*. There is a similarity between the fortifications of Hattusas and Mycenae, Tiryns and other Greek cities, but it would be premature to think of a possible relation here. The Hittite predilection for stone finds expression not only in the fine workmanship of their carefully constructed stone walls, but especially in the way the walls followed the irregular contours of this mountainous countryside.

Temples, cities and citadels of the land of Hatti crumbled away into ruins shortly after 1200 BC. Kings and nobles with their chariots, accompanied by vassals and the common people, the whole of the Hittite nation was swallowed up by the onrush of new peoples. Hittite myths and legends strayed to other parts, where they were transformed and lost their original identity. All that remained of Hittite culture flowed into the main stream of ever-changing tradition of which we also form a part. It was only in this modern era that Hittite culture was rediscovered and that the silent ruins spoke again.

Plate 47
Monumental shrine at a spring near Eflatun Pinar

The sculptured shrine at Eflatun Pinar is one of the strangest monuments of Hittite Anatolia. It lies on the south-western slopes of the plateau, slightly to the east of Lake Beyşehir in a district on the very edge of the Hittite lands. Nevertheless it lies within the Hittite cultural sphere.

This monument, 23 ft long and 13 ft high stands at the back of a water reservoir fed by an abundant spring. Only the sculptured façade, facing south, remains; one side is completely missing, the other has worn away at the point where it reaches the steep bank. It was a platform overhanging the water's edge. The reliefs are grouped in heraldic symmetry. Two severely damaged seated figures represent a pair of deities, a male god to the left, and to the right a goddess flanked on either side by two figures standing on the shoulders of two more figures who support a winged sun-disc. On the outside of this scene are four more figures. The bottom figures have bulls' feet and tails but human bodies and bearded faces, whereas the figures on top, dressed in long robes open to the waist, have lions' heads. They support a heavy lintel decorated with only a large winged sun-disc. Each square block is filled with a figure, only the two winged sun discs above the deities share one oblong block. This meant a careful planning and precise workmanship on the part of the stonemasons.

The meaning of this monument, pieced together after long and careful study, is still not at all clear. It is possible that it may have been part of a sacred well, even if the weir and the lake itself are of a much later date. The deities and flanking figures would therefore represent earth and water spirits. The winged sun-disc seems to contradict this theory and indicate a sun god and goddess. But for whatever purpose the monument was erected, the large sun-disc stretching across the whole width of the scene seems to preclude any superstructure or free-standing statues as has been suggested lately.

The structure itself is unique. The precision with which the blocks are fitted together and the quality of the workmanship represent the best of Hittite stone wall construction. The heraldic composition shows an affinity with the aedicula or cartouches on the royal seals of the fourteenth and thirteenth century and the monuments at Eflatun Pinar can therefore hardly be earlier than about 1400 BC, but still within the Hittite Empire period. Combined with the expansion of Hittite influence towards the south-west it follows that this important example of Hittite architectural art was built during the second half of the thirteenth century.

Plate 48
The Lion Gate, Boghazköy (Hattusas)

Hittite architecture reached its climax at the capital, Hattusas, near the modern village of Boghazköy. Originally a citadel of the third millennium it became the royal residence during the fourteenth and thirteenth centuries. An open residential area grew up along the western slopes and from about 1600 BC onwards when marauding tribes became a continuous threat it was surrounded by a wall. This wall was extended to the south during the thirteenth century and eventually enclosed an area of about 300 acres. The builders made good use of the natural contours of the land and the new wall was brought forwards as far as the southern plateau in a large semicircle and was built on a rampart or glacis to bring it up to the height of the rest of the wall. This part of the enclosure wall was broken by five gateways, three of which are now named after the sculptures which decorate them. At the southernmost point of the wall (Yerkapi), a tunnel running underneath the ramparts made it possible to make surprise sorties on the enemy at what was the most vulnerable point of the walls. The tunnel was lined with stone and vaulted with a rough form of corbelling. The walls and towers were built of roughly dressed cyclopean blocks with a superstructure of mud brick and timber. They were constructed in a series of chambers which were filled with rubble and roofed over to form a continuous battlement on top of the walls. Along the southern wall the weaker parts were protected by a lower wall also strengthened with towers.

As has been said, the walls were pierced by several gates, the most famous of which are the Lion, the Warrior and the Sphinx gates, and the importance of these gates was heightened by sculptures on the door jambs. The gate arch was constructed of large monoliths on top of which were courses of large blocks which inclined inwards slightly to form a parabolic arch, typical of Hittite architecture. The western gate *(plate 48)* is protected by two lions with their front parts only projecting from the stone. Although they snarl and bare their teeth, these creatures are not in the least ferocious. The eastern gate is decorated with the sculpture of an over life-size figure of a warrior with axe and sword (now in the Hittite Museum, Ankara), and the southern gate was decorated with a pair of sphinxes, now in the Archaeological Museum in Istanbul.

Plate 49
The Sphinx Gate at Alaca Hüyük

In the Middle East the earliest settlements date from the eighth or seventh millennium BC. Generally they were established near springs or rivers. Consequently in this mountainous countryside with its dry summers and cold wet winters, there were not many spots suitable for large settlements. This led to the occupation of the same places over many centuries. The main building material of sun-dried mud brick easily disintegrated under the winter rains and was used as foundation for the next building so that the level of occupation was always rising higher and higher. These hillocks to be seen all over the Middle East and Turkey are called in Arabic *tell;* in Persian, *tepe* and in Turkish, *hüyük.* These mounds can be seen today in large quantities on the Anatolian plateau, and very often villages still exist on the mounds or at the foot of them.

Alaca Hüyük lies about 22 miles north of Boghazköy, ancient Hattusas, and at the centre of the land of Hatti. Early on the Sphinx Gate caught the attention of European travellers, but it was not until the twentieth century that it was investigated properly and given its place in the Hittite chronology.

A monumental style in building did not develop in Anatolia before the second millennium BC, long after Mesopotamia, Syria and Egypt and even the Aegean possessed great architecture. It is still not possible to ascertain whether Anatolian architecture really developed out of the style of the fortifications, but so much is certain, that the enormous dimensions of the city gates were unthinkable without the use of cyclopean blocks of stone of the type which had earlier been used in the construction of subterranean postern gates and tunnels. With their corbelled roofs and capstones they differ little from similar structures in the Aegean, for example the 'magazines' at Tiryns *(plate 66).*

Monumental architecture in Anatolia reached its peak in the fourteenth and thirteenth centuries. The construction of the city gates relies on much earlier aboveground structures and the difference lies mainly in the dimensions. The parabolic gateways now have neatly tooled doorjambs, the narrow passages are flanked by mighty towers. At Boghazköy and Alaca Hüyük these door-jambs were decorated with sculpture. At Alaca the half-human, half-lion sphinxes guarding one of the gateways are carved so as to blend with the architectural element. Unlike the lions at Boghazköy, the sphinxes are carved on the inside of the jambs as well. An Egyptian prototype is recognizable but the unity of figure and architecture is typical of Hittite art which has a very special feeling for natural stone and rock.

On the inside of the lefthand jamb is carved a double-headed eagle clutching a hare in each talon, and above this is the very worn figure of a deity. Orthostats lining the bases of the towers (not shown) were also decorated with low-relief scenes of hunting and war. This last method of decoration proved so popular that it was used often on the gateways of the later Hittite and Syro-Hittite cities of northern Syria and Cilicia.

Plate 50
The Rock Sanctuary at Yazilikaya

Five temples have been excavated within the city walls of Hattusas. The largest and, according to tradition the earliest, lies in the lower part of the city. It was dedicated to the weather god of the land of Hatti. The other four, smaller temples are situated in the upper city, which was walled in some time after the thirteenth century. It is not known which deities were worshipped at these temples, but it seems from the general layout that each temple was dedicated to one single deity.

At a distance of about 1¼ miles from the city an open-air sanctuary lies on the slopes of a long valley. Its core consists of an externally insignificant mountain ridge called the 'Inscribed Rock' by the people of Yazilikaya. A spring rises in the immediate neighbourhood and this may have been the reason that this place was chosen for worship. The rocks enclose two chambers of unequal length, their walls covered with reliefs.

During the fourteenth century the entrance to this natural sanctuary was enlarged and a portico and forecourt added as a suitable entry for processions. The inner part of the sanctuary, facing south was thus hidden from profane eyes. Here, between the rocks was the large gallery that served as a holy of holies, the walls decorated with a relief frieze of gods and goddesses. The scene depicts a procession; male figures converge towards the centre from the left, and on the back wall from the right female figures approach (in the shadow) the principal gods, Teshub and Hepat. The most important deities have their names written beside them and are larger than the less important deities.

The 'thousand gods of the land of Hatti' are gathered here for the Spring festival to celebrate the revival of nature after the long, bleak winter. All the gods take part in the celebration; it is the picture of a public festival. The atmosphere of the small side chamber is entirely different. Two winged demons with lion's heads guard the narrow entrance. The chamber itself is narrow and rather dark because of the sheer rock face on either side. The reliefs on the walls face towards the back of the chamber where stood once the statue of the deified King Tudhaliya IV. Protectively embraced by a deity, the king himself takes part in the solemn procession. The god of the underworld with his sword stands between the king and his statue.

This image leaves no doubt that the ancestor of the reigning king was worshipped and that offerings were brought to him and placed in the small niches in the side walls. It now becomes clear why this chamber possessed a separate portal, for the function of this smaller sanctuary was different from that of the main hall. It was a well known Oriental custom to celebrate New Year and Spring festivals outside the city walls, but it is a characteristic Hittite feature to establish the holy of holies in the open air and carve religious friezes in the hidden recesses of the living rock itself.

Plate 47
Monumental shrine at a spring near Eflatun
Pinar

Plate 48
The Lion Gate, Boghazköy (Hattusas)

Plate 49
The Sphinx Gate at Alaca Hüyük

Plate 50
The Rock Sanctuary at Yazilikaya

Minoan Crete

DURING THE SECOND MILLENNIUM BC the eastern Mediterranean was the scene of a brilliant culture which left its mark on the Aegean islands and the Greek mainland, but which was later overshadowed by the splendours of the superseding Greek civilization. Although memories of it lived on in Greek myths and sagas, it was not until the beginning of our century that the existence of a sophisticated culture on the island of Crete during the Bronze Age became once more a reality. Even during the nineteenth century the general belief was that the stories about the island were nothing but reflections of age-old religious superstitions and mythical traditions of Greek and Aegean prehistory. It was the firm belief in the historical accuracy of Homer by a dilettante of genius, Heinrich Schliemann (1822–1890), which altered the whole approach to archaeological research. In the face of all the rigid ideas of the academic world, he proved that the *Iliad*, the epic of the battle of Troy, set down in writing by Homer in its final poetic form during the eighth century, was more than the imaginative work of a great poet and, in fact, contained a nucleus of historical truth about events which took place long before its composition.

In 1870 Schliemann began to dig at the mound of Hissarlik, a village actually built on the mound, in the north-western corner of Turkey near the Dardanelles, and found what he thought to be Homer's Troy. In 1874 he proved to an astonished world that the cyclopean ruins in the Peloponnesus at Mycenae were once the citadel of Agamemnon. Here was proof once and for all that the world of the kings and princes summoned to the great war against King Priam and his sons had been real.

The stories of the glorious reign of King Minos of Crete, who commanded the seas with his powerful fleet, pursued the pirates and made the Greek cities pay tribute, appeared now in a new light, as did the tales of the Labyrinth at Knossos and its monster, the Minotaur. Here too it seemed logical to see a historical core, more so, because it was obvious that the Mycenaean culture in the Peloponnesus and elsewhere on the Greek mainland could never have developed locally in isolation, without help and stimulus from outside.

It was precisely this discovery of the Mycenaean culture of the heroic age that focussed attention on the island of Crete, for although many local cultures flourished in the eastern part of the Mediterranean, none seemed to be the direct ancestor of the Mycenaean civilization. At the time it was known that there had been a pre-Greek culture, but that was all. Some sporadic and unsystematic investigations had been made and the finding of pottery of high artistic value, as well as samples of a pre-Greek script, had attracted the attention of historians and classical scholars. It was Sir Arthur

Evans who uncovered for the first time the creative power of Minoan Crete in all its amazing wealth.

In 1900 he started work at Knossos, the site of the mythical Labyrinth and the palace of Minos. The treasures rescued from the many-thousand year-old ruins surpassed the keenest expectations and had the same exciting impact as the discoveries of Schliemann thirty years earlier. Soon after, Italian archaeologists began excavating at Phaestos and Hagia Triada, in the southern part of the Mesara plain, and a French expedition examined the ruins of the palace at Mallia, east of Knossos, while English, American and Greek scholars worked elsewhere. Under their hands the history of the island came to life again. The Greek sagas of the thalassocracy of Minos were found to be based on historical fact; the cultural and political superiority of Crete in the eastern Mediterranean during the greater part of the second millennium BC was irrefutably proved. Its history could be traced from its beginning in the Early Minoan period (c. 3000 BC), through the Middle Minoan and Late Minoan to its final downfall during the Late Minoan III period in about 1100 BC.

The power and wealth of Crete and the unique character of its culture were mainly the result of its favourable position in the eastern Mediterranean. The island forms a long and narrow barrier to the southern part of the Aegean Sea. It lies half-way between the chain of islands connecting Asia Minor with the rugged coast of the Peloponnesus. Like the whole of the Aegean, Crete once formed part of a land bridge linking Asia with Europe which sank into the sea at a very early date in the earth's history. The island has all the characteristics of a highland, with bleak mountain tops where the snow never melts (Mt Ida, the mythical birthplace of Zeus, reaches a height of 7000 ft) and valleys where the hot sun produces typical Mediterranean conditions. This contrast between rugged mountains and fertile valleys must have been an endless source of inspiration to the people of the ancient world.

The population was mainly restricted to the valleys and coastal plains, and it is here that most of the palaces and cities are situated. The surrounding sea was extremely rich in fish, a welcome addition to a meagre agriculture, and the island was a busy centre of trade and maritime intercourse. Little wonder that the art of the islanders was full of motifs of aquatic life, and that vase painting shows flying fish between coral-reefs, water-snails and octopus. It must have been pleasant to live in the palaces and mansions overlooking the sea and feel the coolness of its breezes tempering the heat of the summer day. The sea was the natural element of the Cretans, and to the sea they owed their enormous wealth and political power.

At the beginning Cretan life was very simple and at first there was nothing to show that it would rise to heights equal to the cultures of Mesopotamia or Egypt. Traces of the Neolithic period (until c. 3000 BC) buried under 26 feet of earth at Knossos and not yet fully explored, do not indicate that the island possessed at that time a higher culture than the other Aegean islands. In fact, there are many indications that it was culturally isolated and fairly backwards compared to the Cyclades and the mainland.

This holds good for the period of the fifth and fourth millennia. There are some indications of connections with Egypt during this period, but it is more likely that the Cretans had closer affinities with their Aegean and eastern neighbours. We know so little about the origins of the earliest inhabitants of the island that there is little point in prolonged speculation. One thing, however, is clear—that the Minoan culture is an indigenous phenomenon and enjoyed unbroken evolution from the Stone Age to the height of its development.

As has been said, wide Aegean connections must be recognized, for it is not very likely that the Cretans could have reached this high standard unaided. There are many reasons why Crete necessarily became the cultural centre of the Aegean world. From the outset the Aegean culture was divided into small units: Greece, the Cyclades, the western littoral of Asia Minor and Crete, but the determining factor was not so much the geographical situation as the introduction of metal, which came from the Asiatic mainland. As the use of metal reached Crete first, it took the leading position from then onwards. The use of metal, first copper, later bronze, brought a fundamental change in the way of life, so far-reaching that all the old values had to be reappraised. Wealth and power were no longer based exclusively on landed property. New crafts and professions came into being, the social structure became more differentiated. Old crafts acquired new aspects, trade was intensified, raw materials and finished products were exchanged, an industrial revolution took place. Tin was imported from Anatolia, copper from Cyprus. The Aegean enlarged its horizons and mingled with foreign merchants and came into contact with Asian and Egyptian cultures.

For a long time it was generally believed that the change following the use of metal was the result of an Anatolian invasion of the island. This, however, does not seem the case. Crete seems to have been affected much earlier than the other Aegean islands by the 'metal shock' and entered the Chalcolithic period about 2800 BC or even earlier. Slowly at first, but more and more intensively later, it went through the initial stages of its own independent culture. Its geographical position was now of the utmost importance for the expanding over-seas trade. Cultural influences from all directions met on the island and radiated to the more backward parts of the Aegean. Gradually Crete loosened its ties with the other islands and contacts with eastern cultures paved the way to a magnificent future.

The history of the earliest period, the so-called Early Minoan period, is relatively well-known and needs no explanation here. It seems more important to stress the fact that Minoan culture was the wholly independent expression of the way of life of an indigenous population. Extraneous influences may have enriched the island materially, but the Bronze Age period grew out of the preceding Neolithic period without a break in tradition and without any indication of any forced or peaceful intrusion by foreign people. And although Crete was open to influences from outside, it transformed foreign motifs and techniques into something entirely Cretan. From Egypt came the technique of making vessels out of extremely hard stone, from there also the Cretans learned to mark their property with stamp seals and the art of seal-cutting in steatite or bone with figural or abstract designs. It was through Egypt that the Cretans became acquainted with many animal and human motifs. Stimulated by Egyptian example they developed a distinctive script, from which evolved the abstract linear script. During the third millennium Cretan pottery and stone ware was already distinguished by strongly contrasting colours, lively decorative patterns and naturalistic painting alien to Oriental and Egyptian taste, and they never lost their taste for natural forms and free-style decoration. Their seal engravings are often masterpieces of miniature figure carving and show the same free flowing style.

The unbroken continuity of Cretan culture is strongly underlined by the study of religion, cult, funerary rites and the formal principles of architecture. If the Minoan culture had not developed undisturbed from its Neolithic beginnings, but had been conditioned by Oriental or Egyptian migrations, then it would be unthinkable that these alien populations would have been content with merely political power and would have refrained from imposing their own religious ideas and cults upon the subjugated native population. Crete would never have retained original nature worship. But all the available sources confirm a continuation of the age-old worship of the mother goddess, the life-giving fertility deity since Neolithic times, venerated throughout the Aegean and Asia Minor. Her images and idols dating well into the second millennium were found in a number of places, in shrines or often buried with the dead.

The cult of the mother goddess became more elaborate during the Early Bronze Age. The bull appears now for the first time in ritual as a sacrificial animal. The bull-game may have been part of the offerings rites, while the double-axe appears, perhaps as the symbol of the ritual slaying of the sacred bull. It was much later, not before c. 1700 BC, that a kind of Pantheon was created. Beside female deities representing the great mother goddess, appear male divinities, although they never usurp the female supremacy.

Cretan religion did not include the monumental cult-statue. The few large statues found on the island are of the Late Minoan period when Mycenaean influences were already apparent; and these probably belonged to special sects and were in no way connected with the official cult. Instead of large cult statues we find small delicate figurines in faience, terracotta and chryselephantine, and lively representations of cult ceremonies, scenes of the bull-game, symbols of the chase and capture of the sacrificial animal, priests and priestesses officiating before an altar flanked by the ceremonial double-headed axe. Somehow there is a complete lack of monumental sculpture. The kings were not immortalized in large works of marble or stone. The desire to assure through massive ever-lasting sculpture a corporeal immortality and victory over death seems not to have concerned them, they did not feel the need for monumental tombs built for eternity, like the Egyptians, who were obsessed by the fear of annihilation and dissolution.

This characteristic feature of Cretan religion may be one of the reasons for the lack of temple architecture. There are, however, signs enough that the cult itself required a centre; this could simply be an altar or even a tree. There were open sanctuaries and shrines on hilltops and mountain sides, but these were never enhanced by gateways and enclosing walls. Even in the vast palaces of the great Minoan days, there were only unobtrusive shrines hidden in crypts, often so small that only the officiating priest could enter. The oldest cult places, during the third and second millennium, were caves, and it could well be that the palace-crypt was an imitation of these holy places. They were not so much the dwellings of the gods as the place of their epiphany. From the cave and palace-crypt it was not a great step to the point where the palace itself became the sacred shrine, and in the legend of the Labyrinth and the Minotaur, the sanctity of the Cretan palace finds its mythological expression. The word labyrinth is a reminiscence of the cult of the double-axe *(labrys)*. For the Greeks who saw the intricate palaces with their many rooms, staircases and halls, it became the word for 'maze', while Greek imagination created the monster Minotaur from the memories of the powerful tyrant Minos and the cult of the sacred bull.

Cretan funerary customs were much the same as in other areas of the Mediterranean. Ornaments and pottery were buried with the dead, indicating the firm belief that life did not end with death, which meant the beginning of a new life. In the matter of tomb building the Cretans went their own way, not primarily because of special ideas of life and death, but to imitate the usual dwelling houses. Everywhere on the island, but especially in the Mesara plain, there are circular vaulted tombs, which were in use for a while at the turn of the second millennium, and which are typically Cretan. Smaller tombs of similar shape are found on the neighbouring Cyclades. Built of undressed stone set in clay and without any architectural embellishment, they are probably imitations of the natural caves which were originally used for Neolithic interments. It is very likely that the earliest settlers themselves lived in caves, which are found abundantly on the island. The vaulted tombs remained in use long after houses and palaces were being built on a rectangular plan with flat roofs. The reason for this is not difficult to see. Tradition in all things connected with the care for the dead would cling to old-established rites and thus the cave-substitute would be felt as pre-eminently suitable for the last resting place. But the main reason was a practical one: the Cretan vaulted tomb, often with a diameter of up to 42 ft, was not a grave monument for one single person of high rank, but a communal grave, and for that purpose the round, high-roofed structure was very convenient.

It is impossible to say whether the actual vault itself had any special religious meaning, but it is certain that special rites were performed near the graves. Small rectangular chambers beside the entrance invariably faced eastwards. The form which these rites took is totally unknown, but they were probably much the same as the cult of the gods. There are even indications of memorial services, but at the same time, the idea must have been to raise the dead to join in cult and offering ceremonies.

From the early second millennium onwards, the vaulted tombs were superseded by rectangular burial chambers carved out of the natural rock, or built in stone, again imitating the domestic two-roomed house with flat roof. Graves with many chambers have been found, but these were built for influential aristocratic families. Still there are no instances of a monumental grave architecture comparable to that of the Egyptians. Strangely enough, it seems that it was not these later graves, but the earlier vaulted ones which may have suggested the design of the famous Mycenaean tholos tombs of the thirteenth century *(plates 60, 61)* and their influence may have reached eventually as far as the Etruscan vault *(plates 67, 68)*.

Cretan culture found its most brilliant expression in the architecture of the royal palaces and houses of rich merchants and landowners. The plates with corresponding text describe in detail the excavated ruins and explain the architectural details. A short historical sketch will suffice here.

The first 'palace period' coinciding with the advanced Bronze Age on the island, began when early in the second millennium, the first palaces were built at Knossos and a little later at Mallia and Phaestos. The old palaces were destroyed about 1700 BC and new palaces built immediately afterwards. The Aegean islands lie within the area of major earthquake activity, and consequently there are frequent signs of collapse and rebuilding. The Middle Minoan and the first part of the Late Minoan periods saw the greatest achievements of the Cretan creative genius and the highest point of the island's prosperity, but even this era did not pass without trouble.

Most of the Minoan population centres show signs of several destructions by fire and earthquake, and subsequent rebuilding, even during the greatest days of Minoan power and influence. In the first Late Minoan period there may have been an invasion from the Greek mainland; for a short period Knossos flourished again showing signs of Mycenaean influence. This is the period of the 'Palace Style' in vase-painting, when the formerly naturalistic designs became stylized. The tablets written in Linear B script date from this period. At the end of Late Minoan II there seems to have been an immense cataclysm, the nature of which is completely unknown, from which Minoan civilization never really recovered. During the last phase of the Late Minoan III period, the remains of the palace were occupied, but the great creative period of Minoan culture was over, and their civilization, now heavily diluted by alien elements, was gradually relegated to legend.

These Late Minoan palaces differed considerably from the original buildings of the early palace period. Frequent destruction by earthquakes and fires, and alterations of plan to comply with new requirements changed them often beyond recognition. Although the island must have been open to attacks from outside, no precautions were ever taken against invasion, and there are no signs of fortifications. It is possible that the island itself remained peaceful, and that the Cretan fleet was strong enough to rule the surrounding waters, so that there was no need for massive city walls and other defences.

This command of the seas is reflected in the great artistic and material wealth of the Minoan palaces, far surpassing their comparatively unimportant position as political, religious and economic centre of only one small island. Their wealth can only be explained against the background of a world seapower with far-flung connections, free from competition, while political stability and artistic and religious traditions flowed on in one unbroken line. Although the royal families of Crete lived in palaces at Mallia, Phaestos, and elsewhere, and seem to have granted some priority to Knossos, it is interesting to see how the common people lived beside the splendour of these royal palaces. There was a sharp dividing line between the relatively small ruling class, courtiers and landowning nobility, and the humble farmer, fisherman and craftsman. Excavations at Gournia have brought to light some living-quarters of the townspeople, but still we do not know very much about conditions of the commoners. These houses are built very close together, like honeycombs in a bee-hive, and had only a few very small rooms. Some were built of stone and clay, others in wattle and daub supported by beams. The roofs were flat. Clusters of houses were built around small open courts, and although much smaller, resembled the layout of the lofty palaces of their overlords. But beside the artistic magnificence of the palaces, the Minoan townships are insignificant and provincial. Even so the inhabitants of these modest townhouses did not represent the lowest social class. There must have been a large number of slaves and bondsmen to form the army of labourers necessary for the service of the royal palaces.

Within the palaces a courtly life existed. When one studies the frescoes at Knossos *(plate 56)*, the fine vase-painting, the elegant figurines and the palatial architecture, one is reminded of the European courts of the Baroque and Rococo. The same refinement, playful elegance and overcultivation, the same joyful sensuality are here, but they spring from a vastly different source. Cretan culture was the outcome of a natural growth, secure in itself and not in any way darkened by the thought of impending disaster, whereas the Baroque was the expression of a feeling of spiritual insecurity.

During his excavations, Sir Arthur Evans discovered a hoard of tablets written in a linear script, which he called 'Linear B' in contrast to the earlier script known as 'Linear A'. Linear B script replaced the older Linear A at some date as yet undetermined but probably about 1400. In 1952 Michael Ventris succeeded in the decipherment of the Linear B tablets which were now conclusively proved to be written in an early Greek dialect. Now the fact that Greek was spoken and written at that time in Crete can only mean that the mighty war-lords of the Peloponnesus and the Greek mainland had some influence on the island, at least at Knossos. This must have happened very suddenly, without much fighting, for life on Crete seems to have gone on much as before.

In whatever manner the final destruction occurred, whether through the forces of nature or by the hand of man, the ruined palaces were not inhabited any more, and so concluded one of the loveliest and most graceful of all Mediterranean cultures. The palaces never rose again; Crete sank into provincial insignificance. The hegemony over the Aegean passed to its Mycenaean conquerers, who were greatly influenced by Minoan culture and transformed it into their own.

Plate 51
The ruins of the palace at Phaestos, with the
plain of Mesara and Mt Kophinos to the east

The palace of Phaestos, begun during the
first decades of the twentieth century BC
shows the basic essentials of Minoan
architecture, which, although there were
many variations on the theme, did not
change throughout its long history. The
numerous ruins of the Early Palace Style
(about 2000–1700 BC) make it possible to
perceive a feeling of continuity in the
architecture. This early palace, destroyed
and rebuilt at least three times, already
shows the basic elements of Minoan palace
architecture in the grouping of rooms
around a central courtyard.

Curved lines are practically unknown in
the ground-plans of Minoan palaces, and this
seems strange indeed considering the almost
exaggerated Cretan preference for a lively
interplay of free-moving lines and shapes
(plate 56) in vase and mural-painting. On
closer consideration, however, the difference is not so striking, since the exuberant
curves used in decorative art are always
carefully limited within horizontal and
vertical planes, which give a stabilizing
effect. The same principles operate in
reverse with Minoan architecture; behind
the avowed angularity there is a wealth of
movement. The rooms are not arranged
along one single axis, but twist and turn to
draw the eye towards ever new vistas,
without however degenerating into a con-
fusing disarray. There is always a well
defined central point, an oblong court (right
of centre of the picture). The Minoan court
is not a space left open in the centre of the
building, but is the starting point from
which the other rooms radiate. The relation
between the court and buildings is here
'conjunctive' while in Mesopotamia and
Egypt it can be called 'injunctive'.

Plate 52
Partial reconstruction of the palace at Knossos.
Columns, beams and walls

It seems strange that the Minoan palace architects did not make any use of the corbel vault, although this form of construction was known and not *a priori* alien to Minoan aesthetic feeling. Presumably the technical difficulties were too great; the vault is more suitable for a massive style of building, but can easily be adapted to a lighter and more elegant form of architecture. Moreover it would be difficult to reconcile the arched vault with the Minoans' customary technique of panel work with its vertical and horizontal lines. Even the later part of the palace did not break away from the original style of stone and brick panels alternating with heavy wooden beams and the columns and piers, constructions derived from primitive house-buildings.

The free-standing piers also derive from wooden prototypes. They are rectangular and made of wood or are a projecting continuation of stone walls. Slender and elegant columns were not strong enough to support two or more storeys and were only used where a less heavy load had to be carried, for instance on staircases, covered galleries *(plate 53)* and light entrance halls. The Cretan column has an exceptional shape from which the builders of the seventeenth century onwards never deviated and which became a characteristic element of all Cretan architecture. It stands on a low flat base of an unornamented round or square shape. The wooden shaft is smooth, never very tall and becomes wider at the top. The capital consists of a ring, groove and heavy cushion firmly bonded to a second groove which ends in a square abacus. The Doric capital is similar in shape and could well have evolved from the Cretan capital via those of Mycenae. The Cretan column, however, which decreases in circumference towards the base, is quite unique. Was it a device to emphasize the heavy burden against which the short column had to set its full strength? Or was it done for the visual effect, to counteract the loss of volume that a straight shaft seems to suffer through foreshortening? Because it was made of wood, it may also have been a method of preventing the base from rotting from water dripping down the column. In making the base narrower than the top, the rainwater would fall clear of the column shaft. The exact reason is not known. But it is certain that the Cretan column was more than merely an architectural element, it had a mystic significance. The column formed an integral part of a cult and as a free-standing pillar it had a definite religious function *(plate 53)*. It is possible to believe, even without actual proof, that the Cretan column retained some of its symbolism when it entered the service of architecture.

Plate 53
North Propylon and Pillar Hall leading to
the north of the central court, Knossos

In the discussion of the general principles of Minoan architecture (caption to plate 51) it has already been mentioned that both architecture and painting followed the same rules. The curving, swirling movement in mural and vase-painting is matched by the complexity of spatial composition in the palaces, never repetitive, but always finding some new direction of movement.

The same lighthearted treatment is found where one would have expected a dignified monumentality, namely in the entrance porticoes. The Egyptians, Babylonians and Greeks saw in the entrance gates the architectural link between an amorphous outer wall and the dignity of the royal presence, the place where foreign ambassadors were received with all the pomp and glory of the occasion, where the common folk stood in awe before an immensely regal grandeur. Not so the Minoans. They rejected an idea of monumentality, preferring light structures, pleasing to the eye, playful in their devious ways to the palace interior. Typical examples are the east entrance to the palace of Knossos (not shown), the famous 'stepped portico' *(plate 54)* and the North Propylon *(plate 53)*.

This propylon was constructed about the seventeenth century BC and has been partly reconstructed under the supervision of Sir Arthur Evans. Following the road from the west, one entered first a fairly narrow gatehouse and walked between a double line of columns. The entrance did not give immediate access to the central court, but the road turned at right angles and the visitor climbed a gently rising ramp between high pillars. If he had not changed direction but walked straight ahead, he then would have entered the 'great hall of pillars' of which the picture shows the bases. It may have been a reception hall. The restored and only partly original west wall of the ramp, with a similar structure along the east wall, gives a good impression of the narrowness of the passage. This is accentuated still more by the position of the gallery on a high bastion, beckoning the visitor from on high and lifting him up towards the delights that awaited him in the palace.

Plate 54
The 'Stepped Portico' and southern elevation of the palace, Knossos

During the sixteenth century BC and probably after the old palace had been heavily damaged, a new stairway 263 ft long was built along the south wing. It took the place of a much smaller gatehouse and formed the link between a valley road from the south-east and the palace higher up on the hillside.

This road reached the stairway over a viaduct with nine arches one of which is just visible in the picture. Its 'false' arch is 26 ft high, 10 ft wide and spans a narrow ravine. It precedes the great aqueducts and bridges of the Romans by more than fifteen centuries and shows the considerable engineering skill of the Minoan builders, although there are only a few examples of arch construction in Crete. The stairway, known as the 'stepped portico' reveals even more than the North Propylon *(plate 53)* the Minoan preference for complicated movements and continuous change of direction. The stairs climb the gentle slope to the palace in two stages, linked by a level passage at right angles to the direction of the stairs. Although only the lower courses of the parapets are still standing, the reconstruction sketch after Evans is on the whole well founded. The mouldings on the cornices are traditional and often depicted on murals. Several fragments have been found nearby and can easily be pieced together. The horn shape, a common feature of Minoan architecture, indicates the importance of the Minoan bull cult and these can be understood as abstract symbols of the sacred bull. Their occurrence in such great numbers on a processional stairway makes it reasonable to assume that the palace itself was also a temple, the dwelling of the great Mother-goddess in whose honour the bull games and bull sacrifices were held. It would be highly unlikely indeed, that these horn symbols were just a meaningless decoration in a society so deeply steeped in cult and religion.

The Minoan palaces did not face inwards behind heavy blind walls, but as the picture shows, they favoured the open façade with pillared galleries and colonnades giving the structure an appearance of great lightness and elegance with a rich interplay of light and shadow.

According to Greek tradition it was Sosastros of Cnidos in the third century BC who invented the multistoreyed house construction. But they did not know that the Minoan architects had mastered this technique more than 1400 years earlier. The architects of the Middle Minoan period (after 1700 BC) experimented freely in this field, especially at Knossos. The Grand Staircase must have served several floors, since it comprises four flights in an excellent state of preservation, and part of a fifth with only the columns needing reconstruction. The best example of multistorey architecture is in the east wing. Built on several levels against the slope of the hill facing the valley of the Kairatos, the first and second floors lie actually beneath the level of the great central hall. The north wing contained magazines and workshops, while the state rooms and royal domestic apartments were in the south wing, separated from the every day activities of artists and workman, as is the Oriental custom.

The problem of linking the different storeys was solved by stairwells. The $11\frac{1}{2}$ ft difference in level was overcome either by straight flights of stairs or by interrupted stairs. The stairs of the north wing were dark and narrow and bore no resemblance to the stairwell of the royal apartments shown in this picture. A central area surrounded by a colonnade serves as a shaft for light and air. The most westward columns follow the line of the interrupted stairs to the first floor. A similar arrangement followed for the next three flights. It is not difficult to imagine the pleasing effect of these stairs, winding around the well up the height of the building. However, the lightwell was not created as a focal point. The general idea of the central stairwell is not that of rest, but of movement through it towards the stairs. And in the same way as the Stepped Portico, the movement is also determined by changing lines of direction.

Plate 56
The dolphin frieze in the Queen's room, Knossos

The imagination of the excavators and the zeal of the restorers were fired by the parts of the multistoreyed east wing of the palace of Knossos which could be restored, and especially by those rooms which could not have been anything else but the royal apartments. The room seen in the picture, measuring 20 × 14 ft and 11 ft high, has with some probability been called the Queen's room. A section of the north wall is shown. It belonged to the complex dating from the sixteenth century.

At first glance the room does not appear very regal nor very comfortable, but it must have been pleasantly cool and shady in the heat of a Cretan summer. It is completely cut off from the outside world and receives light indirectly from a colonnade opening onto a light well on the south and east side. The north wall has two doors, the left leading through a dark passage towards a large reception hall. Through the door on the right narrow stairs to the next floor are visible. A window-like opening into a small closet takes up most of the west wall. In the last period of the palace it was used as a bathroom. A further passage led to a very modern looking water-closet.

This apartment, connected as it was in every direction with the surrounding rooms, formed a suitable centre of family life, although the many breaks in its walls spoiled the spatial effect. The al-fresco frieze gives the room its intimate character. A shoal of fishes, dominated by beautiful and elegant dolphins, is swimming in an aquarium-like sea. This decoration, and the dado of rosettes below it framing the door, were applied over the earlier strip of running spirals, very little of which remains. In its design however, and its relation to the architecture it complies with the general principles employed by the Minoans. Although only a small part of the original fresco survives and there construction is rather doubtful, the treatment of the subject is clearly impressionistic. The fishes swim around in an unrealistic sea of yellow ochre, the rocky banks take on strange bulbous shapes, the slender bodies of the dolphins are treated as flat forms, but the painting as a whole breathes a free and lively delight in nature, in sharp contrast with every other earlier or contemporary form of art in neighbouring countries. The contrast with Egyptian style is particularly strong. The Egyptian and early Greek artist was not interested in naturalistic representation, but gave his subject a symbolic meaning, Minoan art, however, was not 'idyllic' as the later Hellenistic naturalism. It was first and foremost ornamental. This dolphin frieze does not give the illusion of a real seascape, it has no spatial depth and all the elements of the design are drawn on the same plane.

Plate 57
Store-rooms in the west wing, Knossos

The Minoan palaces were not only royal residences and centres of administration and cult, but also of industry and trade. In the west wing alone there were more than twenty magazines, far more than was necessary for the storage of the daily needs of the large court. The magazines were built in the basements along a corridor 263 ft long running north to south. They received light, if any, through narrow slits. They have been kept intact buried under the rubble of the superstructure, together with the large storage jars, *pithoi*, which are often as tall as a man and decorated with cord and wavy line designs. The heavy rims and handles made them easy to seal and move. In the centre is a row of stone-lined pits probably used for the storage of precious goods and used as strong rooms. Judging by the numerous magazines the wealth stored in the palaces must have been enormous. It was the material background for the luxurious living of the Minoan grandees. Minoan trade overseas was widespread and the Cretan mastery of the seas unchallenged. Wealth may also have come from tributes and compulsory labour of the common people who lived in humble conditions beside the splendour of their masters.

Plate 58
Stepped road, Gournia

Our knowledge of the living conditions of the common people is rather fragmentary for the great palaces have drawn most of the attention of the archaeologists. What little we know of the life of the proletariat comes mostly from a few excavations in the eastern part of the island in the neighbourhood of some small towns.

Gournia, on the bay of Mirabello, is a good example of a Cretan town in the late palace era, the sixteenth century. The townspeople were sailors, fishermen and artisans and lived in houses of two or three storeys with small rooms. The ground floor walls were mostly of stone bonded with clay, the upper floors of brick and beam panelwork. A light-well in the centre, sometimes open and sometimes covered with a lantern roof, provided light and air. Clustered together against the hillside like honeycombs in a hive, the houses were divided by two fairly wide ring roads and several twisting alleyways. The alleys, mostly stepped because of the steep hillside, led to the summit of the hill on which the town stands. Here there was a small palace, which was either the country seat of the lesser nobility or the residence of the head of the district. This palace was built on the same lines as the royal palace, with a public court and a miniature shrine and 'Theatral Area'. The apartments grouped round a central court, together with the fact that the houses of the townspeople seem to press in from three sides towards the dominating palace underline once more the general centralizing trend in Minoan architecture.

Plate 51
*The ruins of the palace at Phaestos, with the
plain of Mesara and Mt Kophinos to the east*

Plate 52
Partial reconstruction of the palace at Knossos.
Columns, beams and walls

Plate 53
North Propylon and Pillar Hall leading to the
north of the central court, Knossos

Plate 54
The 'Stepped Portico' and southern elevation
of the palace, Knossos

Plate 55
The Grand Staircase in the east wing of the
palace, Knossos. (Reconstruction)

Plate 56
The dolphin frieze in the Queen's room, Knossos

Plate 57
Store-rooms in the west wing, Knossos

Plate 58
Stepped road, Gournia

Mycenaean Greece *Plates 59 - 66*

ON LEAVING THE GAY, courtly and peaceful atmosphere of Minoan Crete for the Greek mainland, one meets a vastly different world, a world which has only been opened up since the important discoveries of Heinrich Schliemann in the nineteenth century and the subsequent research of countless scholars from many lands. Through their ceaseless efforts a lost civilization has been rediscovered which is called after its main centre, Mycenae in the Argive plain. The most important towns at this time in the Peloponnesus were Mycenae, Tiryns on the Gulf of Argos, Orchomenos in Arcadia, 'Sandy Pylos', the seat of Nestor on the south-western seashore and Thebes in Boeotia. It was here that the princes lived who knew Crete and marvelled at its accomplishments. From here the legendary heroes of the *Iliad* sailed to Troy.

The Mycenaeans seem to have appeared in Greece early in the second millennium BC. The first settlements seem to have been quite modest, but during the thirteenth century their culture reached its peak and spread its influence throughout the whole of the Aegean until its end was brought about by the great Dorian invasion.

Except for its primitive beginning, the Mycenaean culture has two distinct aspects. For its artistic heritage it leaned heavily on the culture of Crete, so much so that it seems as if the Mycenaeans, not content with mere imports, deliberately adopted Minoan art forms instead of improving on their own native skills and traditions. But by imitating Minoan style, it failed to develop along its own separate and individual lines. It seemed only too obvious that Minoan art, though greatly admired, was not really compatible with the Mycenaean character and indeed for a long time the general impression was that Mycenaean art was nothing more than a degeneration of Minoan art by a people incapable of reaching the same height. This, however, is not altogether true. Even if there is a certain deterioration under the hands of the Mycenaean artists and the Cretan sense of form and colour became somewhat barbaric once on the Greek mainland, on closer inspection it is apparent that Minoan influence was superficial as it was too alien ever to express true Mycenaean temperament. This voluntary taking over of Minoan styles is only a secondary aspect of Mycenaean culture, which was sometimes capable of expressing itself in its own native medium, more of which will be discussed later. It is enough to say that this dependence upon Crete was only natural. It was primarily the result of the political and cultural situation prevailing in the Aegean area during the second millennium and the historical background of the Mycenaeans themselves.

The Mycenaeans belonged to a different ethnic group from the autochthonous people, and were probably the first Indo-European speaking peoples to enter the

Greek mainland and the Peloponnesus, first in small numbers, gradually establishing themselves as overlords of the indigenous population. Their origin is still very uncertain, but there are many indications that their homeland lay somewhere in Asia Minor, and that they formed the most westerly branch of a general movement of Indo-Europeans throughout Western Asia and the regions of the eastern Mediterranean. These Indo-European speaking groups probably coming from the Eurasian steppes, reached Anatolia and the rest of Asia Minor at the beginning of the second millennium. One of these groups, known as the Hittites, were destined to create one of the great empires of the ancient world (cf. page 189). The intruders into the Greek mainland may have been a branch of this movement. The people from Gutium, for over a century the bane of the Sumerians at the end of the third millennium, may not have been Indo-Europeans themselves, but could have been in the vanguard of a general displacement of populations.

The early history of Greece can be divided into three main periods: Early, Middle and Late Helladic. Between the Early and Middle Helladic periods there is a definite break in culture, an indication of the arrival of an intrusive people, while the Late Helladic follows the Middle Helladic without any noticeable disturbance. The Indo-European invaders arrived early in the second millennium bringing their own primitive culture (Middle Helladic) with them, and overran the survivors of the Early Helladic period. After the seventeenth century BC the Middle Helladic developed into the Late Helladic, which was the heyday of Mycenaean culture. Some connections with Crete were established, which can be deduced from the appearance of the Linear B script both in Crete and the Peloponnesus.

The introduction of a new racial element in the Aegean had long-lasting consequences. Unlike Crete, which did not lie on the direct route of invasion and consequently could develop peacefully, the indigenous Bronze Age culture on the Greek mainland was forcibly interrupted. The earlier population, though by no means obliterated, and numerically superior to the invaders, sank into political and social insignificance, while the new overlords formed only a thin upper crust. This again is in marked contrast to the situation in Crete, where although the division between the ruling class and common people was sharp, it was social rather than ethnic.

The Greek invaders had an extremely warlike history behind them. Long and hazardous migrations, conquests and perpetual dangers in foreign parts had left their mark. The discipline necessary in hostile countries, the continuous risks of revolt of the subjugated population had determined their thoughts, customs and ideas, and this attitude continued even into later more peaceful centuries. No doubt their origin influenced their mental approach, but not enough of their background is known to be more explicit.

The masculine, strong and militant spirit, a delight in warlike prowess, in the dangers of the hunt and the possession of precious weapons, all reflects their early conditions of ever-impending danger and tense vigilance. The aim of the Mycenaean chieftains, those 'Achaean' kings and princes of Homer, was to perform glorious deeds and to be remembered by their fame, not by material wealth and a long, uneventful life. They did not build open palaces along the sea shores, but strong-walled citadels at strategic points. They were a warlike race and continuous quarrels between the dynasties may have caused them to retire at an early stage to their eyries in the mountains. It is amazing that the stronghold at Thebes is the only one to show signs of damage at the beginning of the fourteenth century, and this was probably the result of one of these internal feuds since at that time Mycenaean power was not in any way threatened from outside; the citadels of the Peloponnesus, on the other hand, built practically within sight of each other, did not suffer any damage. From this we can only conclude that the Mycenaean lords of this date lived fairly peacefully together.

Whether the relations between the Greek heroes of the Homeric epics really mirror Mycenaean conditions, or whether they are the fiction of a much later period is a matter for conjecture.

While the Mycenaeans showed great independence in city-planning and building, the question remains as to why they surrendered so completely to Crete in matters of art. It seems only natural that a people tentatively settling in a foreign land and coming into contact with a superior culture, should be influenced in this way. Crete, at this time, was the centre of cultural life in the Aegean, and the Mycenaeans admired what they saw and everything Cretan became fashionable. As the Romans became the heirs to classical Greece, so the Mycenaeans fell under the spell of the brilliant Minoan civilization. What they themselves lacked in sophistication, they found in this opulent and resplendent island.

Although the invasion of Indo-European speaking peoples took place at the beginning of the second millennium, it was not until the turn of the seventeenth and sixteenth centuries that Minoan influence was noticeable on the Greek mainland. The Middle Helladic period, that is the first period after the invasion, was still fairly primitive. There are, however, archaeological indications that the social structure was well formed and wealth and power already concentrated in a few 'royal' families.

At the same time also, Crete extended its sphere of political and commercial interests to the north-western part of the Aegean, following a more stable situation on the mainland. It is at this time that Cretan imports, pottery, weapons and jewellery appeared in the mainland towns. For a long while it has been thought that the many Minoan objects were brought to the Greek mainland as loot by pirates. This may have been the case at a later date, when the Mycenaeans tried to break the Cretan maritime supremacy, but it was certainly not so in the beginning. The first impact of Crete upon Mycenaean art was brought about peacefully. There is no other explanation to account for the many goods found in Mycenae, Tiryns and elsewhere, which have proved to be the work of Cretan craftsmen.

But although the Mycenaean culture took so much from the older Cretan civilization, it would be unjust to deny them a certain individuality. It seems rather as though the Mycenaeans had at first thrown the mantle of a foreign civilization around their own shoulders through an inability to find their own bearings, and later kept it on out of tradition. But noticeable variations in style, although clumsy at times, were a sign of a gradual loosening of the Minoan bonds and the emergence of an independent Mycenaean art style.

One aspect of Mycenaean thought which differed completely from the Cretan can be seen in their care for the dead and in grave monuments. Among the earliest graves are the shaft-graves found in Mycenae itself dating from the seventeenth and sixteenth centuries. The correct dating has been made possible by the finding of known Minoan ware along with some primitive Minyan ware which the invaders brought with them. At a later date, perhaps in the thirteenth century, six of these earlier graves were enclosed within a circle of upright stone slabs and incorporated inside the city walls. Another cemetery, comprising twenty-four graves, formed an enclosed ring outside the city walls. Some of the funerary equipment found, although very close to Minoan models, is of Mycenaean workmanship, and again emphasizes the unimaginative submission with which the Mycenaeans followed Minoan examples.

Burials in shaft-graves were not a new feature, but were known long before the coming of the Indo-European Mycenaeans. The dead were interred without coffins in deep shafts, cut into the relatively soft rock, the walls at the bottom lined with stone and covered with a wooden roof topped with stone slabs, and the pit filled up with earth. The idea of graves as a dwelling place for the dead goes very far back and is in itself an indication that the early Mycenaeans had already established religious practices and beliefs.

Because of the gold vessels, costly inlaid daggers, helmets and other weapons found within these graves, it is quite obvious that they belonged to powerful and noble families. When Schliemann discovered the grave-circle in 1876 he thought he had found the grave of Agamemnon, the leader of the Greek expedition to Troy, and although modern scholars realize that it is of a considerably earlier date than the Trojan war, this grave must have belonged to some high-ranking prince. One of the most amazing finds were the gold funerary masks, which show a definite attempt to portray the individual features of the dead person. The idea behind this practice which is unique to the shaft-grave dynasty, may have been to defy death by the very nature of the indestructible gold and to assure the dead of an eternal life. It is difficult to know where to look for a prototype of this custom, for in Crete and in other parts of the Aegean world, death masks are unknown. Egyptian mummies of the Middle Kingdom had gold masks or painted portraits and some death masks have been found in Western Asiatic graves. There were connections at this time with Egypt through trading and mercenary services, and the Mycenaeans may well have imitated an Egyptian practice. However, the important point is that it indicates a belief in an individual life after death, but it is not certain whether they attributed a special life-giving force to the gold, as did the Egyptians.

In this active care for the dead the Mycenaeans differed from the Minoans for although they also tended their dead, they were not concerned with the individual and his fate as expressed in the death masks.

Only a few of the bodies in the shaft-graves seem to have worn masks, none of whom were women. Only the leader, highest in rank, was worthy of the shining gold masks which in the next world might herald his honour and glory. Glory in this earthly existence was not enough, his reputation must follow him after death. This same idea was expressed in the stelae placed on the graves. These stelae carved in low-relief with ornamental and figural designs kept alive the memory of noble deeds. This again is typically un-Minoan and belongs to the customs of a different race. It is possible to see here the first traces of the later Greek cult of eponymous heroes. 'The dead ancestor becomes the strong venerable one (hero means strong), in the cult the hero is the strong man after death, endowed with a greater, because a ghostly, strength'. The carvings on the stelae represent the deeds through which the dead person secured his prominent place in life and could claim veneration after death. These stelae retained their aura of sanctity through the centuries and when, during the thirteenth century, the shaft-graves were incorporated within the walls and surrounded by stone slabs, the stelae were reverently replaced.

It was not so much the man himself, but his personal achievements that were the objects of veneration—his martial deeds and his successful encounters with wild animals in the chase. These are the main themes depicted on the stelae, and it was by these glorious deeds that the ancestor wished to be remembered. For this reason also the dead person did not descend empty-handed to his grave, but surrounded by the daggers, rapiers and swords, which had once been his delight on earth. This masculine, robust aspect of Mycenaean life continued in the funerary customs, when, after the late sixteenth century, instead of the shaft-graves, the Mycenaeans began to construct the beehive-shaped corbel-vaulted burial chambers or *tholoi*, perhaps following Cretan examples *(plates 60–62)*. The grave stela was now unnecessary, for the tholoi, hidden beneath enormous mounds, themselves formed a monument for the dead. During the centuries they became larger and more impressive until during the thirteenth century, the greatest unsupported vaults of the ancient world were erected. These Mycenaean tholoi became a monument of great architectural merit, and a fitting addition to the Mycenaean citadel.

Although the beginnings of these citadels cannot be traced, it is possible to tell how the early chieftains lived. The tremendous size of the Late Mycenaean city walls must have had a modest beginning. But however humble the start, everywhere the same manly self-confidence and courage is found in everything they created, in all their actions, whether it was in the construction of their formidable citadels and monumental tombs, or in their great commercial and military exploits abroad.

The palaces of the Mycenaean kings were decorated with colourful frescoes in Minoan style, and these palaces probably became the treasure-houses for products of many lands, and the refined and courtly way of life based on that of the Minoans. (The flounced Minoan skirts and wavy tresses became high fashion for ladies in the Mycenaean courts.) But this was after all superficial. It was only a sophisticated veil over the true Mycenaean character, which is best expressed in the image of the warrior with mighty armour, the intrepid huntsman and—if the ever-present goblets and gold cups are to be taken into account—also hard drinker.

It would be most unusual if this same spirit were not reflected in the character of their religion. But unfortunately there is not a great deal of information about Mycenaean cult and we have to rely on fresco painting and sculpture. From the sources at our disposal it is clear that already in the shaft-grave period 'Minoization' was far advanced and persisted until the final period. The position of the lions on the famous Lion Gate at Mycenae of the thirteenth century *(plate 64)* shows strong Minoan affinities. That other gods did exist, is in itself no proof that Mycenaean religious traditions differed in any way from the Minoan. There is one factor, however, which does seem to indicate a divergence from Cretan usage. The Mycenaean palaces possessed cult chambers in the Minoan manner, but they sometimes contained fairly large images which may have been cult-statues. The bodily presence of the deity in a monumental image was completely alien to the Minoan tradition. That the deity now appeared as a being with a large image, is more than a minor change in religion. It is the expression of a quite different feeling, one that is not satisfied with a purely spiritual partnership between god and man, but needs to look upon an imposing object of worship.

On the whole Minoan tradition had too strong a hold on the mainland to encourage the development of temple architecture; the cult chambers were never more than part of the palaces. But it may be that there is a gap in our knowledge, for in recent years one single example of a free-standing cult chamber has come to light which could well have been the beginning of the development of temple construction. This was found under the Greek temple of Demeter at Eleusis, and is Late Mycenaean.

This is not the place to decide whether or not there is a connection between this tenuous evidence from Eleusis and elsewhere with the religion of classical Greece. It is only of interest in order to stress the fact that the cult of the gods, whether in palaces or in separate structures, was never as important to the Mycenaeans as it was to the Minoans and later again to the Greeks of the classical period. Beside the cult of the dead, for which no effort was too great, it took only second place. The religious feeling of the Mycenaeans was mainly centred on hero worship, and this hero worship was practised at graves, not in temples.

The basic elements for temple architecture, if indeed it existed in Late Mycenaean times, were not given time to develop, when this culture was brought to an abrupt end during the twelfth century by the Dorian invasion. But the palaces, citadels and the vaulted tombs show clearly enough what they could accomplish architecturally. Merged with the new population as an element of the Ionians in Asia Minor during the classical period, they influenced the magnificent Ionian style. Thus it seems that the Mycenaeans were by no means at the end of their evolution when disaster overtook them.

It was shortly after the middle of the thirteenth century that the first waves of of land-hungry hordes penetrated from the North, and like the Mycenaeans they spoke an Indo-European language. Even the Mycenaeans saw the invaders before their walls, as traces of destruction outside the city walls of houses show. The citadel itself withstood the first onslaught. Pylos was destroyed, but some other towns survived. However, the Dorian flood ebbed away and took another direction through the Troad and Asia Minor towards Egypt.

But the whole atmosphere had changed, the impending danger hung like a storm cloud; the former security had vanished. The city walls were hastily reinforced and enlarged and fortified retreats like Gla were built. All the Mycenaean lands were preparing to withstand the next storm which was to burst forth with such ferocity in the second half of the twelfth century.

The citadels were destroyed, the people subjugated and the coastal regions of Asia Minor underwent the same fate as that which the Mycenaeans themselves had brought to the flourishing empire of Minos some centuries earlier.

Plate 59
The Grave-circle, Mycenae

While the Mycenaean culture during the fourteenth and thirteenth centuries BC was a time of great achievements in architecture —citadel, palace and graves—the preceding period from the seventeenth century onwards shows a very different picture. At this stage Mycenaean arts show only Minoan influence; there are as yet no cyclopean constructions.

The difference between the Helladic and Mycenaean cultures, a reflection of the shift in political power in the area of the Aegean, was not as abrupt as it now seems from a distance of thousands of years. There are also too many gaps in our knowledge of that crucial period to be able to give a clear picture of the real sequence of events. But it is certain that the splendid strongholds at Mycenae, Tiryns and Pylos of the fourteenth and thirteenth centuries could never have been built without fore-runners on a much humbler scale. However, these earlier buildings, if in fact they ever did exist, have been totally destroyed. Few structures are left from the Helladic period besides the royal graves, faithfully kept intact by later generations as hallowed places of ancestor worship.

At the beginning of the Mycenaean grave architecture stand the so-called 'shaft-graves'. Box-shaped chambers sunk in the ground or rocks, they continued an ancient tradition: that they were not so much a grave as a dwelling for the dead in the midst of the living. The largest and richest of these shaft-graves were found near the citadels of Mycenae and belong to the seventeenth and sixteenth century. There were two grave circles some 333 ft apart; the one nearest to the citadel was probably the grave of a royal dynasty, the other was probably that of the lesser members of the royal family. The royal circle contained six separate graves (the largest 22 ft long and 13 ft wide). When in 1876 Schliemann found the rich grave furniture—gold embossed weapons, jewellery and golden death masks—he believed he had discovered the grave of Agamemnon and his family. Although nobody connects these graves any longer with the king of the Homeric cycle, much of the glittering pageantry in which the Homeric heroes took such pride is brought to life by these rich grave goods.

During the thirteenth century this circle of graves was incorporated within the extended city walls, a platform was built over the graves and the carved stelae raised to the new level but kept in position over the individual graves. The whole area was then surrounded by a double circle of stone orthostats (the diameter was 92 ft) and thus became a fitting place for worship. Ancestor worship and hero worship played an essential part in Mycenaean thinking. Although these shaft-graves are interesting in the history of religion, they did not possess any monumentality; hidden as they were underground and marked only by a carved stela, they hardly deserve the name of architecture. The shafts were lined with dry-stone masonry and covered with heavy boards and finally stone slabs. There is no sign of any plastering or painting.

Plate 60
Early Mycenaean tholos, Pylos

The relatively primitive and barbaric Mycenaeans of the earliest period fell completely
under the spell of the elegant and gay life of
the Cretans. Not satisfied with emulating
the splendour of the Cretan palaces and
importing fine Minoan ware, they adopted
ideas and customs intrinsically alien to
them. The lure of the Cretan way of life
was such that it even coloured Mycenaean
religion and cult. This 'Minoization' can
be observed better than anywhere else in
the change-over from the old established
shaft-graves to the tholoi, the beehive
graves that seem to have their origin in the
vaulted communal graves on the island at
the turn of the third and second millennia.

It would be tempting to connect this
apparent break in tradition with a dynastic
change, but for the fact that similar tholos
tombs have been found in the western part
of the Peloponnesus, at Pylos, either contemporary with or preceding the earliest of
the nine tholoi at Mycenae. Whatever caused
this change, it is hardly possible that it
could have happened without a simultaneous
change in cult.

The shaft-graves were subterranean
chambers sunk vertically in the ground
without any ceremonial entrance *(dromos)*
or portal. Only stelae, and at Mycenae at
least a ring of orthostats, indicated the place
of interment where the ancestors of the clan
may have been worshipped. The tholoi, on
the other hand, are quite different. Like the
fairly small, heavily damaged tomb near
Pylos (sixteenth or fifteenth century) they
are usually built into a hillside, on a circular
plan with a pointed roof. A long open
passage or *dromos* leads up to the entrance.
These buildings were not free-standing, but
were covered by an artificial mound leaving
only the end of the dromos visible. Although
full of chthonic allusions their bearing upon
the world of the living was much greater
than that of the shaft-graves.

Visible from afar, these beehive-shaped
tombs were considerable monuments and
with their long corridor created a permanent
focal point for the cult of the dead and even
may have been used as temples.

Not much is known about the Mycenaean
cult of the dead, but it probably differed
from Minoan ideas and ritual. Even the fact
that the Mycenaean tomb was not a collective grave used over the centuries, but
the last resting place for a royal family, or
one king only with his consort, gives it a
different meaning. The Mycenaean tomb
was a fitting expression of the greatness and
glory of the king and it is no wonder that
the vaulted tomb was preferred to the old
shaft-grave for a royal monument.

Plate 61
Late Mycenaean tomb, 'The Treasury of
Atreus', Mycenae

The vaulted tomb remained in use until the thirteenth century along with the rock-cut chamber tomb, which already occurs earlier in the Peloponnesus and was probably borrowed from Crete. Well-to-do members of the aristocracy, and even the common people were customarily buried in chamber tombs, and the great tholoi, so impressive to see, and so difficult and expensive to build, were probably reserved solely for the ruling family. The larger and the more monumental the vaulted tomb became, the more difficult its construction. The immense dimensions of these tombs is shown in the picture of the 'Treasury of Atreus', which is in reality a royal tomb. Built at the beginning of the thirteenth century, the tomb, 42½ ft high and 47½ ft in diameter, is the largest unsupported vault in antiquity before the Roman Pantheon. Thirty-three courses of enormous stone blocks were laid with great skill and precision so that each course slightly overlapped the one before in ever decreasing circles ending with a final capstone. The blocks were then carefully chiselled to achieve a smooth surface. The entrance is 16½ ft high and gives a good idea of the size of the stone blocks, which often weighed many tons. But they are nothing compared with the size of the monolithic lintel used over the doorway. The one over the door of the Treasury of Atreus is 26 ft wide, more than 16 ft deep and 4 ft high and its weight has been estimated as over 120 tons.

These huge stone buildings, constructed with equipment so primitive in our eyes, pose the usual question of the reason behind such a laborious enterprise. The reason cannot have been only the urge to create on a superhuman scale—this could have been achieved in a much simpler form—but must lie deeper and spring from a very special relationship with the raw material. Stone, the everlasting, indestructible material given by nature itself. Behind the cyclopean tomb there was the same challenge to nature, the same longing for security and durability that inspired the megalith builders and the builders of the Egyptian pyramids.

How do we then explain the fact that the actual burial chamber in the Treasury of Atreus was cut out of the rock? Was it that its creators did not have faith in a man-made structure, however solid, and preferred to entrust their dead to the living rock itself? We see the same in one other tomb at Orchomenos in Boeotia, probably erected by the same builder.

Plate 62
Entrance of the so-called 'Treasury of Atreus',
Mycenae

As was customary in all Mycenaean tombs, the 'Treasury of Atreus' has a long entrance passage *(dromos)* running between walls of large stone blocks which gradually rise up to the full height of the tholos. This passage leads to the entrance façade with its 16 ft high door with a slight entasis towards the top. Behind the door lies an anteroom 16 ft deep. A relieving triangle was left above the door through the whole thickness of the wall to relieve the pressure of the immense superstructure upon the lintel-stone. The same thing goes for the tapering of the sides of the doorway, although this may have been done to enhance the height of the entrance. The relieving triangle, however, had also another function. What we see today is only the frame of what was once a splendidly ornamented monumental entrance. On either side of the door stood engaged columns of a green stone with a formal ornamentation in relief. The fastening holes are still visible. These columns supported a false second storey, heavily encrusted with different coloured stones, ornamented with a relief that probably filled the triangle in the same manner as the lions on the Lion Gate.

Even if the actual theme of the reliefs remains guesswork, it is fairly certain that the portal was adorned with all the exuberant splendour the Mycenaeans so much admired in the Minoan palaces. It seems that except for some ornamental bronze studs, the inner chamber was left unadorned. Only the powerful language of stone and the monumentality of the vault reigned here.

Plate 63
Ruins of the citadel of Mycenae at the foot of Mt Elias

While the Mycenaeans imitated their Cretan neighbours in all ways of life and furnished their palaces with fine Cretan ware, vying with each other in costly collections, the conditions under which they lived were vastly different. Always on the alert against attacks, it was not open palaces which they needed, but strongholds perched like eyries on high ground, with a clear view all around. Thus the Mycenaeans created large complexes on commanding positions which later became the guiding principle of Roman architecture. The preference for building on high places can also be seen in the light of the same personality cult that made so striking an impression in their monumental tombs and their hero-worship. Since the Minoans did not favour ancestor worship, but professed a a vague nature and Mother-goddess cult, they had no interest in enhancing the status of the king—tribal ancestor—by prominently placed palaces and impressive grave monuments. The Romans with their strong sense of rank and personal eminence followed this Mycenaean trend.

The access to a Mycenaean citadel was not direct, but complicated. A winding road led past heavy walls and magazines to the focal point— the *megaron*, the hall of the chieftain. The *megaron*, with its entrance hall supported by two columns and a single rectangular room, differed sharply from Minoan buildings, but stands at the end of a long history in Aegean and eastern Mediterranean architecture. It was a regular feature in buildings found at Jericho, Troy, and Dimini, and the fact that the Mycenaeans adopted the *megaron* was historically of great importance, for the Greeks made it the basic element in their temple architecture.

Plate 64
The Lion Gate, Mycenae

The citadel of Mycenae was, during the fourteenth and thirteenth centuries, and probably long before, the capital of the Mycenaean world and the seat of a powerful dynasty. It was fortified by an encircling wall of cyclopean masonry, the ruins of which are still standing. So enormous were its stones that the later Greeks imagined them to have been the work of prehistoric giants, the Cyclopes. The 20-ft thick walls were once 33 ft high and crowned with battlements.

The walls belong partly to the fourteenth and partly to the early thirteenth century and the later extension on the south-west, that enclosed the ring of shaft-graves *(plate 59)* was built to safeguard the sacred grave-circle against the growing threat of invaders from the north. The work was, however, not done hastily and there was ample time to build an elaborate main gate—the Lion Gate. This gate can even today conjure up the awe-inspiring impression its majestic dimensions once commanded.

Its grim façade of large stones in neatly dressed ashlar masonry forms the entrance to the fortification and dominates the 65-ft approach to the gate. Flanked on the left by the citadel wall which sealed off the slope of the hillside at that point, and on the right by a bastion, it made a formidable bulwark and covered an approaching enemy on three sides. Four large monoliths frame the gate itself: the threshold, where the grooved sockets for the wooden doors are still visible, two 10-ft high orthostats set with a slight inclination and finally the lintel, weighing 20 tons. The lintel is gently curved at the top and has a width of 15 ft, a height of 4 ft and is 6½ ft thick. The massive stone courses are not continued across the lintel but a relieving triangle was left open into which a sculpture was placed.

This sculpture gave the gate its name.

The general building technique and the large square blocks are reminiscent of the portal of the 'Treasury of Atreus', just outside the city wall *(plate 62)* and it is likely that both constructions, so typical of Mycenaean architecture, were the work of the same builder. In any case these two structures are contemporary, both aim at monumentality and both express that particular feeling for the nature of stone that was characteristic not only of the Mycenaean but of the whole of the pre-Greek period.

The Lion Gate does not owe its fame to its construction or its imposing dimensions, but to the sculpture in relief above the lintel. It is unique of its kind, although there must have been others in existence. The triangle above the door of the 'Treasury of Atreus' was probably filled with a relief and there was a similar gate at Tiryns. However there could never have been very many. On the contrary the absence of any monumental sculpture and the amazingly few examples of small works of sculpture make it unlikely that Mycenaean buildings as a rule possessed sculptural ornamentation. Moreover the lion relief is not meant primarily as ornamentation. It has a deeper symbolic meaning which brings it within the Minoan religious sphere. The two lions rampant, the heads of which are now missing but were probably made of different coloured stone or metal to judge from the rivet holes, are standing with their forefeet on two small objects, probably altars. In the centre between the lions stands the typical Cretan column, a motif well known on the island. Lions often accompany the Magna Mater and the free-standing column, framed by her heraldic lions can be understood as the symbol of the goddess. Here it is not just a formal space filler, or a royal coat of arms, but stood at the focal and most vulnerable point of the citadel, and could invoke divine protection.

Plate 65
*Part of the wall at the east entrance of the
citadel, Tiryns*

Although Tiryns is smaller than Mycenae,
its cyclopean walls are in places even thicker
than those of the capital of the Mycenaean
world. The old citadel with its palaces and
courts was enlarged at the beginning of the
thirteenth century by the addition of a lower
citadel under pressure of threatening attacks,
to serve as a refuge for the rural population
in case of war.

The picture shows the eastern part of the
citadel wall, which at this point is 19½ ft
thick and at others some 26 ft. Between the
earlier wall on the right and the wall of the
lower citadel a space is left open for an
outer gate, the smooth finish of the new wall
indicating its purpose. The difference
between old and new is interesting, although
only superficial. Both are double walls, their
outer shells constructed of large stones; for
the corners especially large blocks were
chosen. The filling consists of rubble and
earth. The earlier wall is constructed with
much greater care and looks elegant compared with the hastily built newer part.
This is, however, not a sign of technical
deterioration. When the citadel of Mycenae
was enlarged, rough cyclopean construction
and carefully tooled blocks were used side
by side. The best work was reserved for
either side of the main gate, because the
gate was not only the weakest point in the
defences, but as the place where princes and
high-ranking personalities were received,
had to present an aesthetic appearance.

This also holds good for Tiryns; the carefully joined blocks are part of the gate, built
after the model of the Lion Gate at Mycenae.
It remains difficult to decide whether the
Mycenaeans invented the cyclopean wall in-
dependently or whether they followed a
widespread fashion, but it is certain that this
technique, apparently primitive, does not
occur at an early stage, but rather towards
the end of the Mycenaean era. Historically
this is not surprising for the mastery of
working in stone was acquired only after a
long evolution, and its possibilities for
monumentality understood.

The cyclopean style of construction was
not restricted to the Mycenaean world.
Early Egyptians, prehistoric builders in
Jordan and Palestine, Malta and western
Europe knew this technique. The cyclopean
nuraghes of Sardinia, although earlier, have
many affinities with Mycenaean architecture, but more with the walls of Hattusas
(Boghazköy) the capital of the Hittite empire.
This strikes one particularly as the prototype of Mycenaean cyclopean architecture,
in spite of many differences *(plate 48)*, which
is all the more likely as the Mycenaeans
were probably familiar with the city walls of
Hattusas. The western seaboard of Asia
Minor was dominated by the Mycenaeans
and thus the Hittite territory bordered on
their sphere of influence. It was believed
formerly that the fortifications of Hattusas
belonged to the fourteenth century BC and
could well have served as model for the
Mycenaean walls. Recent archaeological research however favours a later date for the
Hittite citadel walls and the possibility is not
excluded that it was the Hittites who borrowed the cyclopean building technique
from the Mycenaeans rather than the other
way round.

Plate 66
*Vaulted passage and entrance to the casemates
in the south-east wall, Tiryns*

Mycenaean Greece entered a period of feverish building activity during the thirteenth century. Most of the castles of the chieftains were enlarged and existing fortresses reinforced, for at that time a great unrest troubled the whole of the Aeagean. It was during the second half of that century that foreign tribes, in search of land and spoils invaded the Mycenaean empire and upset the whole structure of the ancient world as far as Egypt. Mycenae itself saw the plundering and pillaging enemy before its gates but, protected by its massive walls, it withstood the onslaught. Nearby Tiryns was probably attacked as well, although there is no definite proof. It is uncertain whether the massive fortifications there were built as a precautionary measure or under threat, after an earlier attack had been repulsed. The attention paid to the safeguarding of the water supply and the building at this time of several fortified retreats (the lower citadel of Tiryns, Gla and others) speak in favour of the latter suggestion.

The Mycenaean citadels were built on hilltops, taking full advantage of the impregnable natural position. The safeguarding of the wells was as important as the strength of the ring walls and gates. It was also necessary to store adequate food supplies in case of siege. For that purpose rows of magazines were built within the south and south-east wall, the least vulnerable places. The passage shown in this plate is about 98 ft long. It gave access to small vaulted storerooms and military depots. Sorties could be made from postern gates at the end of the passage.

Nowhere else is the powerful effect of the cyclopean walls more striking than at Tiryns. Immense blocks rise upwards as if they had grown naturally and not been built by man at all. The weight alone gives the structure the coherence and stability to withstand, nearly undamaged, a span of more than three thousand years.

It is not known how the corbelled arches were constructed but the spaces between the walls were probably first filled with earth which was later removed.

Plate 59
The Grave-circle, Mycenae

Plate 60
Early Mycenaean tholos, Pylos

Plate 61
Late Mycenaean tomb, 'The Treasury of
Atreus', Mycenea

Plate 62
*Entrance of the so-called 'Treasury of Atreus',
Mycenae*

Plate 63
Ruins of the citadel of Mycenae at the foot of
Mt Elias

Plate 64
The Lion Gate, Mycenae

Plate 65
Part of the wall at the east entrance of the citadel, Tiryns

Plate 66
Vaulted passage and entrance to the casemates
in the south-east wall, Tiryns

The Etruscans Plates 67 - 72

THE TUSCI OR ETRUSCI as their Roman neighbours knew them called themselves Rasenna or Rasna and inhabited the central part of Italy between the Arno and the Tiber, and the Apennines and the Tyrrhenian Sea, the region which is now called Tuscany. The history of their culture and its final downfall was played out during the first millennium BC. Although aspects of Etruscan civilization are mirrored in the culture of Rome and consequently were spread over every European civilization following in the footsteps of Rome, we still do not know much about its early history. This seems strange in view of the wealth of facts in our possession from classical sources and through the unceasing work of modern scholars. But however profound the research and however accurate the comparison with the much better known contemporary civilizations of Greece and Rome, the enigma of Etruscan origins, language and religion is so obscured by myths and legends that it remains extremely difficult to extricate true historical fact.

The age-old controversy raging around Etruscan origins would not be of great interest in a work about architecture, were it not for the fact that its nature is closely linked with the question of sources and inner motivations of Etruscan art. Etruscan art is indeed so alien to any contemporary art form despite definite affinities with Greece, and at its core it shows so many independent features, that it becomes imperative to go deeper into the question of the origins.

Before going into details, one point ought to be stressed, namely, that most of what we know about Etruscan culture comes from grave monuments; our knowledge comes from the realm of the dead, and only a pitifully small part from the world of the living. However since life on earth and life after death were closely connected in Etruscan minds, it is fairly certain that the reliefs and frescoes in the tombs give an adequate picture of daily life. Not many Etruscan towns have yet been explored as systematically as the cemeteries, which were carefully placed outside the city boundaries, but archaeological research is steadily progressing and through the confirmation and the study of the literary evidence it has become clear that there was a unity in culture the character of which was homogeneous, albeit many-sided. It would, however, be unrealistic to believe that we can deduce from the forms of these grave monuments all we want to know about secular and religious architecture.

The fact that Etruscan art exhibits so many different aspects led to the theory that it did not grow out of the native Italian soil. It seems to be a synthesis of a variety of cultural influences, both indigenous and foreign. Beside the distinct Italian, so-called Villanovan features and Greek influences, attention has been drawn to the Iron

Age cultures of the Danube, and to those of Western Asia and the pre-Greek world of the Aegean.

Two variant views regarding the origin of the Etruscans have existed since antiquity. According to Herodotus the Etruscans were wanderers, driven by famine from their native homeland of Lydia. The hard-pressed population drew lots to decide which half should remain and which half leave the country. Under the leadership of Prince Tyrrhenus one half went to Smyrna where they built ships to carry them across the sea to new lands. After sailing past many lands they came to the coast of Umbria where they settled and founded new cities. They no longer called themselves Lydians, but Tyrrhenians, after the name of their leader. An important fact is that some peculiarities in the architecture of the Etruscans seem to point towards a connection with the East, especially the tombs, in which an adherence to possibly old-established customs can be seen. The historian Dionysius of Halicarnassus (first century BC) was the first to venture a completely new explanation when he stated that 'the Etruscan people did not emigrate from anywhere, but were always there'. If the theory of an autochthonous Italian population, emerging after a long slumber, is more probable than that of an infiltrating foreign people, then it would be justifiable to claim that the Etruscan people only gradually arose as a political unit from a conglomeration of different ethnical components (Umbrians, Ligurians, Veneti, Latini, Tyrrhenians, Illyrians and Greeks).

Customs belonging to the cult of the dead, religious practices and the names of the gods tend to have their roots deep in antiquity and are not easily changed. They can often be traced beneath superficial changes in culture and the shifting of populations, and indicate a common root. Since the eighth century at the earliest, or perhaps the seventh, a new form of funerary monument appears in parts of the Etruscan area of Italy and only there, while the earlier types of cremation and grave burial still persists. The new graves bear a strong resemblance to the Mycenaean vaulted tombs covered by tumuli. Two explanations are possible for the origin of this kind of grave: the Tyrrhenians could have brought their traditional burial customs with them, or an indigenous people, becoming strong and prosperous, wished to build impressive monuments for their dead leaders and found a suitable style in that of the eastern Mediterranean tombs. While there is so much uncertainty about early Etruscan history it would be very rash to say that this new form of burial meant a complete break in cultural tradition. Changes in burial customs do not necessarily imply an influx of new peoples; this is most readily seen in our modern society with the two customs of inhumation and cremation being practiced simultaneously. So far archaeologists have not found a distinctive break in tradition.

The exact explanation will probably always evade us, but it is certain that the influence of classical Greek art, which became more and more apparent during the seventh century did not play a part in the evolution of Etruscan funerary tombs. They may have benefitted from Greek building experience, yet the corbelled burial chamber did not originate in classical Greece, but rather shows, as already mentioned, a parallel with the Mycenaean tombs.

The Etruscan problem becomes still more complicated when the time factor is taken into consideration. Should we speak of 'Etruscans' in Italy during the turn of the second and first millennia BC, or not until the eighth century? The Etruscan element within the Italian cultures is clearly discernible from the beginning of the seventh century and reached its culmination during the sixth and fifth centuries; by this time Etruria had made itself known from the Alps in the north to the Straits of Messina in the south. There are a number of reasons for the rise of Etruscan power after the seventh century. Economically it developed rapidly through the discovery of copper and iron deposits, which brought great wealth to the small towns and agricultural settlements. Etruscan merchants ruled the western Mediterranean together with the Carthaginians and waged war against Greek shipping. About the sixth century the most important cities formed a loosely-knit confederation of twelve peoples—the Romans speak of *Etrusci populi*—and so gradually they were welded into a political, religious and economic state. And last but not least, Etruria was, through its contacts with the Greek colonies on Italian soil and Sicily, the bridge across which Hellenic art first entered the Italian world. This link was never broken. Greek merchants settled in many Etruscan cities and it was no wonder that their fine arts were greatly admired, and that the existing native arts were profoundly influenced by these newcomers.

Etruscan art was never fully Hellenized, it kept its own character even in sculptural art where Greek influence was most noticeable. The Etruscan artists were so indebted to the Greeks that for a long time all objects of quality were considered to be Greek imports or the work of Greek artists in Italy, the cruder products imitations of Greek models by local artisans, technically inferior and provincial. This is, however, a serious misrepresentation of the true facts. Undoubtedly Greek art was the formal base of Etruscan art, Greek artists were indeed employed in Etruria and there were many Greek imports. But much of the essence of Etruscan art is alien to Greek ideas, there are even distinct anti-classical tendencies which often seem primitive and barbaric. While following Greek formulae Etruscan art remained the expression of its own characteristics during the whole of its existence from the eighth until the first century BC, and it was strong enough to influence even the work of Greek artists settled in Etruria.

In following first Corinthian (orientalizing) principles, then Ionian and later Attic and Hellenistic models, the Etruscan artists seem to be completely dependent on Greek art forms. But this evolution of style did not destroy their own purposeful progress. But however ready the Etruscans were to take advantage of the Hellenic spirit and to make use of Greek forms, the driving force was their highly individual attitude towards all aspects of life, death and the life hereafter. This is essentially the reason why the pure classic spirit remained alien to the Etruscans.

When Greek art achieved its final canon of beauty, free from trivialities and the idiosyncrasies of individual artists, a beauty that was timeless, reposing in itself, when everything, including architecture obeyed the law of a universal harmony of number and measure, at that moment Etruscan art, unable to follow, went a different way. The Etruscan mind could not follow the wonderful freedom from fear of the realities of time and death inherent in Greek thinking. The Etruscan was too much in the grasp of mysterious divine powers and hidden forces of destiny; he believed the power of the dead was too strong to permit him to act by his own free will. He was always consulting supernatural powers whose will he tried to read in the entrails of sacrificial animals, in the flight of birds or the colour and direction of lightning. Few other human societies were to such a degree conscious of their own mortality, the death of the individual and the downfall of their world than the Etruscans. They lived constantly under the shadow of death, and death was no more than a passing over into an enhanced, divine, and therefore desirable existence. Life on earth with all its pleasures was only a prelude to an enchanted life hereafter. The Greek creative impulse which was never overwhelmed by the thought of death while striving after spiritual and bodily perfection in this life had no meaning for the Etruscans. In this light it becomes clear why the Etruscans lavished so much care on their graves in the earlier period. The often weird demonaical features of their art, which are all the more apparent when they found themselves having to fight for their liberty and their very existence succumbing in the end to the superior might of Rome, indicate a change in their ideas of the afterworld to a dark place to be feared.

Greek influence is less noticeable in Etruscan architecture than in painting and sculpture. The reason does not lie primarily in the fact that Etruscan temple and grave architecture had already found its own style before Greek impact was strongly felt; more influential is the fact that where temple architecture is intrinsically an expression of indigenous religious ideas, it does not yield easily to foreign influences. It performs a specific task within its own realm of thought. Only a complete Hellenization of the Etruscan people would have paved the way for a wholesale transference of Greek architecture. But as we have seen this was not the case. Although many superficial elements remind us of Greek temple building, Etruscan architecture maintained its own distinct style. Architectural art is more formal and cannot express ideas and thoughts in different ways without losing its inner meaning. While painting and sculpture act through a medium of forms more or less realistic or stylized, derived from nature, architecture—that is spatial and corporeal structures—is the immediate realization of abstract ideas. It is for this reason that the architectural arts give the best insight into Etruscan thinking. Plates 67 to 71 describe fully the many forms of funerary monuments, their origin, meaning and architectural details. A few general remarks will suffice here.

Two features are of special interest: first of all, the care lavished on the building and furnishing of the graves, comparable with Egypt; and secondly, the surprising variation in style and internal arrangement of space. The grave is the abode of the dead who now have passed on to a much richer life details of which are painted in glowing colours on the walls. There is music and dance, fishing and wrestling, there are gay banqueting scenes, ducks picking crumbs from beneath the table. Man and wife are seen reclining affectionately beside each other. Where, in all this, is the sting of death?

The funerary chamber was built after the plan of dwelling-houses, where local traditions played an important part. The dead were either laid to rest on funerary couches or in the case of cremation in an urn shaped in human form with the features of the dead person clearly portrayed. The dead were not however confined to their tombs; they entered into the underworld through a symbolically indicated door, through which they could always return to the tomb. Here in these tombs their families honoured them and provided them with nourishment.

All that remains of Etruscan temple buildings are the stone platforms on which the wooden superstructures stood, and quantities of terracotta antefixes. The Etruscan temple was a fairly compact building on a square ground plan. The wooden super-structure rose from a high stone platform. The gently sloping roof with a wide overhang had cornices decorated with polychrome terracotta antefixes and acroteria which terminated the guttering. The cella was fairly small; at a later date this was divided into three for the worship of a trinity, like the Roman temple of Jupiter, Juno and Minerva on the Capitol. The worshipper entered through a wide portico with supporting columns. The front columns were spaced wider apart than those at the sides, in order to give an uninterrupted view of the cult statue within the cella.

The longitudinal axis was still further stressed by the wide steps leading up to the entrance. In this respect Etruscan temples differ from the Greek ones, because the colonnade of the Greek temple was accessible from all sides, the columns equally spaced all round, without any marked direction or emphasis on the length as with the Etruscan buildings. Considering this fundamental difference in purpose it would be impossible to see the Etruscan temple as an imitation of the Greek. Indeed, it is throughout a native creation, although the origins are still hidden and the examples known are of the time when Greek influence was being felt. Moreover the connection between temple and tomb is too obvious to be ignored. How else could the similarity be explained between the raised temple platform and the yard-high stone podium of the tumuli-graves and their entrances which have similarly decorated cornices. Both serve the same purpose—to raise the sacred dwelling above the common level of the secular buildings of the city. The roughly square ante-chambers before the resting place of the dead fulfil the same purpose as the columned hall in front of the dwelling of the god. There are many more similarities, for both grave and temple are places of worship.

The historical importance of Etruscan art and culture is considerable. Rome was the heir to all that was Etruscan. The name 'Rome' is itself Etruscan. The insignia of the Roman magistrate, the *fasces*, symbol of the power over life and death; the Roman pantheon; Roman gladiatorial games—all originated in Etruria. The Romans took over so many cult practices that it is difficult to decide which are original Roman and which Etruscan. In the field of architecture the Romans learned more from their neighbours than from the Greeks. The Roman temple was based on the Etruscan principle of direction towards the cella which was later carried even further in Christian church building. The tumulus grave of the Emperor Augustus and the impressive monument of Hadrian both have their prototype in Etruscan grave architecture.

Plate 67
Vaulted tomb near Populonia

Populonia, called Fufluna by the Etruscans (probably after the wine-god Fufluns) and known by the Greeks as Popluna, was one of the earliest settlements in Etruria. It was the only town near the sea and at a later date was famous for its smelting furnaces where the iron ore from Elba was smelted. The legends mentioned by Herodotus say that it was here that the Tyrrhenians from Lydia first landed on Italian soil. Whether this is true or not, the fact remains that it was at Populonia that some of the earliest Etruscan tombs were situated.

The Etruscan vaulted tombs date from the seventh century to the second half of the sixth century BC and are all built on much the same plan. A narrow passage led into a square grave-chamber with an unsupported vaulted ceiling surrounded by a circular outer wall. This wall was as high as a man and finished with an overhanging cornice that served as protection against the rain and made a striking division between the wall and the mound of earth above. This circular structure was surrounded by a pavement which was used for the funeral processions when members of the family came to honour the dead and brought offerings. The Etruscans felt the dead to be very near to them. They believed that after transformation in the grave, the dead lived on in higher spheres and maintained the closest contact with the living, and could protect them in return for care and veneration. And so the graves were everlasting dwellings for the dead as well as memorial and cult centres. Standing together in cemeteries they were an integral part of the world of the living.

The builders of these graves did not aim at any particular aesthetic effect. The great monumental impact was achieved by the austerity of the circular wall, and its stone mass formed a barrier to protect the dead during their transition to the new life in the next world. The circular grave walls seem to go back to remote antiquity. They are found in the pre-Etruscan Villanovan culture. At Vetulonia, not far from Populonia, numerous stone rings *(circoli interrotti)* have been found around several small urn graves of one family or clan. Sometimes the ring was simply a wooden fence or a row of stakes. But all the same whether wood or stone, these circles belong to the same category as the later Etruscan ring walls and show an Etruscan connection with earlier cultures on Italian soil.

Plate 68
The vaulted tomb of Casal Marittimo

The relatively small and intimate grave of Casal Marittimo (10 ft 9 in. in diameter, and 6 ft 10 in. high) was built in the sixth century BC. In 1900 it was moved from its original site and re-erected in the garden of the Archaeological Museum at Florence. With its stone plinth and corbelled vault it belongs to the same class as the magnificent tholos graves of the Mycenaean princes and the European megalithic graves. It therefore seems to give weight to Herodotus' theory about an eastern Mediterranean origin of the Tyrrhenians *(plates 45 and 61)*.

The problem of the transmission of this style of vault is extremely complicated. How could it travel from Greece into central Italy? It is difficult to assume an immediate link, the gap in time is too great. Between the latest vaults in the eastern Mediterranean, the Mycenaean tholoi belonging to the thirteenth century and the earliest representatives of the same type in Etruria not earlier than the seventh century, there is a time lapse of several centuries. There is the possibility that a few insignificant vault constructions on the island of Sardinia and elsewhere could help to bridge the gap. Nevertheless the similarity in form and technique cannot be entirely accidental.

The Etruscan tomb possessed, in common with earlier examples, a gently sloping *dromos* and was hidden under a tumulus. Moreover the vault was only used in grave architecture as far as is known at present; but then, very little is known about Etruscan secular building. The best explanation is that immigrants from the East took their own building techniques and feeling for spatial form with them to Italy, and were unwilling to abandon age-old traditions, especially with regard to the cult of the dead. The urn burials and fossa graves of the existing Italian cultures had no appeal for them. The only feature the newcomers may have borrowed is the exterior stone plinth *(plate 67)*. A further question arises as to why the Etruscans kept for so long to the vaulted tomb. One possible answer is supplied by a late but reliable tradition, which says that the Etruscans endeavoured to create a subterranean imitation of the vault of heaven. The Marittimo tomb could well be such a stone 'heaven', where the dead entered into a new life.

An oblong pillar, tapering towards the top stands in the centre of the tomb. It is technically unnecessary and could be removed without any danger to the stability of the building; similar and larger vaults are without a central support. The only explanation then lies in its symbolic meaning. It is, perhaps, the axis of the earth, supporting the universe, the vault. Or on the other hand it may be the Tree of Life, an image certainly not unfamiliar to the Etruscans.

Plate 69
Grave chamber of the 'Grande tumulo dei letti funebri', near Populonia

The 'tomb of the stone beds', which has a surface area of 59 ft, has been severely damaged. Only the carefully pointed stone walls of the square burial chamber ($15\frac{1}{2} \times 15\frac{1}{2}$ ft), a part of the sloping entrance passage and parts of the couches on which the dead were laid to rest, and which give the tomb its name, still exist. This seventh-century grave was probably covered by a corbelled roof like other, better preserved tombs in the neighbourhood *(plate 68)*. But although in deplorable condition, the grave furniture is most interesting. A row of stone benches against the wall imitate wooden bedsteads with turned feet. Stone slabs, now missing, would have covered the beds. It was a family grave fitted out for the burial of six couples. The Etruscans liked to bury the dead in the company of their loved ones, so that they could imagine that the dead had not really died, only been transformed. This custom, founded on a strong family feeling and a deeply-felt relationship with the deceased, poses several riddles.

These communal graves often contained a large number of burials. Many years must have passed before the long shafts were completely filled and with each new burial the walled-up door had to be re-opened. This could not possibly be done without damage to the bodies already laid to rest, which postulates some means of preservation against decay that would automatically follow the admission of fresh air into the tomb. It is highly improbable that the Etruscans, so particular in their care for the dead, would not have used some kind of embalming process, but it remains a mystery as to how it was done. However, they certainly did not use the Egyptian technique and the preserving agents were only active for a short period, for bones and whole skeletons showing no trace of successful preservation were found in the undisturbed graves exactly as they were once laid. If the Etruscans imagined life after death as a disembodied ghostly existence beyond the grave, and the primeval idea of the 'living corpse' was far from their thoughts, then it is difficult to understand why they took such great care in shaping the bier like the couch on which the dead spent so many happy hours in convivial delights during their lifetime. There are many other indications as well that the Etruscans did not think of life after death as a purely spiritual existence, but very material indeed. Therefore they must at least have attempted the preservation of the bodily remains.

The 'tumulus of the funerary beds' is interesting for yet another reason. The masonry was of a high standard and the walls of carefully shaped tufa were built without any kind of bonding. The blocks are not only set in straight courses but interlock to give greater stability to the structure.

Plate 70
Funerary couch in the 'tomba dei relievi'
near Cerveteri

The aim of the Etruscan tomb was to provide a dwelling for the dead where he could return at will, and the very human desire to take with him as many familiar objects as possible into a strange world beyond the grave, caused the change from monumental tholoi to homely dwelling places, even though it could only be a simple imitation.

Only the graves of high-ranking families were equipped with all the luxuries of their stately homes. The flat gently pitched roof imitated the wood construction used in real houses so accurately that it gives a good idea of the excellent workmanship of the Etruscan carpenters. The task of the grave builder, however, was not as difficult as it seems at first glance, for these dwellings of the dead were not free-standing stone structures, but hollowed out of the rock. They are caves and belong technically-speaking to the realm of monolithic plastic art rather than to architecture. The famous 'tomb of the reliefs', dating from the third century BC and thus when Etruria had long lost its independence to Rome, is one of the best examples of this kind of monolithic building.

The chamber itself is rectangular, its roof a copy of a wooden ceiling, the ridge beam of which is just visible in the picture. It is supported by two rectangular columns, while the side walls are decorated with engaged pillars, fluted like Greek columns. The funerary couches are situated in niches between the pillars. The old-fashioned capital are of special interest. With their high spiralled leaf-volutes they are reminiscent of the Aeolic capital, often found in the eastern Mediterranean and the forerunner of the Ionic capital. This striking resemblance may be a coincidence; on the other hand it may be yet another proof of an eastern origin of the Etruscan people. In any case it shows how conservative the Etruscans were in spite of their readiness to borrow art forms from every point of the compass.

The 'tomb of the reliefs' owes its great fame to the pious rendering of all the objects that had made life on earth so enjoyable and without which the life hereafter would have lacked many comforts. On the walls above the niches, on the surfaces of the pillars, wherever there was space, the possessions of the deceased were represented in relief, true to form and colour. There are jars and bowls, mirrors, fishing tackle and all kinds of utensils. Armour and weapons however are the most frequent subjects of the reliefs. There is a complete arsenal of daggers, swords, helmets, shields and greaves, a sign of the warlike prowess of the race. And no wonder, for during the fourth and third centuries the Etruscans were continuously exposed to merciless attacks from Rome.

The wealthy family whose tomb was so sumptuously adorned felt the same oppressive threat as the rest of the Etruscan people, a threat not to be glossed over by the peaceful idyll of the head of this family and his consort. Although the long walking-stick beside the couch, the elegant sandals on the footstool, the bedstead with gold and silver ornaments, or the writing case on the bureau beside the bed, breathe a homely atmosphere, there is also a darker side. The demon of the Underworld with his serpentine feet, his sword of judgement ready, and the three-headed hell-hound Cerberus show that the Etruscan image of the Underworld was not one of unmixed pleasure.

Plate 71
Aedicula-grave, Populonia

After the sixth century the traditional
vaulted tomb disappeared and the style of
grave took on a new form, which had
already been foreshadowed in earlier rock-
graves. In the neighbourhood of Populonia
and only there, small, rectangular aboveground dwellings for the dead made their
appearance. With projecting cornices and
gabled roofs decorated with painted terracotta antefixes, they were imitations in
miniature of the great temples. The belief
in the divine nature of the dead could not be
expressed more charmingly than in these
temple-graves and with their exquisite workmanship they link, even more than the
tumuli, the world of the living with the
realm of the dead.

Plate 72
Porta all' Arco, Volterra

Etruscan secular and sacred architecture—house, city and temple building—is represented by far fewer survivals than the grave architecture. Many of the ancient ruins lie hidden under modern buildings, and many more have been pulled down and used for other purposes, so that a great amount of work is still to be done on undisturbed sites. When the strange Etruscan culture first became an object of study, the main interest was in the funerary monuments and only lately has much attention been focussed onto the other aspects of Etruscan life.

However, we are not completely in the dark. Classical writers have left a good deal of information and there are many ruins still to bear witness to the lost splendour. Parts of an enormous wall that once defended Volterra, the Etruscan Velathri, against marauding bands are still standing. The walls which were once 5½ miles long and between 10 and 16½ ft thick were built towards the end of the fifth century BC. A lower, inner wall surrounded the acropolis. The outer wall had ten gates, one of which, the 'Porta all' Arco', withstood the centuries undamaged. It is constructed of tufa and the arch is of travertine. The part of the wall adjoining the gate was rebuilt during the Middle Ages in small masonry. The gate itself, more than 26 ft deep, is the earliest example in Italy of the true arch and dates as it stands from the early second century BC; some parts of it may be as early as the third century BC. The Etruscans transmitted the technique of building an arch with wedge-shaped blocks to the Romans, but it is not certain where and how they themselves acquired this knowledge. At the base and the top of the arch there are projections of black tufa. These are now so badly eroded as to be unrecognizable but were probably the masks of gods or demons entrusted with the protection of the city.

Volterra, like the other great Etruscan cities, was built on a hill and fortified, a type of location especially popular during the time of general unrest and Roman attacks. The foundation ceremonies of an Etruscan city were strictly prescribed, and were known to the Romans as '*etruscus ritus*'. The first step was to decide on the site by consulting the omens. Then, in solemn procession a furrow was cut with a plough-share of pure copper, drawn by a white bull and a white heifer. This furrow symbolically indicated the moat, and the soil cast inward the future wall. Nobody was allowed to step over this sacred furrow. Where a gate was to be built, the plough was lifted and carried across *(portare)*, thereby leaving a profane space for entry and exit *(porta)*. In the centre of the consecrated area a deep well, the *mundus*, was cut, was closed with a stone cover, and only opened at special festive days when the souls of the dead could visit the light of day *(mundus patet)*. The main road from east to west was called the *decumanus* and the *cardo* ran from north to south. Between the *decumanus* and *cardo* other roads were built, separating the *insulae* of houses. The usual house form was that of the *atrium* type, later to be adopted by the Romans.

Plate 67
Vaulted tomb near Populonia

Plate 68
The vaulted tomb of Casal Marittimo

Plate 69
Grave chamber of the 'Grande tumulo dei letti
funebri', near Populonia

Plate 70
Funerary couch in the 'tomba dei relievi' near
Cerveteri

Plate 71
Aedicula-grave, Populonia

Plate 72
Porta all' Arco, Volterra

Central and South America *Plates 73 - 108*

IT WAS ONLY AT A FAIRLY RECENT DATE that the arts and cultures of the two American continents attracted the attention of historians and archaeologists, but since then professional interest has steadily increased. Systematic research on the origins of these extraordinary civilizations was started towards the end of the nineteenth century, but there are still many enigmas and gaps in our knowledge, and so any attempt at a satisfactory reconstruction of the earliest stages can only be tentative. But with some reserve it can be said that this picture of the ancient American cultures is on the whole accurate.

The history of American civilization shows little affinity with that of the Old World. American culture in an advanced stage does not extend over so long a span of centuries as does that of the Near East; it does not possess the same versatility and wealth of creative impulses. It would be wrong, however, to deny its people some talent. The single artistic creations of the American cultural sphere compare very favourably with those of the ancient world, and if a certain monotony is perceived, the reason does not lie primarily in the lack of competence, but rather in the peculiar historical evolution of the two continents and their people.

To do full justice to the American cultural history one must remember that its evolution was cut short at its height, when at the beginning of the sixteenth century European conquerors arrived in search of gold and under the banner of the Cross destroyed the power and splendour of the American Indian empires. The native way of life and philosophy was disrupted and with European colonization came the end of any indigenous Indian creative power. The local culture was too rigid and too alien in structure and spirit to the newcomers, to serve as a basis on which to build the foundations of a New World culture.

The Indian cultures were only short-lived compared with the civilizations of Egypt and Mesopotamia which covered a span of many thousands of years. The advanced cultures of Central America lasted for no more than eight hundred years until their downfall in the sixteenth century AD. Moreover the Indian civilization never reached the same dimensions, but was restricted to the narrow strip of land connecting the two continents, with its greatest focal point in the modern states of Mexico, Guatemala, Honduras and Salvador. Another centre was the narrow coastal regions and highlands of the Middle Andes covering the greater part of modern Peru. How did it come about that exactly in these parts of the Americas and only these did a high level of culture develop, and that its creators never seriously attempted to extend their influence further afield? This problem calls for an explanation, for it concerns the very essence of the ancient Indian cultures.

It could not be said that favourable natural and climatic conditions caused the influx of population, for especially in Peru the natural conditions were far from clement. With its barren coastal plain and rugged mountains it certainly was not an alluring paradise. Anthropologists are agreed that the first settlers were of a Proto-Mongoloid type whose homeland lay in Asia and that they entered the North American continent via the Bering Straits and Alaska. They were hunters and food-gatherers and lived a nomadic existence following the game they hunted. Gradually small groups spread over the whole of the continent until they reached Central America and the Andes about ten or twelve thousand years ago. There are soil-tilling groups all over South America. Even in the tropical forest zone many tribes practise shifting cultivation. Conversely in Mexico (the Gulf coast and the Maya territory) the location of the fields was changed every few years in a system of shifting horticulture, and these people can truly be called civilized. The Peruvian coast, too, supported an urban population.

Agriculture developed at various times in different parts of the Americas. The first attempts at plant domestication in coastal Peru appear to have been made about 4000–2500 BC and the importance of agriculture gradually increased with the addition of new food plants. It was probably not until about 750 BC that subsistence in Peru was based entirely on cultivated plants, though agriculture was an important factor by 1200 BC or even earlier. In Mexico the process was just as gradual, though here it began much earlier. The first steps were taken about 7000–5000 BC, and agriculture increased in importance until between 3400 and 2300 BC domesticated plants supplied 25 per cent of the diet in the Tehuacan valley; from then on, dependence on farming increased, bringing with it larger and more permanent settlements.

A more leisurely life, when the harvest was gathered in and the future secured for one more year, gave time for thoughts higher than those of mere day-to-day necessities. Technical skills developed, the spiritual horizon widened, the social structure divided itself into classes. Manners and customs became more refined, religious thinking enriched. Gradually the foundations were laid for a higher level of culture and arts.

For unknown reasons this only happened in Central America and Peru, and it is difficult to understand why these cultures did not expand more widely. Increase of population can be a major factor in causing migrations, but we know nothing of these pressures in the American Indian world. There were, inevitably, some natural catastrophes such as earthquakes, volcanic eruptions and famines, but the destruction they caused was on a localized scale and no major migrations seem to have resulted. Finally, the Indian world had no opportunities to come into contact with other cultures. There were no trade connections and commercial exchanges with neighbouring countries, such as those which favoured the spread of cultures in Asia and Europe, and the Peruvian and Mesoamerican cycles always remained separate. So although there was some trading between the various native cultures, they developed largely within themselves in isolation. For this reason also it can be seen that all

American Indian cultures sprang from the same roots, although outwardly they may appear very different from each other. Small communities lived together in comparative isolation, so that through constant interbreeding sharply defined types evolved. These tribal groups acquired specific customs and ideas, a great diversity of dialects developed, but basically all the American Indian people belong to the same ethnical strain.

The religion of the Indians was, for all its local divergences, fundamentally a nature religion. Then there is the fact of their craftmanship, so amazing in view of the fact that they never fully advanced beyond a neolithic technology although gold, silver and later copper, and in the Andes at least bronze, were known. Although our knowledge of ancient American pre and early history is still far from complete, the archaeological discoveries corroborate the material and cultural coherence of the Indian civilizations. While the main stream divided into two separate branches—the culture of Central America and that of Peru—the differences are mostly due to variations in climate and natural surroundings, though there must, of course, have been human reasons at least as powerful as those produced by environment.

Archaeologically the Central Andes includes, besides modern Peru, also a part of Ecuador in the north and Bolivia and Chile in the south. The low coastal area, some hundreds of miles long, is the region of the greatest aridity in the world. The Humboldt current, sweeping along the Peruvian coast, prevents any precipitation. It is a desert of rock and sand; but in the river valleys where fresh water comes down from the mountains irrigation was practised, and large populations flourished. It was in these valleys and estuaries that the villages were built, and the 'coastal cultures' developed in contrast with the 'highland cultures'. Parallel with the coast line rises the great mountain range of the Andes. It forms a complete barrier between the narrow Pacific strip in the west and the enormous basin of the Amazon and its tributaries to the east. Although not lacking in water, the isolated table lands and numerous valleys were still less desirable for human habitation. The altitude of the plateaux, known as *punas*, made them unsuitable for agriculture, as only potatoes and maize can grow there at altitudes up to 12000 feet and above that, quinoa. But they were excellent pastures for the native herds of llamas and alpacas which provided wool and were used as pack animals. The steep and narrow upper reaches of the rivers were fertile but these too presented great difficulties for cultivation. The steeper slopes were terraced, and these terraces still form a prominent feature of the landscape. Another grave disadvantage was the excessive variation in day and night temperatures, which was greater in the rare atmosphere of the highlands than at sea level.

It is no great wonder that these harsh natural conditions had a lasting effect on the people and their culture. The difficulties under which the Peruvian people laboured caused them to concentrate more than the Central American Indians on the improvement of techniques for supporting life. An ever-expanding population urgently needed more agricultural lands. Extensive irrigation works were built to bring water to the arid deserts. These could only be constructed and maintained through the cooperation of the settlers under a central organization. It was on these foundations that communities developed which grew into the many famous cities along the coast. These irrigation works and terraces are, besides the beautiful textiles and rich ceramics, the most outstanding features of the Peruvian civilization.

While the Andean cities were on the whole built to be lived in and to give shelter, many of those of Central America were ceremonial centres. Here stood the temples, palaces, living-quarters of the priests, rest-houses for the many pilgrims who flocked to the city on feast days. There were altar precincts, and courts for the ball-games. There were social centres, which kept the solidarity of the tribes alive; sacred places comparable with Delphi and Olympia in the Greek world. The Central American Indians did not need to fight for every inch of living space like their Andean brothers. The soil on which they lived was more fertile and a greater variety of plants could be cultivated; the climate was milder; the forests were rich in game. Because of this there was ample leisure for the spiritual side of life and for producing works of art. But the lowland forest country of the Gulf coast and the Maya lands inevitably has its own limitations; clearings are soon exhausted and new fields have to be reclaimed. Family groups, even whole village communities moved from place to place in search of fresh acres. This made living in large towns impossible and led to a decentralization of the population. The scattered settlements however were closely linked by tribal ties and neighbourly connections, and of course by the unity of their religion and ritual. The social life of the tribe found its highest expression in an elaborate cult for which the people met in the sacred temple-cities. The magnificent temples, the symbolic picture writing, the amazingly accurate calendar and a method of astronomy designed for ritualistic purpose, all show the supreme importance of communal rites, ceremonies and cult. A powerful priesthood recruited from every tribe performed the many ceremonies, but their influence was not strong enough to overcome the political antagonism that existed between the different peoples. It happened more than once that the sacred city of a tribe did not survive the loss of independence of its members, and with the disappearance of the tribe, the tribal deities also died. The tribal sanctuaries fell into disrepair and the conquerors built a new ceremonial centre for their own gods.

The Inca empire, which lasted barely a century, developed during the fifteenth century AD. Originally a small tribe with its centre in Cuzco, situated in the central highlands of Peru, it rapidly spread its power over all the Peruvian peoples from Ecuador in the north to central Chile, a distance of nearly 3000 miles. They established a well-balanced social order, a uniform tax system and compulsory military service. The Quechua language of the conquerors became the official language. The Inca emperor was an absolute ruler; he was worshipped as *Intip Cori* (Son of the Sun) and *Sapay Inca* (the only and highest Inca). The worship of the Sun was the official religion. An influential nobility formed the vast army of officials necessary for the administration of the empire. An excellent information service and a widespread network of roads kept the far-flung communications open and contributed greatly to the success of Inca rule. It was undoubtedly the organizing genius of the Incas, their martial prowess and love of conquest that created the only real empire in the New World. But this empire could never have existed without the age-long experience in civic organization of the coastal tribes (cf. page 299).

The empire of the Tenochcas, the true exemplars of the Aztec culture, was totally different from the centralized Inca state. Where the Incas created a united state, incorporating many formerly independent units, the Tenochcas were content with levying tribute from the subjugated tribes. Besides tribute and captives, the Aztecs were interested in securing themselves against rebellion and in establishing their over-all control over subject states. They had the right to exact taxes and to impose governors and garrisons as they thought necessary, but they never had a centralized government on the Inca pattern. One of the reasons may have been that they could not free themselves from the old theocratic tribal system. The claims of cult and religious ceremony were too strong to leave room for the construction and political organization of a large empire. It is typical that the Aztecs went to war not only to conquer more land or exact tribute, although Aztec economy relied heavily on the contributions of subject cities, but to capture prisoners to be sacrified by their thousands on the altars of the Aztec gods. The well-being of the tribe depended on the favour of the gods and that favour could only be gained by sacrificing what was most precious—human life. The Aztecs undoubtedly possessed far greater power than the preceding tribal theocracies, their leaders assumed imperial status, and displayed an excessive luxury in the capital Tenochtitlan (Mexico City), but this did not alter the fact that it was ultimately the gods who ruled. Everyone, high or low, played a part in the complicated ritual. Even the highest priest had his strict duties so that the interests of the state and religion were inseparably interwoven.

The Aztec king (Tlacatecutli) was elected, but once in power he held a position of supreme importance. In the earlier stages of Aztec rule he was an absolute monarch, though sometimes he accepted advice from the tribal counsellors and in particular, from the official known as the Cihuacoatl. In later Aztec times the Cihuacoatl acted as vice-Emperor, and his powers were civil rather than religious. He dealt with financial matters, patronage and promotions, legal appeals, and acted as head of state when there was an interregnum.

It would be futile to speculate how far the Incas and Aztecs might eventually have evolved had it not been for the intervention of the Spanish conquest. They certainly had not yet reached their apogee. And it is equally certain that it was not primarily through ethnical, physical and psychological factors that the two cultures showed such a wide divergence; the main reason lay in the different natural conditions of the two regions.

The mature Aztec civilization takes much of its character from the earlier great cultures of Mexico. During the Archaic period, which ended at about 1500 BC the inhabitants of Mexico had learned to cultivate the standard food plants and had begun to turn from nomadic or semi-nomadic life to a farming existence in settled villages. The succeeding 'Formative period', lasting from about 1500 BC to the third century of our era, was marked by the introduction of pottery and by an improvement in agricultural methods which led to the establishment of large villages. By the end of this period some of these villages could better be called little towns and the first temple pyramids had appeared. Most of these farming communities were hardly civilized but some of the more advanced Formative peoples, especially the Olmecs of La Venta and other sites on the Gulf Coast and the first inhabitants of Monte Albán in Oaxaca, were building elaborate ceremonial centres, creating fine sculpture in stone, and carving inscriptions in hieroglyphics. From these roots grew the great civilizations of the Classic period; namely the cultures of Teotihuacán in the north-eastern part of the Valley of Mexico *(plates 74, 75)*, the Totonacs of Veracruz *(plate 81)*, and Zapotecs in the state of Oaxaca *(plates 76–80)*, and the Maya in south-eastern Mexico, Guatemala and Honduras *(plates 82–91)*. Of all the Classic civilizations, that of the Maya was probably the richest and most productive of artistic and architectural achievement. Their main building technique was that of rubble masonry plastered with pulverized limestone cement, finished with a facing of carefully worked stone. This facing was sometimes ornamented with painted stucco and sometimes glazed with a solution made from the bark of the *chocom* tree which, when polished, has a shiny water-tight brick-red finish. The splendid temples and palaces of the Maya have two distinguishing characteristics which are unique in Central America—the corbelled arch and the 'false façade' at roof level. These, like so many of the architectural elements of the ancient world, probably evolved from simple peasant huts of wood, thatch and adobe. The steeply-pitched thatch of these huts may well be the prototype of the corbelled arch. This construction, however, will not stand unless it is cantilevered by a considerable weight on either side, which may have led to the introduction of the elaborately carved and latticed roof-façades so highly favoured by the Maya.

Their world was ruled entirely by the priesthood, at whose command fantastic temple-pyramids were raised and years of tireless labour expended on the carving of countless intricate stone monuments, using no tools but those of a neolithic level of technology, and endless human patience. The priests, in their turn, were ruled in their every move by the most inexorable and all-powerful influence in the Central American civilizations—the calendar. At a very early date this calendar was worked out with an astonishing degree of accuracy, and every aspect of Maya life was pervaded by its power. Each city was a closely-knit community of interdependent units, and down to the smallest detail their lives were strictly ordered by the passing days and months, the intricate symbols of which are so ubiquitous a feature of Maya art. In common with the other Classic civilizations which fill the period AD 300–900, literacy was normal among the Maya, and the arts of painting and sculpture were fully mature.

A series of widespread disturbances brought the Classic period to an end. The Post-Classic phase, which lasts until the Conquest, is at first a period of confusion. The various Mexican peoples tried to take advantage of the breakdown of the old order by regrouping to form new and militaristic states. Barbarian peoples entered Mexico from the arid lands to the north and added a new strain to the old culture. Eventually a new unifying force emerged in the civilization of the Toltecs who had their capital at Tula, and in the legends of the later inhabitants of Mexico the period of Toltec rule is regarded as a sort of 'golden age'. Several Mexican dynasties, among them the Aztecs, claimed descent from the Toltecs, and although this is not true in any ethnic sense there is certainly cultural continuity.

It could hardly be otherwise. When the Toltec state came to a violent end there followed another period of confusion with fresh barbarian incursions. The last primitive tribe to enter the Valley of Mexico was the one we call the Aztecs. They arrived as farmers, rough and uncivilized in their ways, violent in their habits and un-popular with their neighbours, but by making skilful use of the disturbed political situation they were able to build up a great empire. The culture of the Aztecs derives largely from the more advanced peoples among whom they settled—especially the survivors of the old Toltec state and the Mixtec groups of Oaxaca. But successful statecraft does not necessarily lead to the production of great art. There must have been a living force to stimulate the creation of Aztec art. And here, as in all early cultures, this creative force was worship and cult. A religion cannot spring up spontaneously; spiritual structures cannot be built in a single day; they grow slowly over the centuries, through the experiences of countless generations, experiences which must have been drawn from a root common to all South American Indian peoples. Where this initial impulse came from will, perhaps, always remain hidden. The religion-directed art of the Aztecs seems to have had very little interest in abstract aesthetics, and their everyday utensils and furnishing were strictly functional, achieving elegance only accidentally. Their highly-organized society, was, however, divided into clearly defined classes, the richer of whom were able to wear ornaments of gold (one of the few metals known to the Aztecs), jade and turquoise. They produced exquisite 'feather mosaics' and worked the spectacular plumes of the *quetzal* bird into the insignia of rank. But all their most impressive productions were the architectural monuments dedicated to the service of their demanding and ever-watchful gods.

Of the early Mexican peoples perhaps the most important were the creators of the recently discovered La Venta culture which belongs to the middle Formative period of southern Mexico, Veracruz and Tabasco. In the historical period this part of the Gulf coast was inhibited by the *Olmecs*, the 'people of the Rubber Country', and by extension archaeologists have used the term to describe the earlier culture. This, however, is unjustified for nothing is known about the Gulf coast tribes during the Formative period, and to avoid confusion it is best to call the culture after its most important archaeological site, La Venta.

Some centuries earlier than the other Central American peoples the La Venta people had created a religious art of a very high standard. Characteristic are stone heads more than 6 ft high carved in an extremely hard stone, not quarried locally. They all have the same swollen and infantile features with thick-lipped mouths, slightly open. The images of their gods have strange jaguar-like faces. Small jades and a late stela are inscribed with hieroglyphs and calendric formulae. They built pyramids and stepped platforms as temples and altars. The technical skill and formal patterns of their sculpture are very remarkable and could only be the work of a gifted people who were probably already in the grip of a fully developed religious system under the leadership of priest-kings. This La Venta culture had a great influence on its neighbours. Similar infantile features appear on carved slabs from Monte Albán, the first temple-city. The Totonacs of Veracruz followed La Venta artforms and probably many religious and ritual customs. The Formative cultures of the Mexican valley were influenced by La Venta. There seems also to have been a close connection with the Mayas. The La Venta hieroglyphs and calendar systems resemble those of the early Maya culture, but there is a mystery here for the dates written in Maya hieroglyphs seem to be earlier than those inscribed on the Maya monuments themselves. The relationship between La Venta and the Maya cultures is not at all clear. Early Maya sculptures on the temple at Uaxactun (Guatemala) show a definite similarity with the La Venta sculptures. The same round jaguar faces which are not typical of later Maya art, appear here.

With such a lack of evidence it is impossible to define the part played by the La Venta culture in the evolution of the other Central American Indian cultures. Situated in the midst of other people living on a more primitive level, its example may have provided a lively stimulus, great enough to explain the sudden upsurge of art everywhere in Central America.

The captions to the plates 73–100 describe the main features of the Central American cultures in detail. It is sufficient here to point out the impersonal quality and the continuity of tradition of Indian art. There is comparatively little difference between early and late work. Where Western art evolves from the conventionalized, stylized forms of a primitive period, through a continuous process towards the complex, lively and naturalistic patterns of its final stage, Central American art is stationary. This stagnation is understandable when one considers how deeply art was enslaved by religion. After having reached a final system, religious ideas and ritual customs did not permit any changes and therefore religious art was strictly confined within its established form. The visual representation of a deity could not be varied to accentuate one or the other aspect of his power. The image was dogmatically fixed. The Indian artist was not free, as his European counterpart was, to express any emotions. There was no room for personal feeling in a rigid doctrine, for although the gods could be influenced for the good of the community, they remained remote. There was no bond of 'love with every passion blending' between god and man.

Similarly, architecture was restricted by tradition. Except for minor local variations, it too shows how all Indian art sprang from a common root. The basic plan of the cult centre remained unaltered through the centuries. It was and remained an open-air altar or temple placed on a high terraced pyramid, to which a single stairway gave access. Only in a few instances were there more stairs *(plates 73, 74)*. This was the generally accepted canon, for as Tacitus, describing the traditionalism of Roman temple building, remarked: 'The gods do not suffer changes gladly'.

The temple platform is not exclusive to the Central American cultures, it is also the usual form of sacred architecture in the Andes, which is not so strange as it might seem considering the conformity in religious thinking. In the Northern Peruvian highlands and on the north coast there appeared a new cultural style called 'Chavín', after its most important site, Chavín de Huántar. Starting in about the tenth century BC, it showed great uniformity in style and its influence was to spread far. The chief god of the Chavín culture has the same feline features as the Olmec deities of La Venta—the head of a jaguar or puma with terrifying fangs joined to a human body, or sometimes that of a condor—and the Peruvian culture shares certain other traits with the cultures of the Formative period in Central America. Like La Venta, Chavín was a ceremonial centre, for the valley in which it lies is not wide enough to sustain a large population, and it was probably a place of pilgrimage. Here too were terraced temple platforms as well as many other striking similarities with La Venta.

These by themselves are too slender an argument for calling Chavín an offshoot of La Venta, although the two cultures certainly overlap in time. Moreover certain basic features of the Olmec culture, like writing and calendrics, are not represented in Chavín. Until recently the Chavín complex had no recognizable antecedents in Peru, but excavations at Kotosh, on the eastern slope of the Andes, have revealed an earlier stage in which the pottery, though not of true Chavín type, is beginning to take on Chavín features. There are signs also of Olmec influence, and the level is dated to slightly before 1000 BC. Immediately above this stratum is another with pure Chavín artifacts. Outside Peru, the closest parallels for Chavín ware are to be found in the pottery from Tlatilco, a site of the Formative period in the Valley of Mexico. The influence of the La Venta culture is strongly felt at Tlatilco, and it is likely that there was contact between Mexico and Peru by way of the Pacific coast where ocean-going rafts and dugouts were known to have been used in later times. At a date close to the start of the Chavín phase, a new and improved type of maize is introduced into Peru which, like the types previously grown in the country, probably came from Mexico. In between the two main centres, recent work on the coast of Ecuador has shown that this region had contacts with both Mexico and Peru, but more research is still needed along the Pacific coast route.

The Chavín culture seems to have been more than just a tribal culture; signs of Chavín influence are found throughout the whole of Peru, though they differ considerably in detail. Some scholars believe that immigrants from the Andean highlands brought it to the coast, others, that it was established by a superior tribe from the north. It is probably more correct to speak of a widespread religious movement and not of a homogeneous culture. The common factor of the Chavín culture is its characteristic form of art, subordinated here as elsewhere entirely to religion. A feline, puma or jaguar deity was worshipped here, represented in a typical curvilinear style. However, by about 500 BC the Chavín culture had disintegrated, and continued only in many local cultures.

The Mochica culture, which flourished between AD 200 and 800, in the valleys of the Moche and the Chicama in north Peru, is one of the most interesting cultures to follow the Chavín. These people erected enormous pyramids built of mud brick (adobe), the only material available in the valleys. The most imposing ruins in the Moche valley are known as the Temple of the Sun and the Temple of the Moon. Like their counterparts, the Mesopotamian ziggurats, they are in a pitiful state of neglect, but the sheer massiveness of these impressive monuments speaks still of the achievements of the past. As we have seen, the history of the Peruvian peoples was determined by secular and political events, but the influence of a common religion cannot be overlooked. This does not mean that art and culture found their mainspring in the religion of which they are the spiritual manifestation, as in every early stage of human evolution. It would be better to say that a common religion was the medium through which ideas spread. And these ideas were expressed in a common artistic language. If it is correct to see the Chavín culture as the result of a pan-Peruvian faith, then it would be the first example in Andean history of the spread of a culture through spiritual communication alone.

A second example of this trend can be seen in the Tiahuanaco period. Mystery and legends surround the imposing ruins of Tiahuanaco, near Lake Titicaca on the Bolivian highlands (plate 101). This culture seems to have developed in Bolivia during the first centuries of our era and for a long time had only limited distribution. Then, in the early ninth and the tenth centuries, came an expansion which brought Tiahuanaco traits from the highlands down to the coast where the local post-Chavín cultures, Mochica, Nazca, Recuay, etc., were superseded by a distinctively coastal version of Tiahuanaco. It is not so much the historical problem of this amazing theocratic culture that concerns us here as the question of how it was possible for this culture to impose its style on the whole of the Peruvian world and so bring about a certain unity of culture. Some call this period 'expansionist', but this term implies a forceful invasion and a pan-Peruvian domination on the part of the Tiahaunaco people which is unlikely in view of the relative independence of the local cultures. It may have been that the expansion of their influence was due to the introduction of bronze; it is a fact that the copper and tin mines of the southern highlands and Bolivia are of great antiquity. But the material benefits from the introduction of metal were not the main cause of the spread of the Tiahuanaco culture. The standard of living did not materially rise in the Andes, new technical skills did not develop. The expansion of Tiahuanaco was not a result of a widespread trade in metals. It can only be explained as the diffusion of religious ideas. Tiahuanaco itself was a ceremonial centre. Missionaries may have gone out to spread a religion, which was, for reasons unknown, more attractive than the old beliefs. There appears, to, too have been a renewed expansion of Tiahuanaco influence at a later date, this time probably backed up by military force.

The influence of the gods of Tiahanaco waned during the thirteenth to fourteenth centuries. Local traditions again became strong and over the whole of the Andes region independent states formed, following the same pattern as that which had formed after the breakdown of the Chavín culture. The new 'empires'—Chimu, Cuismancu, Chincha and others—were the creations of warlike tribal chiefs.

Civic organization was in the hands of a few noble families who held hereditary office. The common people lived in carefully planned settlements and towns along the riverbanks. Irrigation schemes, canals and other public works made cooperation essential and thus a kind of state collectivism sprang up. And on these foundations was built the great empire of the fifteenth century—that of the Inca.

Plate 73
Archaic stepped pyramid, Cuicuilco, Mexico

It was during the first centuries of the Christian era that the Indian cultures of Central America rose to a rare and amazing height and emerged as fully developed, mature entities with pronounced individual characteristics. This revolutionary upsurge had its roots in the so-called Archaic and Formative cultures, which have now, by radiocarbon dating methods, been traced back beyond the fifth millennium BC. Agriculture, the art of pottery making and weaving laid the foundations on which a high standard of culture could develop. The first evidence for ceremonial architecture belongs to the late Formative period. However, there are only a few remains, and although archaeological research is still going on, the greater part has been irretrievably lost.

The stepped pyramid of Cuicuilco near Tlatileo in the Mexican Valley, is probably the oldest ceremonial building of Mesoamerica and belongs to the late Formative period. It consists of a circular mound (40 ft in diameter and 65 ft high) and rises up in four stages in decreasing circumference. Built about 500–300 BC, it was the work of the whole population, spurred on by religious zeal and the command of a priesthood in whose hands the people's fate lay. They created this great mound out of sand and rubble and faced its sides with stones as protection against the wind and rain. An altar for the gods stood on the summit and possibly also a temple, in the same way as their descendants later built their pyramids. It was enlarged at least once. Roughly constructed stairs led up the east side from stage to stage to the platform, and on the west side there was probably a ramp.

All the elements of the classical Indian temple pyramid are present here and with it the ideas and religious concepts inherent in its formal construction. Walter Krickeberg, one of the leading experts on Central American cultures, rightly interpreted the stepped pyramid as a symbol of the sky which the Indian people saw as a mountain and not as a vault. They imagined the sun to climb up to the summit in the morning and descend again in the afternoon. The four steps of the pyramid symbolize the rising and setting of the sun. But whatever the right interpretation may be of the pyramid form, Mexican pyramids have the same intrinsic meaning as those of the ancient Orient. As with the Mesopotamian temple towers, they were intended to raise the sacred places of worship above the level of everyday life and bring them nearer to the divine beings.

The picture shows the lowest stage, battered and reinforced with stones. The wide ditch is the result of excavations. At about AD 300 the pyramid was enclosed in a yard-thick layer of *pedregal*, a volcanic sediment caused by the eruption of the nearby volcano. Molten lava flowed around the site, killing the local people and destroying their homes.

Plate 74
The Teotihuacán culture.
The Pyramid of the Sun, Teotihuacán, Mexico

The Teotihuacán culture is probably the earliest truly civilized culture in Central Mexico, but it cannot be connected with a definite Indian tribe such as the Maya, Zapotecs, Totonacs or Aztecs. We do not even know the name of the people who, between the second and seventh centuries AD, built a city covering more that three square miles, which was the most splendid if not the largest of ancient Mexico. Their disappearance was as sudden as their first entry and their buildings are, even in ruins, still breathtakingly beautiful. What the spade of the archaeologist has recovered and the zeal of the restorers replaced—not always accurately—is magnificent and it is small wonder that the Aztecs gave it the name 'Teotihuacán' which means "the place where gods are made". The myths say that it was here that the gods sacrificed themselves for the good of mankind, and they wrongly believed the pyramids to be the burial place of bygone kings. This is a historical error for it was in its time no necropolis, but a glittering temple-city full of life and one of the few towns where sacred and profane buildings stood side by side.

The Pyramid of the Sun dominates the town. The enormous structure now rises up in five stages, each sloping at a different angle, to a height of 210 ft with sides 700 ft long at the base. The pyramid ends in a fairly large platform on which a temple once stood. A broad staircase tapering towards the top leads to the platform. The restorers, in their endeavour to preserve as much as possible of the mud-brick ruins, have given it an inaccurate shape (originally it had only four tiers) so that the pyramid as it stands today does not give a true picture of the original Teotihuacán construction. Where today it has a solid mantle of stone, reminiscent of the Egyptian stone pyramids, it was originally probably covered with a thick layer of plaster, painted in brilliant colours. Then it must have looked very bright and gaudy in the strong southern light, but now its solid mass, although impressive, is unimaginative and heavy. As the centre-piece of an immense precinct, surrounded by smaller buildings, the pyramid is a testimony of the inconceivable power of the priest-kings of Teotihuacán and its people's religious faith, that can move mountains.

Without the help of carts or wagons, they carried the sun-dried bricks needed for the solid structure of more than a million cubic feet, and piled them up layer upon layer. The pyramid seems to be built in one continuous effort as it was originally planned and not as in so many cases by over-building an already existing smaller construction. Test tunnelling has proved this without any doubt. It is not known to which deity the immense structure was erected, but, in spite of its name, there is no proof that it was a temple for the sun god, as the Aztecs who themselves worshipped the sun, believed. The old legends, however, are the only evidence we have for their dedication.

Plate 75
The Teotihuacán culture.
The so-called Pyramid-temple of Quetzalcóatl,
Teotihuacán, Mexico

Teotihuacán was famous not only for the Pyramid of the Sun and its smaller companion, the Pyramid of the Moon, but also for the temple precinct within the 'citadel'. This temple has been much altered but is now partly restored in its original form and much of its ornamentation has been saved. The pyramid was built in six stages each becoming shallower in height towards the top. Its façade represents the best that Indian art has ever created. The *adobe* core was hidden behind perpendicular courses of stone blocks separated by projecting cornices and decorated with sculptured friezes identical for each of the six stages.

Terrifying feathered serpent heads alternate with demoniacal masks with saucer-like staring eyes. The bodies of the scaly serpents gods fill the friezes in low relief. In the background are snails and seashells of Carribean varieties which seem to indicate that these gods lived in the sea or were associated with water. This sacred mound was once glowing with paint, traces of which have been found, and the sinuous serpents once glared at the onlooker with eyes of burnished obsidian. Although the figures on the friezes were undoubtedly deities, it is still a much debated question as to which gods they represent. The feathered serpent is identified by some as the god whom the Aztecs called 'Quetzalcoatl', the benefactor of mankind, god of life, of wind, the planet Venus and the morning. The mask with the staring eyes is almost certainly an early representation of the Aztec god Tláloc, a rain and water deity.

It is likely that this people, who must have been agriculturalists, connected their supreme god with the life-giving qualities of water rather than with the scorching, hostile sun as did the later Aztecs. The Teotihuacán people seem to have been keen observers of the orbits of the stars and seasons of the year. It has been calculated that 366 sculptured heads filled the friezes and this number comes too near to the days of the years calculated by the Aztecs as 365, to be accidental. Moreover the Pyramid of the Sun at Teotihuacán, like those of sun-worshipping tribes, is orientated towards the west with a declination of 17° to the north and points towards the setting sun at its highest point on the ecliptic. This seems indeed to indicate a sun worship, but as Krickeberg rightly remarks, this very date inaugurates the beginning of the rainy season in the Mesa Central and although they left no calendric notations, the people of Teotihuacán must have felt a close association with the passing of the seasons. Their supreme god was probably a rain god, who as master of the crops was then more powerful than his Aztec successor Tláloc.

Plate 76
The Zapotecs.
The temple-city, Monte Albán, Mexico

At the beginning of written records, the peoples of the Valley of Oaxaca in southern Mexico were speaking a language called Zapotec. It is uncertain at what time Zapotec-speakers reached this part of the country, but there is no major disturbance in the archaeological record from the founding of Monte Albán to the time when Zapotec is known to have been spoken. It is therefore possible that the people spoke Zapotec from the beginning, but excavations at the ceremonial centre of Monte Albán show a very long period of occupation which can be divided into five phases. Of these, the flourishing third and decadent fourth periods can safely be called Zapotec, and the fifth and last is linked with the Mixtecs.

The site of Monte Albán is near the city of Oaxaca in the Mexican state of the same name and lies on a hill which rises to a height of 1310 feet above the valley floor. The earliest remains (Monte Albán I) include the Temple of the *Danzantes*, a stone-faced platform into the outside of which are set stone slabs with incised human figures. These have the round heads and thick lips typical of Olmec art, and Monte Albán I must span the period 800–350 BC.

The greatest period of Monte Alban culture was undoubtedly the first 'Zapotec' phase, Monte Albán III, which lasted from the first century AD until about 950. The hill was levelled off, and on the terraces thus created were erected a great number of temples and courts, stairways and colonnades.

The picture gives a view over the whole of the area seen from the north. In the foreground is a sunken courtyard with a building of unknown function in the centre. To the south stands a small platform orientated on an east-west axis, but its superstructure has completely vanished. The heavy circular column-bases are an exceptional feature, as piers and columns do not form a basic part of Zapotec architecture. This platform was reached from two sides by unusually broad stairs, a feature repeated on most of the Monte Albán buildings. Behind the colonnade lies a rectangular court (655 × 1100 feet), bounded on the south side by a large platform with an as yet unexplored pyramid temple and on the east and west sides by several detached temple buildings. Within the central court there are ruins of a group of buildings apparently used for astronomical observations.

Monte Albán was preeminently a religious centre and, unlike Teotihuacán, there are no traces in the areas excavated to date of dwelling houses, not even living-quarters for the priesthood, as in most other temple cities. These, however, may lie in the unexcavated outskirts. One structure could be interpreted as a palace; it perhaps only came to life on days of ceremonial festivals and was undoubtedly a place of pilgrimage. During Monte Albán III the slopes of the hill became a huge graveyard, now an inexhaustible field of study. Another theory has been brought forward, namely, that individual cities or larger Zapotec communities each built their own private sanctuaries here in the same manner as the members of the Greek *amphictyones* built temples and treasures at Delphi.

There is however as yet no final explanation for the problem of Monte Albán.

Plate 77
The Zapotecs.
Entrance façade of the palace with the colonnade,
Mitla, Mexico

Around the year AD one thousand, Phase III at Monte Albán came to an end and the site, with all its sacred buildings, was abandoned by the Zapotecs. During Period IV, which lasted until about 1300, or 1350, no new buildings were constructed but the site remained sacred and both burials and offerings were still made there. Eventually (Period V) Monte Albán was re-occupied by the Mixtecs who occasionally buried their own dead in tombs built during the great days of Zapotec civilization. When Monte Albán was abandoned, the Zapotecs seem to have retreated towards Mitla, about 6 miles south-east of Monte Albán, and made this into their new centre. The well-preserved buildings at Mitla however differ in form and design and even purpose from those of Monte Albán. What one meets here

are not temple pyramids but sprawling low buildings with flat roofs centred around courtyards, not at all in keeping with ritual and ceremonial requirements. They can only be interpreted as priestly or royal palaces.

There are five separate complexes, of which the palace with the colonnade sometimes called 'government house', is the most prominent and the best preserved. A hall 122 ft long, and 23 ft wide is divided into two by a colonnade from the entrance. It is placed transversely on a level platform. Three fairly low doorways lead into a square forecourt that lies secluded from the outside world framed by isolated side buildings. A short flight of stairs stretching across the three doors, leads from the concreted court into the palace itself. At the back of the transverse hall there lies another square court *(plate 78)* enclosed on all sides by small chambers. Its only entrance is through a narrow passage, which gives it an intimate character. It could well belong to the royal apartments or that of the high-priest and his retinue.

Plate 78
The Zapotecs.
Interior of the hall of the columns Mitla,
Mexico

The most important palace at Mitla, dwelling of the Zapotec king or high-priest,
received its name from the row of columns
in the centre of the entrance hall. These
columns may have been necessary for the
support of a flat roof over the wide hall. The
six columns have no bases or capitals and
were made of trachyte, a volcanic rock found
abundantly in the neighbourhood. It was an
easy medium in which to work, while at
the same time very strong. The column,
never a basic architectural element in the
Zapotec repertory, was presumably used
only for structural reasons, both here and
at Monte Albán *(plate 76)*.

Within the Central American region Mitla
architecture is unique in its use of monolithic columns, both in the method of
execution and style. The surface of the
columns may have been relieved by a web of
geometric decoration *(plate 79)* but this
would not, in fact, detract from their
megalithic weight. If the builders of Mitla
had not been conscious of the natural
properties of stone and recognized it as a
means of creating for eternity, it would be
difficult to understand why they took such
inordinate trouble to cut blocks often
weighing more than 23 tons with only stone
implements, and then transport them over
large distances with such primitive aids,
probably wooden rollers.

Their task may have been made easier
because trachyte breaks up into large seg-
ments and this may also have been the reason
why they chose to erect these enormous
monoliths instead of cutting them down to
smaller sizes. This explanation, however, is
not entirely convincing, for the pieces of
stone mosaic used in 150 or so of the surviving carved panels which decorated the
walls were cut in all shapes and sizes.

Plate 79
The Zapotecs.
Details from the inner court of the palace with the colonnade, Mitla, Mexico

The stone ornamentation which covers nearly all the walls of this building, looking like so many finely woven carpets, is exceptionally charming.

Friezes set in plain projecting frames fill the walls in richly varying patterns. The technical skill they show is as great as the inventiveness of the formal design. Nearly a hundred thousand stones must have been cut to size and accurately fitted into a continuous pattern. The stonemasons of Mitla fulfilled this difficult task in an unsurpassed manner. No joints are visible, the patterns blend faultlessly and it is difficult to know what to admire most, the supreme skill or the fact that the people of Mitla had at their disposal only the simplest stone implements.

The construction of the inner court perhaps shows the influence of Teotihuacán architecture, although Mitla is several centuries later and is contemporary with the Toltec capital at Tula in the Valley of Mexico. At Mitla, as in Teotihuacán the plinths were left plain and slightly tapering, while the ornamentation was reserved for the vertical walls. The same sort of deep-set decoration within frames also occurs at Teotihuacán, especially on the Quetzalcoatl temple *(plate 75)*. The origin of the design is difficult to assess. Its continuous direction, whether in a 'Grecian meander' or formalized scroll, sweeps in one uninterrupted movement along the walls. Zapotec weaving and wood carving of which no specimens now exist, may have served as models for the stone carvers.

The formal patterns vaguely recall animal shapes such as the serpent or jaguar in extremely abstract lines. And it is possible that a people as devout as the Zapotecs, where ritual observations ruled every act and the priests were all powerful, saw an inner meaning in a design that to us seems an aniconic ornament.

Plate 80
The Zapotecs.
Crypt of the palace, Mitla, Mexico

No other Indian people showed greater piety towards the dead than the Zapotecs. The sacred city on Monte Albán *(plate 76)* was surrounded by innumerable tombs, hewn in the rock or built as crypts under the temple foundations. They were underground chamber-tombs, decorated with relief mosaics or mural-painting on plastered walls. Relief was also used on the door-jambs and lintels of the entrances leading down into the graves. There are many indications that the Zapotecs believed in an after-life and that it was the custom to celebrate a second ceremonial burial when the flesh had rotted away, after which the tomb was finally closed. Sometimes the tomb contained only one body but more often it was a collective grave.

In later days the simple chamber grave gave way to a cruciform crypt. Under two of the buildings, which frame the second court of the palace with the colonnade, similar crypts have been found. They are also carefully fitted with decorated panels. At the intersection of the two arms of the cross a column supports a monolithic coping stone (on the picture just visible in the shadow). The Spanish monk Francisco de Burgoa, in the second half of the seventeenth century described similar crypts, but his stories are rather exaggerated. He had seen crypts, now located near the palace of columns, of enormous dimensions. He mentions thirty Spanish miles. Allegedly these gave access to a subterranean cave where innumerable bodies of sacrificed captives and men killed in war were hidden behind a heavy stone slab. Not a trace, however, of such a cave or passage has been found during modern excavations and the cruciform chamber has more modest dimensions than Burgoa led us to believe. But he was right when he said that these tombs were for the interment of high-ranking personalities such as the high-priest or the king, who, during their lifetime lived in the palace.

Plate 73
Archaic stepped pyramid, Cuicuilco, Mexico

Plate 74
The Teotihuacán culture.
The Pyramid of the Sun, Teotihuacán, Mexico

Plate 75
The Teotihuacán culture.
The so-called Pyramid-temple of Quetzalcóatl,
Teotihuacán, Mexico

Plate 76
The Zapotecs.
The temple-city, Monte Albán, Mexico

Plate 77
The Zapotecs.
Entrance façade of the palace with the colonnade,
Mitla, Mexico

Plate 78
The Zapotecs.
Interior of the hall of the columns, Mitla,
Mexico

Plate 79
The Zapotecs.
Details from the inner court of the palace with
the colonnade, Mitla, Mexico

Plate 80
The Zapotecs
Crypt of the palace, Mitla, Mexico

Plate 81
The Totonacs.
The Great Temple, El Tajín, Mexico

The culture of the Totonacs, a people living on the northern shores of the Gulf of Mexico, is on the whole more recent than that of Teotihuacán and overlaps with the Zapotec period of Monte Albán. It may have begun during the Early Classic period, but the peak of its activity was about AD 600–300 and sites continued to be occupied until the thirteenth century. Formerly it was believed that the Totonacs were the same people as the legendary Olmecs, the founders of the earliest great culture of Central America. There is indeed a certain formal affinity, but not enough to conclude that the Totonacs were the direct descendants of the Olmecs of the La Venta culture, although the Totonac country lies immediately to the north of La Venta. Olmec influence can also be traced in the Maya and earliest Monte Albán cultures. The 'Totonac' culture is also called 'Tajín' after its most important site, and 'Classic Veracruz' after the state in which it is most commonly found.

The Totonac culture also seems to have erupted suddenly with works of unsurpassed perfection. The city of El Tajín was the religious centre of the early Totonacs. Its extensive ruins have not yet been fully explored. Like the Maya temple cities it had been overgrown by dense jungle and thus saved from complete destruction. Our knowledge, except for a few small buildings, is still confined to the main structure known since 1785, the Great Temple. It was known locally as 'Tajín' and therefore gave its name to the town.

The architectural features repeated in all its seven stages are more typical Totonac than its general shape. Other cultures, including the Maya, used the niche as an ornamental element, but the Totonacs made this motif a basic feature of their architecture in general, and in particular of the Tajín pyramid. Its seven stages, the highest of which is in fact a temple, are broken up by the niches in the vertical part of each terrace. It has been suggested that the niches once contained cult statues, but this is not likely, because it was against all Indian customs to unite architecture and sculpture in this way. A very steep staircase leads up to the summit from a relatively small forecourt surrounded by low buildings. The stairway however is not contemporary with the main structure but was added later; some of the niches have disappeared under the ramp. The great depth of the stair risers reminds one immediately of the stylobate of a Greek temple. These are of super-human dimensions so that only the gods can stride up them. The small projecting niches in the stairs may have had a special ceremonial purpose. Lamps or torches may have guided the way to the summit. The whole plan of the temple was ruled by cult. Like the figures on the temple of Quetzalcoatl at Teotihuacán *(plate 75)* the 365 niches are correlated with the calendar year which the Totonacs probably borrowed from the La Venta people. The formalized snake ornaments on the balustrades represent the god of El Tajín. It would be reasonably safe to assume that the god of Tajín was the rain-god Quetzalcoátl of the Teotihuacán people. The word Tajín means lightning and the rain-god could well appear as a thundercloud.

Plate 82
The Maya.
The Great Jaguar Temple, Tikal, Guatemala

When we speak of the lost cultures of the Americas we think in the first place of the Mayas. Although the Maya population of today is still of pure Indian blood, the high culture that made their name immortal has long since gone—literally drowned in the tropical jungle. Here we touch on one of the mysteries of this people, so mysterious, and so highly gifted, who abandoned their cities about AD 900, those grand centres of theocratic civilization. There are more than a hundred towns lost in the rank vegetation of the tropical forest although there are no signs of tribal war or invasion of a foreign people. Every temple or palace built since the third century AD, the beginning of the Classical period of the Maya culture, in Guatemala and the Honduras shared this fate, and for this reason scholars and archaeologists have been able to reawaken many of them again from their long sleep.

Many conjectures have been brought forward as to the cause of this general exodus. It has been suggested that perhaps epidemics decimated the population, or that changes in climate made the further cultivation of the soil impossible. The explanation of J. Eric S. Thompson, in his time the greatest expert on Maya culture, seems to be the most credible. He sees it as the result of a peasant revolution against the harsh rule of a priesthood exploiting the peasants through forced labour and heavy tributes. The temples, as is clear even now in their ruinous condition, must have been built with the blood and sweat of the ordinary people. And as the rival cities vied with each other in magnificence, such enormous sacrifices must have weighed too heavily on the people, and at last, in spite of their piety, they revolted, abandoned their fields and left the priests to their fate. Whatever the correct explanation, without the religious zeal and fanaticism of the Maya priesthood, these astonishing structures could never have been raised.

Architecture was the foremost expression of their piety and Tikal, only one of the recently discovered Maya centres, can be understood in this light. Its temple pyramids grew into soaring terraced mountains, in the same spirit as the sky-scraping spires of the Gothic cathedrals. The Jaguar Temple reaches a height of nearly 230 feet and the steepness of the nine terraces of the partly restored pyramid as well as the unbroken flight of stairs to the crowning temple, were created by the same burning zeal that inspired the builders of the medieval churches.

Plate 83
The Maya.
The Temple of the Sun, Palenque, Mexico

Of the more than one hundred Maya cities that have been discovered—and undoubtedly more pyramids, temples and altars are still hidden under centuries-old forests—the majority are characterized by distinct local nuances, although the general shape and ornamentation of the temple pyramids does not vary. But as the tribal cult centres did not assume more than regional significance their buildings show a clear cut individuality.

Characteristic of Tikal *(plate 82)* is the great height and elegant shape of its pyramid. Palenque, in the Mexican state of Chiapas, is famous for its rich ornamentation in stucco and stone and for the lightness of its buildings. Its temples and palaces do not impress by their sheer weight and excessive dimensions, but rather by the great variety of colourful, although badly damaged, figural and ornamental reliefs. Stucco workers and masons went to work wherever there was room and enhanced by their art the dignity of their temples.

The Temple of the Sun stands on a platform raised on a truncated pyramid of four stages. Its upright walls conform with the general principles of Maya building. It has an open portico, leading to an anteroom in front of the cella. This gives the otherwise windowless body of the building an open aspect, with above it the heavy steep roof. Its superstructure of trelliswork also occurs in other Maya temples and formed the background of rich stucco decoration. It probably had also some cult purpose.

Plate 84
The Maya.
Stairway of the House of the Magician,
Uxmal, Yucatán

The temple pyramid of the House of the Magician at Uxmal is one of the later works of Maya classical architecture (twelfth to early thirteenth century AD). It is an example of the 'veneer-technique', typical of west Yucatán. A core of solid cement and stone is covered with richly decorated stone slabs, not unlike a veneer of wood. Except for this technical detail, the House of the Magician does not differ much from the usual pattern. The usual external stairway with relief decoration leads to the high temple, either side of which is carved with the masks of the god Chac, a rain-god, whose prestige was so high with the Maya peasantry, that his image appears on practically every sacred building. His turned-up trunk soon became a *leitmotiv* of all Maya art.

Looking at the picture one can feel something of the emotion the Maya people must have experienced when, standing at the foot of the pyramid, they took part in the ceremonies, more guessing than seeing what happened, for the rites were performed by the priests in the cella of the temple on the summit, high above the common people. But the solemn procession of the priests in their colourful robes must have been well calculated to induce a suitably reverential frame of mind in the onlookers.

Plate 85
The Maya.
House of the Virgins, Chichén Itzá, Yucatán

A fate that seems to us atrocious, but to the Maya laudable and even desirable awaited, according to an old tradition, the occupants of this towerlike building. Specially selected maidens were kept in this completely windowless building only accessible by a few narrow doors. In seclusion and abstinence they prepared themselves for their final sacrifice of atonement to the rain-god.

The rain-god dominates the corners of the building with his up-turned trunk, a motif found in nearly all Maya architecture *(plate 84)*.

The House of the Virgins contains most of the main Maya elements. The plinths of the Mexican structures were slightly battered, while the Maya preferred the perpendicular base. The Maya showed a marked liking for weighty horizontal frames consisting of two or more parallel courses with ornamental interstices. The centre is deep-set while the outer courses project sharply. This idea of horizontal dividing lines, consequently observed even in the high pyramid temples, is represented harmoniously in the House of the Virgins. It seems that the Maya architects were conscious of this sense of movement, for by leaving the substructure unadorned, they thereby stressed its supporting function and optically lightened the building with a false roof façade with open-work ornamentation.

The Nunnery at Uxmal was built around a courtyard and consisted of four groups of buildings. The façade of the main building facing the inner court is a fine showpiece of Maya ornamentation. As in so many Maya buildings an elaborate façade hides the roof. This façade consists of a series of gables decorated in regular horizontal bands, the central motif of which is composed of grotesque masks of the rain-god Chac. The S-shaped trunk, threatening teeth and deep-set, saucerlike eyes, repeated over and over again, have sometimes been called baroque, but one has to be careful when comparing Maya decorative forms with European art forms. True, this tower of masks seems to have much in common with European baroque in the wealth of detail which completely covers the surface area, but it adheres to quite different formal principles.

Nothing of the exuberant movement and the fluidity of the late baroque is present in the Maya style, nor the sheer force of upward thrust that characterizes baroque columns. What we encounter here is a monotonous repetition of horizontal bands with separate sculptural elements which do not allow any freedom of movement or lively energy. Horizontality and verticality are nearly balanced but because of the height of the gables above the horizontal lines of the lower structure, the vertical line is on the whole predominant.

However, in spite of the continuous repetition there is no lack of inventiveness. The sculptures themselves show a great variety of detail. The duplication of the same mask was probably deliberate and the priests on whose orders the work was executed aimed at a clear understanding of the all-pervading power of the deity.

Plate 87
The Maya.
*Detail of the Palace of the Governor, Uxmal,
Yucatán*

Next to the four-winged complex of the
Nunnery *(plate 86)* the Palace of the
Governor is considered one of the major
buildings, not only of the city of Uxmal, but
of the whole school of late Maya architecture
in Yucatán. This exceptionally beautiful
corner of the palace gives a good idea of the
technical skill and artistry of the builders,
stone masons and sculptors—a wonder of
ingenuity when one considers that the
people who created this work knew only
stone implements. The palace of the governor is another example of the veneer
technique that we have already seen in plate
84. It consists here of accurately joined
square stone blocks attached to the perpendicular wall and the incurved pointed
arch typical of Maya construction, and covers
a solid core of rough rubble and mortar.
This treatment continues in the triple
cornice and in the relief frieze above, which
is composed of a great number of small
blocks. The frieze of rain-god motifs and
serpents alternating with meanders does
nothing to lighten the massive weight of
the building. Maya architecture, except for a
few instances such as Palenque, did not as a
rule favour light open buildings, but preferred a compact and massive structure.

Plate 88
The Maya.
The Great Gate, Labna, Yucatán

The Maya people built few monumental
gateways, and the one at Labna is about the
only surviving specimen. This is difficult to
explain and it does not *a priori* follow from
this that the Maya did not know the true
arch (of the Roman type) but only the
'false' arch. It is true that it is not easy to
span a large area with a corbel arch, but the
building at Labna shows that it was not
primarily technical difficulties that prevented
the creation of gateways. Other people, the
Mycenaeans for example, knew only the
false arch but still succeeded in creating imposing gateways. Presumably the Maya simply lacked the incentive to build entrance
gates. Their temple complex and cities were
not enclosed within walls, which would
have needed gates, but were built on terraces and linked by open courts, and therefore had no use for gateways or propylons.
The element *par excellence* of Maya architecture was the stairway, and these were
built on a truly monumental scale.

The gate at Labna is an ornamental showpiece of the highest rank. In the wings on
either side of the central porch are small
chambers and above these are two symmetrical balconies, but these are only false
façades in the form of a Maya dwelling with
thatched roof. On either side they are
flanked by trellis panels which again show
the great skill of the Maya artisans in hand-
ling their stone tools.

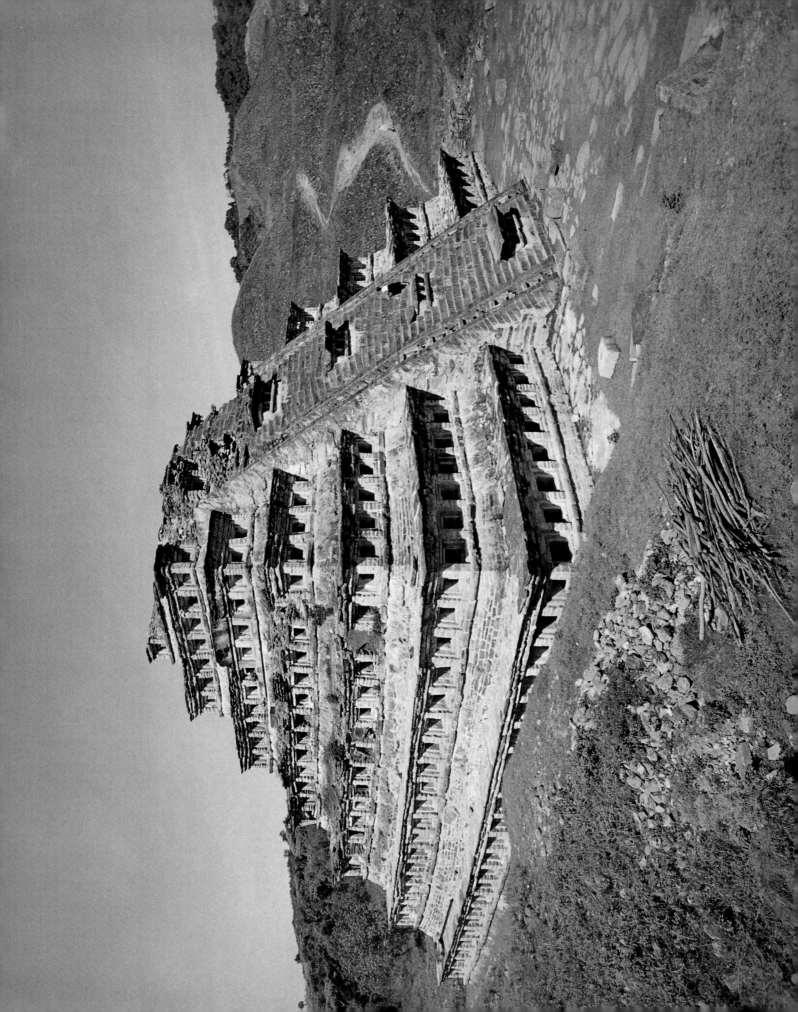

Plate 81
The Totonacs.
The Great Temple, El Tajín, Mexico

Plate 82
The Maya.
The Great Jaguar Temple, Tikal, Guatemala

Plate 83
The Maya.
The Temple of the Sun, Palenque, Mexico

Plate 84
The Maya.
Stairway of the House of the Magician, Uxmal,
Yucatán

Plate 85
The Maya.
House of the Virgins, Chichén Itzá, Yucatán

Plate 86
The Maya.
Rain-god masks on the main building of the
Nunnery, Uxmal, Yucatán

Plate 87
The Maya
Detail of the Palace of the Governor, Uxmal,
Yucatán

Plate 88
The Maya.
The Great Gate, Labna, Yucatán

Plate 89
The Maya.
The five-storeyed temple, Edzná, Mexico

It is not strictly correct to call this structure, fascinating though its mass and proportions are, a five-storeyed building, because it has no interior and thus no storeys in the proper sense. Although they frequently built in layers the Maya seldom placed storey upon storey, and the famous tower at Palenque, which is four storeys high with an interior staircase, is unique.

The multi-storeyed effect of the temple at Edzná is only an illusion; in reality it is a solid pyramid built in five layers surrounded on every platform by narrow arched galleries which open outwards, with narrow doors and slender rectangular windows, but without any interior.

This method of gallery construction and the absence of real interiors arises probably from a technical aspect of Maya architecture. It was customary to cover enclosed spaces with arched roofs instead of horizontal ceilings of wood or stone *(plate 88)*. The false or corbelled arch is unsuitable for spanning a large space, particularly when the arch, triangular in section, had to bear the whole load of high crowning gables and the flat roofs.

Plate 90
The Maya.
The Palace, Sayil, Yucatán

The Palace of Sayil, one of the most beautiful examples of Maya architecture, rises up in three broad terraces. External stairways lead from storey to storey and although the core of the pyramid-shaped building is solid it is surrounded by a series of one hundred arched chambers. The ground floor is heavily damaged and not fully excavated, but narrow galleries are visible at regular intervals intersected by cross walls. Its frontage was probably as richly decorated as that of the first floor. This main façade consists of a series of alternating narrow and wide windows, the wide ones divided by two interposed columns, which give it an unusual lightness and airiness, a marked contrast to the almost blind walls of the superstructure.

The dividing elements between the openings are mock pillars, imitations in stone of wooden pillars. It is easy to overlook the fact that Maya stoneworking frequently imitates wooden models. In Sayil this is obvious, and undoubtedly much of the Maya ornamentation in stucco and stone, executed with such great assurance, followed the patterns of the almost completely lost art of the woodworkers. This also applies to the Chac masks and serpent reliefs of the cornice above the pillared galleries, alternating with reed-like bars. Some finely cut wooden lintels found in a good state of preservation at Tikal point to a likely connection.

The building at Sayil, a temple according to its plan, is nevertheless called a palace, mainly because of the absence of a surmounting shrine. It was probably never meant as a royal residence, although it is possible that the priests lived here during festivals. But as the festivals, ceremonies and rites occurred very frequently the palace would never have been left unoccupied for long. The Maya kings and nobles probably lived in large wooden houses with thatched roofs in the immediate neighbourhood of the temples.

Plate 91
The Maya.
Court for ritual ball-games, Copan, Honduras

It is a sign of the generally peace-loving character of the Maya and their absolute faith in the power of the gods that the spacious temple city of Copan, the second largest of the known Maya cities, did not possess walls or any other kind of fortification althought it was so near the edge of the Maya territory.

This city still flourished during the ninth century AD and had many splendid temple pyramids, large palaces and other buildings, but suddenly, without leaving any evidence of the reason, its people left and the town was eventually overrun by the jungle. Its buildings have suffered grievously by the jungle because the builders had used an inferior mixture of clay and chalk for bonding which did not last. The high pyramids fell into ruins but a fairly low building, the court for the ball-games, has survived practically intact and it has been possible to make a fairly reliable reconstruction of what had almost been destroyed by the forces of nature.

The ball-game, known to most of the Indian people of Central America, was popularized by the Aztecs and deteriorated into a sporting event, but originally it was connected with a cult ritual. It could not have been otherwise, for these courts were situated within the temple precincts and magnificently laid out in the shape of an I. They had sloping ramps (the later Toltecs and Aztecs preferred perpendicular walls) and small temple buildings were attached to them where before or after the games sacrifices were made. The game required great skill and endurance, and the point was to knock a rubber ball weighing $4\frac{1}{2}$ lbs through a small ring using only the elbows, wrists and hips. It could be very difficult indeed to score a hit. The players seem to have been protected by wearing heavy leather aprons and other guards. Whatever were the rules of the game, the purpose was undoubtedly to perform acts that found favour in the eyes of the gods, or to divine their will.

Plate 92
The Toltecs.
Temple of Quetzalcoatl, Tula, Mexico

The moment the Toltecs appeared from the north on the Mexican plateau, the nature of the Mexican culture changed radically. It was relatively late when this mysterious people asserted themselves, their art and their culture, but with their arrival the Classical theocratic epoch gave place to a militant period lasting until Aztec times.

The chronicles mention the years between 908 and 1168 as the Toltec period, which has been confirmed by archaeological research. A profound change in philosophy took place with the rise and final victory of the great gods of the sky, especially the sun-god. The old gods, in spite of their strange and sinister features were after all vegetation gods, well disposed towards the peaceful peasant population. They were however not strong enough to withstand the new deities, created by a hard and militant spirit, and soon sank into a state of meaningless shadow existence. There are many other signs of this wind of change. A militaristic trend becomes apparent in the reliefs and sculpture of Central Mexico during this time. An aggressive, almost tormenting tone is struck, and more and more the manly soldier is represented in art as a symbol of the bloodthirstiness of the sky gods, in whose wake came unrest, war and internecine strife. The theocratic priest-king lost his absolute power to the supreme commander or, as with the Toltecs, to a military caste.

War became the main preoccupation, for the gods of the sun and the stars demanded tribute of human hearts, and the more captives a warrior brought home, the greater the honour. These profound changes in cult and ritual are reflected in the art forms. Not that the religious zeal became any less, on the contrary the great number of newly erected temples speak of ever-increasing fanaticism. Tula, the capital and the religious centre of the Toltecs, was second to none in the ancient sacred cities of the classical period. The Temple of Quetzalcoatl is very impressive and characteristic of the altered mood. Although not the largest, it is the best preserved building at Tula. Partly restored, its low pyramid on a square plan (140 feet long) consists of five stages. Many of the reliefs that once covered the sides have disappeared, but the fastenings are still visible. The grim human-shaped columns and square pillars decorated with reliefs found in the rubble at its foot once supported the flat roof of a crowning temple and have now been re-erected *(cf. plate 78)*. The vastness of this temple and the use of numerous columns and piers are a typical feature of Toltec architecture. A large hall stood at the foot of the pyramid, its flat roof supported by a triple row of columns. This constitutes a new element which we shall meet again in the Toltec Temple of the Warriors at Chichén Itzá *(plate 96)*.

Plate 93
The Toltecs
*Atlantes on the Temple of Quetzalcoatl, Tula,
Mexico*

The Toltec temples on their low pyramidal bases were spacious and needed central supports for the flat roofs. The Toltec architects of this temple and the later temple at Chichén Itzá were not content with the rows of unadorned pillars. The four massive columns of the front row 15 ft high, each constructed of four stone blocks, were carved in the shape of warriors with large heads and thick-set bodies. The fusing of relief (the arms pinned to their bodies as if standing to attention) and sculpture in the round (heads and legs) are reminiscent of early Greek sculpture where similar atlas figures transform the round column into a human shape and give it a certain degree of plasticity without complete freedom.

The functional shape of the Toltec atlas figures is also accentuated by a symmetrical stiffness of the limbs and the lack of facial expression, although the general rigidness may have been lessened by the application of colour, which in some instances is just recognizable.

The true significance of these gigantic figures is not clear. Their technical function is apparent; the high feathered crowns serve as capitals for the heavy wooden beams. But it is unlikely that they represented human warriors, for the simple reason that these figures overshadow the relatively dwarf-like relief figures on the pillars at the back. There is much to be said in favour of the explanation given by Hugo Moedanos, who suggests that these large sculptured columns represent Quetzalcoatl himself. He sees this in the red and white stripes painted on the bodies and the fact that the atlantes carry spears and spear-throwers *(atlatl)*, the weapons of the god.

The atlantes and the pillars with relief ornamentation in the cella constitute a new architectural element, namely that of spatial construction. Free-standing supports mean large interior spaces and the Temple of Quetzalcoatl is one of the earlier examples of an interest not only in compact masses, a purely exterior architecture, but in interior construction. No other Indian people before had attempted this, nor was it attempted later on the same scale. We do not know what inspired the Toltecs to branch out in this new architectural direction, or why their example was not followed by later inhabitants of the region.

Plate 94
The Toltecs.
Relief decoration on a wall of the Temple of
Quetzalcoatl, Tula, Mexico

The north and west sides of the stepped pyramid on which the temple stood were never obscured by additional buildings and were originally surrounded by a wall 7 ft high, of which only the northern part remains in good condition. Both faces are decorated with brightly coloured relief, making this wall a masterpiece of Toltec art. The plinth consists of plain stone blocks, the superstructure has three rows of reliefs framed by plain horizontal bands. The first and third row are made up of continuous stepped meander designs and themselves frame a slightly wider frieze. The uniformly repeated motif of the frieze is a serpent from whose open mouth a human skull with protruding teeth emerges. This gruesome scene may be a symbol of the dual nature of the planet Venus as the morning and evening star, the skeleton symbolizing the journey of the star through the Underworld (which means the period when Venus does not appear in the night sky). This interpretation is fitting for a temple dedicated to the god of the morning star. The same wall still has a crenellated superstructure in which the perforated slabs of stone represent sections of conch shells, but it is not clear whether these too have a symbolic meaning or not. Except for the theme, the building technique of the walls is not without similarities with other cultures. The unadorned plinth and the horizontal friezes show strong Teotihuacán influences *(plate 75)*.

Plate 95
The Toltecs.
The Tower of Caracol, Chichén Itzá, Yucatán

The Tower of Caracol is one of the earliest buildings at Chichén Itzá where Toltec influence can be seen. It is a circular structure, two storeys high, and stands on a double terrace. According to an old tradition it was built by Kukulcan, the legendary priest-king who led the first wave of Toltec immigrants from the north into Yucatán and Chichén Itzá during the tenth century.

A certain ambiguity in architecture and ornamentation vouches for the antiquity of the building, for typical Toltec elements as seen in the later Temple of the Warriors *(plate 96)* and the temple of Kukulcan *(plate 99)* are hardly discernible here. Were it not for the fact that neither the circular tower construction nor the snake ornaments on the stairs were known to the Maya, but occurred frequently in Mexico, the Caracol would be classified as a Maya creation. The plinth lacks the battered shape typical of Toltec and Mexican buildings, and it is also quite vertical like Maya structures. The doors too are narrow as found in the best Maya architecture *(plates 83, 85, 89 and 90)*

and the double storeyed interior with a spiral staircase has the usual Maya arched roof. Most of all it is the decoration that seems to be alien to Toltec art. The cornice, fitting like a girdle around the tower, has strong affinities with Maya architecture. It has sharply projecting courses like Maya buildings. The grotesque masks of the Maya rain-god are also found here and the four serpent-mask panels above each doorway are made of mosaic elements in the Maya fashion.

The reason for all this is perhaps that the early Toltecs (Itzá) wandering into Maya territory, not as conquerors, but in search of new lands, settled next to the old established inhabitants and adapted the far greater skill and experience of the Maya artists to their own taste. In any case it is almost certain that Maya architects assisted in the building of the Caracol and that it was built in the time when the Toltecs had settled in Maya territory.

The tower has a diameter of 36 ft and was equally high. It received its name from the spiral staircase (caracol means snail). To judge from its circular shape and the seven slits that served as windows in the superstructure it may have been an observatory.

Plate 96
The Toltecs.
The Temple of the Warriors, Chichén Itzá,
Yucatán

The chronicles mention the year 1168 as the year in which the Toltecs fell victims to the wars and discords, unrest and uncertainties they themselves had helped to create some centuries earlier. Tula, their splendid ceremonial centre, was abandoned under pressure from the Chichimecs from the north. Some Toltec tribes stayed in Mexico and merged with other tribes. Others however wandered southwards towards the Maya territory, where already in the tenth century, fellow tribesmen had settled under their legendary priest-king Kukulcan, who was in fact an historical figure. These were the masters of Chichén Itzá.

The problems surrounding this original Toltec migration and the person of Kukulcan who after his death was worshipped as the ancient god, Quetzalcoatl, are fraught with difficulties. An early Toltec settlement at Chichén Itzá must be accepted, for the buildings in that city show undeniable affinities with Tula buildings and are, moreover, basically alien to Maya architecture, although Chichén Itzá existed in the sixth century, long before the Toltec arrival.

Tula influence is particularly marked in the largely restored Temple of the Warriors, which looks like a more elaborate version of the Temple of Quetzalcoatl *(plate 92)*. The ground plan of the Chichén Itzá temple is a square with sides of 65½ ft. It stands on a stepped pyramid 37 ft high. A broad flight of stairs leads to the temple. At its foot lies a hall that once had a flat roof supported by endless rows of columns exactly like those at Tula, only larger. It may have served as a market place and council hall. The lost pillars at Tula may have been similar to the rectangular pillars with low relief *(plate 98)* at Chichén Itzá and the Temple of the Warriors, in spite of many individual features was probably very similar to the Temple of Quetzalcoatl. The sculptured pillars at the temple at Tula are repeated on a more impressive scale at Chichén Itzá as feathered serpents. These and many other similarities cannot be mere coincidence; the architects of Tula and Chichén Itzá must have been in contact with each other. Even when the builders of Chichén Itzá borrowed many Maya, so-called Puuc-style elements, most noticeable in the spaciousness of the temple, their basic conception remained Toltec. Where the Maya temple is small and not much more than a cage, the Toltec temple possesses a real interior, with a wide portal. It is divided by a series of columns and an inner wall into two separate chambers.

W. Krickeberg explains the contrast between Maya cage and Toltec hall as the antithesis between two different philosophies and two widely divergent social spheres. While the Maya temple was only accessible to the priest, the Toltec temple was the place where the heads of the clans met and held their councils of war.

Plate 89
The Maya.
The five-storeyed temple, Edzná, Mexico

Plate 90
The Maya.
The Palace, Sayil, Yucatán

Plate 91
The Maya.
Court for ritual ball-games, Copan, Honduras

Plate 92
The Toltecs.
Temple of Quetzalcoatl, Tula, Mexico

Plate 93
The Toltecs.
Atlantes on the Temple of Quetzalcoatl, Tula,
Mexico

Plate 94
The Toltecs.
Relief decoration on a wall of the Temple of
Quetzalcoatl, Tula, Mexico

Plate 95
The Toltecs.
The Tower of Caracol, Chichén Itzá, Yucatán

Plate 96
The Toltecs.
The Temple of the Warriors, Chichén Itzá,
Yucatán

Plate 97
The Toltecs.
Serpent pillars in the portico of the Temple of
the Warriors, Chichén Itzá, Yucatán

The Toltecs, more than any other Indian
people, had a predilection for pillars and
other supporting elements. These serpent
pillars are typical of Toltec architecture.
They stand regularly at temple entrances and
are identical in the fusing together of low
relief, often only incised, with sculpture in
the round. At the Temple of the Warriors
the serpent heads, with wide open mouths
and threatening fangs are carved from a
single block of stone. They rest without
bases on the ground. The pillar itself forms
the body of the serpent, the sinuous movement only indicated by incised lines. The
up-curled tail of the rattle-snake acts as a
capital.

There are several theories about the
symbolic meaning of the snake pillars and
their position at the very entrance of the
temple. The plumed serpent without any
doubt represents Quetzalcoatl-Kukulcan
(plate 75). But it is difficult to say whether
he acts here as guardian and averter of evil,
or whether he is there as the rightful owner
of the sanctuary.

Plate 98
The Toltecs.
Reliefs on the pillars from the hall at the foot
of the Temple of the Warriors, Chichén Itzá,
Yucatán

The great hall of the Warriors at the foot of
the temple on the west side is a masterpiece
of Toltec column architecture and relief
carving. Its sixty pillars, over 8 ft high and
rectangular in shape, once the support of
roof beams, stand in four rows. They consist of enormous blocks joined together
with the help of small stones and owe much
of their fascination to their formalized low
relief decoration. The bases represent the
god of the morning star in the shape of a
human skull between the teeth and protruding tongue of a plumed snake *(plate 94)*.
This forms the pedestal for the main figure,
that of a warrior in all his baroque array of
armour and head-dress. Originally painted
in bright hues, the columns must have
looked like a regiment of valiant soldiers.
The amount of work alone is stupendous,
considering that in all 250 nearly life-size
sculptures were worked with stone tools.
The figures, although identical in design, vary
in detail.

The warlike Toltec spirit found a fitting
expression in this bombastic military procession. While the theocratic cultures of the
classical period preferred to portray their
gods and priests, Toltec imagery is full of
the glory of martial deeds. Not the priest,
but the soldier held the place of honour in
their minds for it was the soldiers whom the
warlike gods of the sky favoured as the
bringer of blood and human hearts without
which the gods and their people could not
thrive.

Plate 99
The Toltecs.
The Castillo, Chichén Itzá, Yucatán

One of the most impressive buildings of Central America is the 'Castillo', the temple pyramid of Kukulcan. Its harmonious proportions and classical form are displayed to the full by modern restoration. Like the Temple of the Warriors it is an example of late Toltec temple architecture at Chichén Itzá, and dates from the twelfth century or even later. The pyramid is built up in nine stages. Open stairs lead in an uninterrupted flight to the summit on all four sides and this symmetry stresses its unorientated compactness. The same symmetry also occurs in other Itzá structures of this period, but is not generally characteristic of Central American architecture. The massive rectangular temple accentuates this impression. Only that fact that the north side of the temple has a triple portal, supported by snake-pillars, while there are only small openings in the other side, indicates the orientation of the building. It is believed that the temple front faces north to be in line with the 'sacred way' leading in a northerly direction towards the sacred Cenote. This was a roundish pool, dedicated to the worship of the rain-god from early Maya days until the Spanish invasion in the sixteenth century. Innumerable precious offerings were found at the bottom of this 65 ft deep and still pool and also remains of human skeletons, for human sacrifices were brought to the rain-god in times of disaster or sickness, throughout the whole of Central America.

The Kukulcan temple may have a connection with this old-established place of pilgrimage, but its construction was determined by the religious conceptions of the sky gods and the numbers of the heavenly bodies. Its nine stages stand for the nine heavens and the 364 steps of the four stairways signify the days of the year, and thus the building can be understood to be a monumental symbol of the universe and all that exists in it.

Plate 100
The Aztecs.
The Temple Pyramid, Tenayuca, Mexico

It seems strange that so little is known about the architecture of the Tenochca or Aztecs, while their customs, religion, the sites of their cities and the history of their people are so well preserved in written documents. Much of the Aztec building activity is recorded in the Indian *codices* of the early Spanish epoch in the sixteenth century and enthusiastic conquistadores described the wonders of the Aztec cities, palaces and temples, in terms which, although admittedly exaggerated, nevertheless conjured up some of their splendour.

The buildings themselves have perished, razed to the ground except for some poor remains and a few better preserved examples. For all their admiration the Spanish conquerors did not hesitate to destroy the centres of Aztec life, especially the capital Tenochtitlan (modern Mexico City), which had seventy or eighty thousand inhabitants in those days. A nomadic tribe of the Tenochca (Tenoch was the head of one clan), one of the Nahua-speaking Indian peoples, arrived (perhaps from the north Mexican steppes or the state of Nayant in the west) in the highly developed Mesa Central, the valley of Mexico, during the fourteenth century.

The capital Tenochtitlan was built in the fourteenth century on an island in Lake Texcoco and gradually extended over several artificial islands. It was only natural that the Aztecs-Tenochca learned from the earlier cultures and were guided by their art-forms and building techniques; thus they became their cultural and political heirs. Keen pupils as they were, they soon surpassed their teachers and probably pressed them into their own service. In any case much of the Aztec architecture is founded on a thousand years of tradition, and a continuation of well-established customs.

A good example is the temple pyramid of Tenayuca excavated in 1925. Tenayuca lies on a bay in Lake Texcoco, north-west of Tenochtitlan. It is built in the usual stepped pyramid form 62 ft high, and covers an area of 196 × 164 ft; it is surrounded by 138 serpent sculptures. The large platform on the summit provided ample space for two temples. According to reports, the temple at Tenochtitlan also consisted of two buildings and it is likely that in both double sanctuaries the same two gods were worshipped, namely the rain god Tlaloc and Huitzilopochtli, a tribal ancestor who became a sun god and the god of war. The fact that the temple axis is orientated to the point on the ecliptic where the sun sets at its highest point indicates a form of sun worship.

On the open-air altars in front of the temple human sacrifices took place during which hundreds or even thousands of captives were often slaughtered to pacify the gods. The Tenayuca pyramid as it is seen today covers at least five and probably six successive constructions of identical shape. Dr. G. C. Vaillant, a prominent American archaeologist, connects the successive stages with the cyclical ceremonies celebrated every fifty-two years. Struck by the recurrent rhythm in nature, the Aztecs imagined that every fifty-two years the world would come to an end. In anticipation they destroyed all their worldly goods and the altar fires were extinguished. When in the fatal year the cataclysm did not happen, the people imagined they were favoured by the gods and saved for another cycle, and great renewal festivals were held. The last of these events can be dated to the year 1507. Counting back through the fifty-two year cycles, the date for the innermost pyramid must fall in the thirteenth century and therefore long before the arrival of the Aztecs. The first two temples and pyramids were built by Chichimecs who later moved their seat of government to Texcoco.

Plate 101
Decadent Tiahuanaco-Inca.
Circular burial tower, Sillustani, near Lake Titicaca

The partly collapsed burial tower, *chullpa*, shown in the picture, lies on the Peruvian-Bolivian border. It is in the neighbourhood of Tiahuanaco, the centre of the theocratic highland culture, that flourished after about AD 300 and extended its influence over most of Peru during the ninth century. After the Tiahuanaco floruit came a period of Decadent Tiahuanaco of unknown duration, though it came to an end before the Incas arrived in 1430–70. Associated pottery finds show that the *chullpas* were not associated with the great period of Tiahuanaco culture, and they date to either the Decadent Tiahuanaco or Inca period, when all Tiahuanaco influence had ceased. The careful stonework of this particular example, the Sillustani *chullpa*, suggests a full Inca date.

Its outer wall is constructed of accurately joined dressed stone blocks, and in spite of the thick-set appearance it is not totally lacking in elegance. Only the Tiahuanaco and later the Inca had this feeling for the nature of stone.

Plate 102
Chimú.
The Ruins of the Chimú capital, Chan Chan,
Peru

The architecture of Peru is difficult to assess with only the help of photographic documentation. It is an established fact that many divergent cultures flourished in the wake of the Chavin period from about 500 BC, and that they had a considerable architecture has been sufficiently substantiated by partly remaining large structures. These are, however, in a piteous state of preservation and so little research has yet been done, that even the worst preserved mounds of say, Mesopotamia, are photogenic compared with what remains of the earliest buildings in the Andes. The reason for this sad state of affairs lies partly in the lack of public interest in these remote monuments and partly in the unstable building material favoured by the original architects. Illicit treasure-hunters, too, have done, and are still doing, considerable damage in spite of strict laws.

Even Tiahuanaco near Lake Titicaca in the Bolivian highlands (cf. p. 306) did not escape this fate, although built of more durable material. There is not enough of this city left for a reliable reconstruction, which can only be done by drawings. But there is no doubt that the Peruvian people, even before the city-building period and the period of small kingdoms during the thirteenth and fourteenth century AD, erected considerable buildings of which the gigantic 'Huaca del Sol', the Temple of the Sun, is one of the most impressive. It is falsely called a stepped pyramid and is 135 ft high and 756 ft long at the base. It was built probably during the sixth century AD, out of a million rectangular *adobe* bricks, by the north Peruvian Moche people in the coastal valley of the same name. Chan Chan, the capital of Chimú in the old Moche territory was also built of mud bricks. The kingdom of Chimú was a flourishing and rigidly organized state and in many aspects set the pattern for the later Inca empire. Chan Chan surpassed anything that the New World has created. In its regular layout it resembled the cities of the Indus cultures *(plate 37)*, and was large enough to house a population of two hundred thousand inhabitants with an area of almost eleven square miles. The palaces, numerous temple pyramids and rectangular housing units are intersected at right angles by straight roads. Squares, walled courtyards and verdant gardens broke the regularity of the town plan without dissolving it. The non-pyramidal temple precincts consisted of a complex of small cult chambers, the housing units, only partly excavated, and the palaces were surrounded by high *adobe* walls. Its people lived in seclusion behind the walls organized in clans or some similar social groups.

Plate 103
Chimú.
Relief on a mud brick wall, Chan Chan, Peru

The ruins of Chan Chan, only partly freed as they are from the sand, cannot give a true impression of the city as it once was. Although built of mud brick, which makes it now look uniformly dull, the walls were originally covered with brightly coloured reliefs. A network of formalized animal shapes (fishes, birds and some undefined four-legged creatures) covered the yellowish-brown *adobe* in broad horizontal bands, alternating with geometrically abstract patterns, similar to the ornamentation on the Chimú pottery. The ornamentation on the lower part of the walls is exceptionally well-preserved because it was buried under a thick layer of sand. The main motif seems to be the serpent, a sacred animal, which probably gave the city its name. As far as is known Chan Chan means 'serpent town'.

Plate 104
The Incas.
Gateway and wall of the fortress of
Sacsayhuamán, Cuzco, Peru

The history, daily life, religion and cult, the political organization and final downfall of the Quechua-speaking people, or Incas of Peru, the founders of the only real empire in ancient ·America, are just as well known as that of the Aztecs. But whereas the Aztec architecture is known mainly from descriptions and a few poor remains (cf. *plate 100*), Inca buildings fared much better. The Incas did not use mud bricks but stone for their public buildings. Moreover many Inca towns, for instance Machu Picchu, remained undiscovered for a long time, hidden in inaccessible mountain locations and therefore were not robbed or used as stone quarries.

The enormous fortress of Sacsayhuamán above the Inca capital, Cuzco, owes its excellent state of preservation mainly to its unbelievably skilful stonework. Huge limestone blocks, some up to twenty feet high, with bevelled edges, are built up in irregular courses, a characteristic of Inca building technique.

The postern gates through the triple line of walls are narrow with heavy monolithic lintels. The door openings become narrower towards the top. The builders liked this trapezoidal shape and it is often found in Inca buildings, perhaps because it allows the use of a shorter lintel, and therefore less shaping and manoeuvring of heavy stone.

Plate 105
The Incas.
Inca bath, Tambo Machay, near Cuzco, Peru

Water from a nearby spring still runs through the granite trough that carries the mountain stream to this Inca well house constructed in three storeys against the steep slope, dated to the fifteenth century. The interpretation as the "bath of the Incas" could possibly be correct, for judging by the carefully constructed reservoir and the neighbourhood of the royal residence at Cuzco, it must have been a building of some importance; but on the other hand it could also be a sacred building and the spring a 'holy well'. The work is of a high standard, especially on the two upper storeys.

That the courses are irregular, and larger and smaller blocks joined seemingly without any pattern, is not a sign of inefficiency. On the contrary, the irregular shape was chosen on purpose and what is called a polygonal building technique is used here. The polygonal blocks are so carefully joined without bonding that the blade of a knife cannot be inserted into the cracks. Formerly it was believed that the polygonal walls were more primitive and always of an earlier date than the regularly coursed stone masonry. Both

techniques however existed side by side at the same time. Regular squared masonry was mostly used on important buildings as for instance the palaces and temples at Cuzco.

Peruvian stone, mostly of an igneous nature, is extremely hard and difficult to work. This may have been one of the reasons why the Inca builders did not always choose to use regular masonry. The volcanic rock had to be shaped with stone tools into rough blocks and then ground down with water and sand into its final rectangular and slightly rounded shape. This was an exhausting business and it is understandable that the more finely executed blocks were only used in special instances.

J. H. Rowe has argued that the polygonal technique was a monumental continuation of an earlier rough stone construction, and the rectangular technique arose from walls made of square cut turfs. This could well be true, for Inca houses were mostly built in these primitive materials. The shallow niches of the "bath" on the ground and second floor are trapezoidal in shape, which together with the heavy monolithic lintel characterizes Inca architecture. The massive stone work and the complete lack of ornamentation heighten the impact of the building.

Plate 106
The Incas.
Wall of the House of the Chosen Women,
Cuzco, Peru

After seeing the fortress of Sacsayhuamán near Cuzco *(plate 104)* or the Inca bath *(plate 105)*, one is impelled to believe that the wall shown in this picture is of a much later date and the result of a long technical evolution.

In reality it was constructed at the same time as the rough walls of the fortress and this particular style of stonework was chosen here because of the importance of the building which justified the extra work involved. The slightly inclined wall is more than 16 ft high. The regular courses of blocks with sunk joints are without mortar. It was once the retaining wall of the famous *Acclai Huasi*, the House of the Chosen Women. Today part of the convent of Santa Catalina, it was in Inca days a convent for girls and young women, chosen as gifts from the emperor to his courtiers and specially honoured warriors. Some were consecrated as *Mamaconas* to the service of the temples and sanctuaries and the most beautiful were thought worthy of the highest honour—to be sacrificed to the gods in times of disaster or on the occasion of very solemn festivals, thus safeguarding the well-being of the Inca and his people. This was considered the greatest honour a woman could attain.

These convents were to be found in many Inca cities, and officials visited the villages at regular intervals to select girls, from all those who had reached the age of ten. This is a good example of the rigid organization of the dictator-ruled state of the Incas.

Plate 107
The Incas.
View of the Inca town of Machu Picchu, Peru

The only undamaged city of the Inca period, Machu Picchu above the Urubamba river, the area from which the last Inca emperor directed the desperate struggle against the Spanish conquerors for almost forty years, was rediscovered in 1911 by Hiram Bingham.

This is not the place to relate the adventurous story of the search for this last Inca stronghold high up in the Andes close to the permanent snow line. It was found in much the same condition as it was when, four hundred years ago, its people left it for the last time. Much has been destroyed by dense undergrowth, wind and weather have taken their toll. The roofs, thatched in Inca fashion, are no longer there, walls have crumbled away, terraces have collapsed. But what remains is truly impressive. The town lies on the mountain which gave it its name, and is situated on a saddle which falls steeply on three sides to the Urubamba, flowing some 1480 ft below, while the fourth side is protected by a cliff. Its temple precincts, housing, and cultivated terraces are built on the ridge and along the sides of a spur. Looking to the north-west one sees, along

a row of houses with painted walls and a semicircular temple, a large field of shallow terraces. This was the town centre. It is enclosed on both sides by temple buildings the most important of which was certainly the one on the little mound to the left which contains the famous sun-stone, judging by the position and its significance. In all directions small stepped paths and terraces interlink, and the steep slopes at the edge of the built-up area and right to the top of Picchu are terraced. These supplied the inhabitants with a diet which was not very varied but obviously quite adequate. Although Machu Picchu seems to have been a refuge for the last true Inca, the descendant of Manco Capac, it was not a fortress like Sacsayhuamán. Its natural advantages were such that the only fortification it needed was a watchtower and gate on the south side, the only weak spot in the defence system.

It is strange that the town was soon abandoned and never resettled. The Spaniards never went so high into the mountains and probably never saw it although its existence was known to them. The findings *in situ*, especially the graves, rule out an epidemic. Bingham suggests that lack of water may have been the cause; the only spring the town possessed may not have been sufficient to support a great increase in population.

Plate 108
The Incas.
The Temple, Machu Picchu, Peru

Machu Picchu was more than one of the last refuges of a persecuted people, it was also a residence worthy of the Inca, son of the Sun. There are no real palaces as such, but the numerous sanctuaries and temples, although minute in dimensions, are among the noblest that Inca architecture created.

The small temple shown in the picture is a splendid example of the stonemason's art in the early sixteenth century. A semi-circular wall was built around an outcrop of rock and a rectangular wall encloses both the half-circle and a larger forecourt. The meaning of the structure is obscure, although the circular wall around the bare rock suggests a sun temple. The customary form of an Inca sun temple was circular.

The agricultural terraces that completely cover the north-western slope towards the Urubamba show the proficiency of the mountain tribes in utilizing every inch of ground at their disposal.

Plate 97
The Toltecs.
Serpent pillars in the portico of the Temple
of the Warriors, Chichén Itzá, Yucatán

Plate 98
The Toltecs.
Reliefs on the pillars from the hall at the foot
of the Temple of the Warriors, Chichén Itzá,
Yucatán

Plate 99
The Toltecs.
The Castillo, Chichén Itzá, Yucatán

Plate 100
The Aztecs.
The Temple Pyramid, Tenayuca, Mexico

Plate 101
Decadent Tiahuanaco-Inca.
Circular burial tower, Sillustani, near Lake
Titicaca

Plate 102
Chimú.
The Ruins of the Chimú capital, Chan Chan,
Peru

Plate 103
Chimú.
Relief on a mud brick wall, Chan Chan, Peru

Plate 104
The Incas.
Gateway and wall of the fortress of
Sacsayhuamán, Cuzco, Peru

Plate 105
The Incas.
Inca bath, Tambo Machay, near Cuzco, Peru

Plate *106*
The Incas.
Wall of the House of the Chosen Women,
Cuzco, Peru

Plate 107
The Incas.
View of the Inca town of Machu Picchu, Peru

Plate *108*
The Incas.
The Temple, Machu Picchu, Peru

ACKNOWLEDGEMENTS

Sources of the colour plates

58, 71, Bavaria-Verlag; 30, Dr E. Brunner-Traut; 54 (reconstruction after Wace), Dr B. Cichy; 39, J. le Doaré; 49, Dr F. Fischer; 14, 15, 17, 31, W. Forman; 6, Dr F. W. Funke; 45, R. Grosjean; 81, 83, 88, 89, 90, 92, I. Groth-Kimball; 52, 57, 62, 73, 78, 80, 85, 86, 91, 96, 97, 98, 104, 105, 108, J. Hartmann; 79, 82, 84, 87, 93, 94, 99, 100, 102, 103, H. Helfritz; 24, 36, Dr H. Hell; 2, 3, 4, 5, 47, 48, 55, 60, 65, Hirmer-Verlag; 51, 63, 64, Holle-Verlag; 33, B. Hungerford and R. Garner; 13, 16, 19, 23, 25, 27, 34, 35, A. F. Kersting; 9, 12, 53, 56, 59, 61, 74, 95, 106, F. A. Mella; 37, 38, courtesy of the Government of Pakistan, Department of Films and Publications; 21, 28, 29, K. Peysan; 50, O. Pferschy; 7, 8, 10, 11, 26, 43, P. Popper; 75, 107, Rapho; 41, H. Saebens; 40, Agencia Salmer; 22, 101, M. Schliessler; 18, 20, 32, Uni-Dia-Verlag; 1, British Museum Photographic Service; 44, J. M. Spiteri; 46, 67, 68, 69, 70, 72, Scala; 42, Professor Waterbolk; 76, 77, FZA.

INDEX

Numbers in italics refer to the illustrations